F.M.Smith
Saint as Reformer

VOLUME 2

F.M.Smith

Saint as Reformer

1874-1946

By Larry E. Hunt

Herald Publishing House,
Independence, Missouri

Library of Congress Cataloging in Publication Data

Hunt, Larry E.
Frederick M. Smith: Saint as reformer, 1874-1946. Volume 2.

Originally presented as the author's thesis (doctoral—Missouri-Columbia, 1978).
Includes bibliographical references.
1. Smith, Frederick Madison, 1874-1946. 2. Mormons—United States—Biography. I. Title.
BX8695.S73H86 289.3'3 [B] 81-7213
ISBN 0-8309-0341-0 AACR2

Printed in the United States of America

CONTENTS

Preface

As a student of United States reform history in the late nineteenth and twentieth centuries, as well as the history of the RLDS church, Dr. Larry E. Hunt found Frederick Madison Smith to be an example of a Saint who was a willing participant in the spirit of reform common to his time. President Smith wrote about contemporary "progressive" themes such as conservation of energy, efficiency, scientific management, professionalization, and centralization in the doctoral dissertation in psychology he prepared for G. Stanley Hall and in his many printed essays in church-sponsored publications. To these he added themes from the church tradition such as "stewardship," and he leaned toward the theocratic side of "theocratic democracy," which was the governing philosophy of the church. Using both theocracy and efficiency, he centralized what he considered to be the ragged, semiautonomous, and inefficient quorums and departments of the church. Many Saints did not understand the "modernizing" tendency of their new president, and they unsuccessfully opposed him. Although the quorums, personnel, finances, and administration of his church were completely centered in his office by 1925, much to his dismay little was accomplished and, in fact, he alienated a portion of the church.

According to Dr. Hunt, in reform external to his institution, President Smith restricted his activities to supporting Victorian morality, extolling the nurturant role of women in the family, and electing "good men" to political offices. He was more concerned with individual character than environment as the primary sources of evil or good and he was more interested in order than social justice. He believed that "true reform" came not from collective groups such as labor or from legislatures, but from enlightened, well-selected people who were good managers for the public. Dr. Hunt builds a plausible argument that President Smith deserves a lasting place in the memory of the Saints not as an autocrat or crank but as a leader squarely in the mainstream of conservative American reform.

While building this thesis, he provides readers with insights into some aspects of this scholar-president's life and thought that have been buried for years under tons of innuendoes: his intellectual development, the "supreme directional control" controversies of the 1920s, his connection with the Masonic Lodge, his encouragement of managerial trusts in the Order of Enoch, and the personal pecadilloes that more often than not overshadowed his substantive goals and achievements. Saints would do well to acquaint themselves with this part of their history.

Paul A. Wellington
Editorial Director
Herald House

Chapter V

THE STRUGGLE FOR ADMINISTRATIVE CENTRALIZATION, 1915-1925

In 1915 most of the 71,000 people of the small church over which Frederick M. Smith was to preside for the next thirty-five years were as aware as their leader that their scriptures and traditions gave them a regenerative and preparatory mission for the kingdom of God, and their faith in the eventual achievement of that mission was strong. They did not, however, accommodate themselves to the new president's more centralized vision of the means to that reign of economic, political, and social justice, particularly in the area of ecclesiastical governance. While most of the Saints were accustomed by practice to congregational, democratic, one-to-one administrative procedures to effect their "common consent," their new president aspired to centralize those procedures in the "First Quorum" of the church[1] for the purpose of greater organizational efficiency in an increasingly complex and interrelated world.

Under more centralized leadership, Fred M. believed the church could better use its small resources, avoid duplication of services, plan its fields of expansion, avoid the diffusion of energy that accompanied haggling, competitive, semiautonomous bureaucracies, and become a more refined instrument for reform activities adjunct to the kingdom mission. His authoritarian personality, the efficiency concept gleaned from his educational experience with G. Stanley Hall, and the more autocratic, centralized governing principles and procedures of the earlier Restoration motivated his desire for this structural, institutional change that he viewed as significant reform. These components, whether appropriated from his religious or secular contexts, approximated the "mugwump style" of other reformers in the America that produced him. His messianism, his appeals for obedience to law and duly constituted authority, his emphasis on the referendum rather than the initiatory power of the people, and his use of the idioms of efficiency, centralization, and order all corresponded to the themes and acts of reformers in the progressive era, particularly those of mugwumpery.

Essentially, what he proposed for his religion and its clerical representatives was a centralized, hierarchical, bureaucratic organization within which the lines of authority were clearly delineated and led directly to him as the sole repository of final authority and guarantor of right direction. As such, the leitmotif of his administration was more attuned to that of his authoritarian grandfather, Joseph Smith, Jr., than that of his democratically inclined father, Joseph III. His rationalizations in support of this position, although often ensconced in the sociological jargon of his time, were simple, modern recapitulations of the themes of the church before its fragmentation in the years 1844 to 1848.

One of the most disputatious of institutional controversies in Fred M.'s ecclesiastical administration derived from his own authoritarian interpretation of governance that was centered in the "supreme directional control" of the Presidency of the church over all its general officers, quorums, and departments. If his vision represented the wave of the future, many of the Saints preferred the familiar paths of the past and fought the new, centralized, authoritarian impetus spearheaded by their leader, only to lose the battle. The majority of his retinue, however, stayed with the church in faith that the man they considered to be the "Lord's anointed" would not fail to lead them into new areas of development, spiritual maturity, and eventually to their coveted kingdom of God on earth.

After the decade of acrimonious controversy starting in 1916 consumed the intellectual and physical vigor of his prime, his wife and early biographer categorically stated that

> the story of life is a succession of plans rejected, ideas thwarted and movements retarded, because those with whom he worked were unable to look forward to the needs of a quarter of a century hence. One of the greatest handicaps . . . among the many he has to meet, is this failure to find men who will look forward with him into the future.[2]

While this judgment reflected her husband's opinion as well, both stopped short of a critical assessment of how and why dissenters could legitimately question the means employed to attain and secure the future to which all—leaders and followers—had pledged their lives and resources. Echoing Thomas Jefferson who often alluded to the idealistic virtues of democracy and the quantitative wisdom inherent in the masses of common people to temper the excesses of potentially Draconian leaders and prevent tyranny, and who upheld the role of the "natural aristocrat" as that of supplementing the ignorance and the crudity of the mutitudes,[3] the majority of the people of the RLDS church sought to maintain a delicate equilibrium between the democratic and theocratic traditions of the Restoration. Those at the ends of that political spectrum, believing that compromise with what they conceived to be revealed truth was intolerably evil, were astounded by the totalitarian implications of his infelicitous phrase, "supreme directional control," and opposed him with all the vigor they could muster.

Theocratic Democracy in the Early Restoration, 1830-1844

The Restoration has often been referred to as an indigenous American movement whose ethos was shaped by the cultural environment within which it was born.[4] While typical of its larger American environment, however, it was simultaneously peculiar, manifesting its own idiosyncratic characteristics.

One area wherein its typicality and peculiarity converged and which would profoundly affect Fred M.'s administration in later years was that of ecclesiastical and civil governance.[5] Restorationism was not simply a religious entity but a corporate body withdrawn and separated in the early nineteenth century from the broader community, yet it shared the democratic value system of the society that gave it birth. At the same time it was also a religious community positing authority in what it believed to be contemporary revelation through a divinely chosen leader and prophet. The church effected a reconciliation of secular democracy with the authority of a divinely inspired leader in a hierarchically structured system dubbed by its adherents with the appellations, "theodemocracy" or "theocratic-democracy."

This structure represented the early Restorationists' attempt to rationalize an authoritative governing system for the church, combining the rule of God with the ratifying power of the people.[6] Joseph Smith, Jr., supplied the simplest definition of his own ideological child. Theocratic-democracy was the political condition wherein "God and the people hold the power to conduct the affairs of men in righteousness."[7] More specifically, theocratic authority generally indicated a divine or religious "legitimating power" which was close to being "singular, absolute and authoritarian," whereas democratic authority implied that these same forces were derivative of, shared by, and at least partially retained by the people being governed. Theocratic authority reached downward from God through priesthood or prophetic utterance, while democratic sanction reached upward from the Saints in their collectively expressed will or "common consent." The theocracy, as such, ultimately inhered in the authority of the Godhead, but its specific expression of will to the church community came primarily through a prophetic spokesman who was "to preside over the whole church, and to be like unto Moses,"[8] and secondarily through a chosen hierarchialized priesthood, selected, ordained, and ranked by the prophet and his councils.[9] Members of the church could express their common consent to, or dissent from, theocratic rule in conference sessions in which they reacted to legislative proposals, priesthood calls, "revelations" presented to the church by the prophet, or voted to sustain the general authorities of the church.[10]

In the words of a recent student of Mormon ecclesiastical governance,

> theocratic authority involved the presentation of the word and will of God through the prophet-president directly and authoritatively, while democratic sanction conveyed the will of the gathered body of believers, their collective conception of truth and testimony of faith. To the degree that democratic authority partook of an expressed divine authority, it did so indirectly, non-prophetically and derivatively.[11]

Even though Mormons saw the power of theocracy and democracy cojoined in a mutually supportive and complementary system, the authority of each was never equivalent, and common consent came to mean coercion by assent. By the 1840s the weighty, bureaucratic theocracy pressed heavily on the submerging democracy until the latter drowned in the murky waters of authoritarianism, a contradiction at last resolved. It was this autocratic resolution, among other things, that the Reorganized church repudiated in its own experience in the later nineteenth century.

Joseph Smith III and Theocratic Democracy in the Reorganized Church 1861 to 1915

Joseph Smith III was to preside over the Reorganized church from 1860 for the next half century. Law, not charismatic personality or authoritarian edict, was the keystone of his administration. He was more at home with scriptural injunction, humanely interpreted, than he was in the ephemeral realms of doctrinal speculation or the contest for power. Moreover, rejecting the exclusiveness of the Mormon past, he led the Reorganized church in a more cautious, temperate path with regard to mission, gathering, governance, and financial practices. To "bring forth and establish Zion" was still the goal of the church, but his zeal was tempered by a more practical, patient nature, and his belief that "republican institutions must prevail until the coming of Christ."[12] The injudicious urgency for the kingdom in the early church was not part of his experience, and his slower approach to that divine state sometimes frustrated older Saints,[13] but his gentle, democratic manner, his respect for law, common sense, and the individual, and his tolerance for dissent more than compensated for what appeared to be lack of enthusiasm. His followers as a corporate body were not always exactly sure what their beliefs were, and they demonstrated a large degree of wary independence. Perpetually on the edge of confusion and dissent, they required less coercion and more persuasion from leadership. In response, he had to grope his way in the "no-man's-land" between latitudinarianism and authoritarianism, often finding himself reprimanded by Saints from both extremes.

Most of the energy and effort of Joseph III and the early Reorganization was expended in coming to terms with the past, developing coherent internal structures as the movement began to centralize and coalesce, and in creating an identity of its own vis-á-vis Utah Mormonism and the negative press surrounding it. Structurally, there were many problems to be resolved, not the least significant of which included governance, but due to the virulent wariness of the new Restoration constituency, their denouement awaited the twentieth century. Centralized, hierarchicalized lines of authority inherent in Mormonism were left fallow by President Smith as he operated from the more democratic side of theocratic democracy. Remembering Nauvoo and his father's autarchy, he mused that the power of one man—or group of men—to rule would endanger the prosperity of the church collectively and the individual liberty of its members. Power exercised by "supreme authority" did not bring men together; it too often fragmented constituencies rather than causing them to "bend together." Therefore, he upheld "the great truth constantly affirmed by the Book of Mormon that the voice of the people should rule."[14] More specifically

> Every organization, whether general, district, or branch, is greater in its entirety than in any one of its parts and possesses the right to reverse or annul, at will, any procedure instituted by its parts without its consent. . . . Should any departure from this order of procedure be indulged, it is the privilege and duty of the organization to veto the movement of its president, should the movement be considered ill-advised or improper. . . . A presiding officer is the servant of the body over which he presides. His duty is to execute the will of that body and when he is no longer willing to do so, he should resign and thus permit the selection of one who has a better conception of such an official duty.[15]

Even though Joseph III operated from this stance, during the first few years of his administration, the Quorum of Twelve and the bishops watched over the new prophet—by his own recommendation—in order to prevent the "one-man rule" he feared.[16] As time passed and the people matured in their confidence in his leadership, however, the institutional structure slowly began to centralize around the authority of his office and person.[17] When challenged by Apostle Zenas H. Gurley, Jr., to guarantee decentralized church governance in 1885, he and the conference affirmed their deeply rooted Restoration tradition that the seat of power in the institution was the prophetic chair of the Presidency.[18]

He was always willing to concede to the Twelve and the Bishopric their respective missionary and financial responsibilities, the last of which the two temporarily shared in the late nineteenth century.[19] It was the Conference of 1894, however, that demonstrated the balances of power were moving more toward the prophet-executive and away from a temporary power-sharing relationship with the other leading quorum. On April 12 the Conference adopted the report of a Joint Council of the Presidency, Twelve, and Quorum of High Priests which affirmed the following:

> The Presidency is the leading quorum in the church. That the duty of presiding over the church devolves on that quorum. That it is the prerogative of the President to preside over the whole church, to bear the responsibility of the care and oversight of the work of the church in all its different departments; and through the constituted officers of the church in their various callings, according to the laws, rules, and regulations in force and recognized by the church.[20]

It was his prerogative to receive and present to the church that which he deemed to be revelation from God, to interpret and teach the principles of previous revelation, to preside over its councils and "General Assemblies," and to counsel and direct the Twelve, the "second quorum" in importance in the administrative hierarchy.[21] Three days later, he presented to the Conference what he and its members agreed to constitute a message inspired of God which included this statement: "The burden of the care of the church is laid on him [the president] who is called to preside over the high priesthood of the church. . . ."[22] The document absolved the Twelve from any further responsibility to watch over the leader or to cooperate with the Bishopric in teaching and administering the financial laws of the institution.[23]

In an editorial in the *Herald* during the following year President Smith quickly disclaimed any desire to exercise the authoritarian privileges of his office at the expense of the democratic "common consent" that was also part of Restoration heritage. Ideally, he believed that the Saints acting in the duly constituted assemblies of the church possessed "the intuition of the Spirit" that made for unity of purpose in leader and follower alike, personal ambitions, interests or influences to the contrary. Furthermore, if "erroneous misunderstanding" led a conference astray, "divine intervention" guaranteed that a "mistake made by a majority will not be permitted to fatally injure the work for the intended good of the whole."[24] In other words, since the voice of the people was not always the voice of God, theocratic wisdom would protect the institution against the possible excesses of democracy. A few years later he added that theocratic authority had been provided the institution for the uplift of the people to "higher conditions" that could not be reached without knowledge "digested, comprehended, intelligently applied." Every official was but a servant of the "common people" to this end, to prepare them for a careful, thoughtful exercise of the privileges and responsibilities of membership.[25]

His son Frederick agreed that one of the roles of leadership in the church was that of educating the people toward the "higher condition" that would eventually fulfill the spiritual, social, and economic mission of the organization. A person of different tastes and experiences, he did not share his father's patience with the erratic course which that nurturant process often required, nor was he as reluctant to exercise the rights he considered to be his as president of the Reorganization.

The Incipient Authoritarianism of Frederick M. Smith

Fred M. began a thirteen-year apprenticeship for the Presidency of the church when he was ordained as counselor to his father in 1902. As time passed and Joseph III succumbed to blindness and the ravages of ill-health, he learned to rely heavily on the young man he had designated as his successor. Fred M., listening closely to his father's judgment, assumed that responsibility with both confidence and candor.[26]

Much to the consternation of other members of the family and typical of his duties, he opened and read even the most personal of communications to his father. He protested to them that there was "nothing objectionable" in this necessary practice, and added:

> If there is anyone in the Church who has a better right to be close to Father in all matters, even pertaining to his personal mail than I have, I do not know it. I do not concede this right even to his present wife. As his probable successor, I cannot concede to anyone the right to be more closely in touch with his affairs than I.[27]

By the end of the first decade of the century he presided over the conferences of the church in his father's stead, attended to mundane administrative matters as well as to those involving interpretation of its laws, and became thoroughly familiar with the legislative structure of the institution. During the same period, he completed two graduate college degrees, edited the *Herald* and the *Journal of History*, revised tracts, lectured at the Stone Church, served on the board of trustees of Graceland College, the Order of Enoch at Independence and

Lamoni, and the newly formed Independence Sanitarium and Hospital, was a member of myriad committees, and traveled on church business.[28]

The administrative milieu in which Fred M. served his internship was fragmented, lacked a clearly defined and generally accepted organizational integrity, and thus facilitated the semiautonomy of the various bureaucracies in the hierarchical governing structure.[29] Among these, the Twelve and the Bishopric were the most notable. While Joseph III strove for a balance of power among the quorums through the restraint inherent in his more democratic and patient nature,[30] Fred M. preferred tight reins for the restless steeds in the church who chose to gallop in their own directions without the signals or whip from the driver's seat.[31] On occasion, his father would exert the authority of the Presidency to preserve the unity of the church or its evolving patterns of belief;[32] with Fred M. that exertion became his modus operandi as he attempted to rationalize its organizational structure. Given the history and tradition of the Restoration movement, his position was not untenable, but the people and priesthood of the Reorganized church were extremely wary of any person who was blatantly authoritarian.

Fred M. addressed his religious constituency on the topic of "obediency," as early as 1903. When God had given a commission to any person to do a particular work, he asserted, "so long as that person is in discharge of that work, his voice should be obeyed . . . as though it was from the Deity himself."[33] In the army of the Lord, as in any army, policies and decisions were not made by the rank and file but by the general or commander-in-chief. Valiant soldiers obeyed those commanders, even if the orders they received had the appearance of ineptitude or sheer folly.[34] He adamantly concluded that

> you can talk of intelligent obedience all you please; but there comes a time in the life of every man, when he can not rely one moment on his intelligence, nor on his mental force, nor on his reason. There are times in the life of every man when he must be led absolutely by faith, blind faith; and it is then that he renders obedience that makes him truly great in the eyes of the Redeemer. And I would to God that the time would hasten when we, as a people . . . would realize the lessons to be learned from the obedience of Abraham . . . so . . . that we can express the sentiment: "Though he slay me, yet will I trust in him."[35]

To implement his goal of enhancing the power of the Presidency through centralizing the function of the bureaucracy in its office while still his father's counselor, Fred M. instituted a monthly and quarterly reporting system for all church appointees and the officers of stakes, districts, and congregations. Church work often faltered, he assumed, due to "a lack of proper cooperation" of the priesthood on all levels; the new system, he hoped, would help insure that cooperation through the central authority of the institution.[36] His interest was first kindled in this method when, as assistant to the church historian in 1896, he sent a circular letter to members of the Quorum of Twelve, requesting that they collect and forward any items of historical interest to the church archives. William H. Kelley received the circular and a note urging his cooperation and stating "we are *now making history*," and "we should *record* it in such a way that those who follow can know it and use it."[37] In 1903, as one of the Presidency, Fred M. again reminded Apostle Kelley that his quarterly reports were overdue,[38] and four years later, when he responded to the apostle's hyperbolic depiction of the report requirement as "usurpation," he described their responses as mere cavil: "I see no reason why there should be any difficulty or any disposition to think the Presidency is usurping power that does not belong to them, or that they are asking more in the way of reports than they should. . . ."[39] By 1913 he was advising all of the quorums in the church to increase their ministerial efforts and "keep in touch by reports with the First Presidency" regarding their accomplishments, activities, problems, and the conditions of their work.[40] At the Conference of 1914 he spoke briefly, vindicating his reporting system. He had received quarterly reports from all but four of seventy districts. The information he took from these indicated to him a pronounced need to increase spiritual nurture in those districts through additional appointee executives from the presidential office.[41]

Fred M. also postulated that the prerogative of appointing local executives for congregations or districts inhered in the Presidency and no other quorum, and that the missionary efforts of the church were carried forth under its auspices. In another circular letter to the Twelve—a quorum that by tradition had an administrative as well as a missionary investiture of authority in the assigned geographical domain of each—he claimed these prior and preemptive appointive rights for the Presidency. The Council of Twelve was the "second quorum" in authority in the church, not the first. Not only could the Presidency appoint local officers from the "high priests and the eldership" and issue licenses to the same, but they could nominate persons for ordination to the latter clerical responsibility.[42] But, he demurred,

> In stating this opinion we do not intend to give it as the expression of a dictatorial decision, or to infringe upon the rights of either of the quorum possibly affected by the opinion if carried out. . . . We feel at present no disposition to strenuously contend for what we believe to be the rights of the Presidency.[43]

Once he became secure as president of the church after 1915, however, he did begin to "seriously contend" for those rights.

The identity quest of the early years of the RLDS church vis-á-vis Utah Mormonism continued well into the twentieth century and provoked a dilemma for Fred M. as he developed his authoritarian rationale. Debates between the two churches focused on the nature of authority, the theological teachings of Joseph Smith, and the divinity—or lack of it—of polygamy. The latter, although no longer officially practiced in Utah, was productive of more acrimonious dialogue than any other issue. When Reed Smoot, a nonpolygamous Mormon apostle, was sent by the Utah legislature to the United States Senate, the public protest over his seating generated an opportunity for the Reorganized Saints to declare themselves and their faith as separate and distinct from Utah Mormonism.[44] On the Smoot issue, Joseph III found a dangerous principle in "the making of any man's religion a cause of war against him when no overt act of outrage against the laws . . . is alleged or proved,"[45] but he himself was less sanguine about the senator's political value to the nation. Ironic in the perspective of his 1903 sermon on "obedience," he saw Smoot "as supine as a dead body, to be moved at the will of his ecclesiastical superiors. . . and cannot truthfully take the oath of office."[46]

He arrived at these conclusions regarding the Mormon senator and his church from his research into the Mormon movement and personal observations during residences in Utah in the early spring, 1904, and most of the year between the Conferences of 1905 and 1906. His first trip to the Mormon state was ostensibly motivated by his desire to attend the family reunion scheduled for early February, but the second was undertaken by direction of his father to become acquainted with the theological and sociological conditions of the former empire, and to "testify to the truth." Both assumed that the public pressure then exerted on the Mormon hierarchy due to the Smoot investigation by the Senate Committee of Privileges and Elections had caused the members of that faith to become more introspective and critical of themselves and their system, and therefore it seemed to them a propitious time to lay the RLDS claims before the "misled" sheep of the flock.[47]

His first visit was consumed by innocuous exchanges of amenities between the distant members of the family—his "Mormon cousins"—and in establishing a measure of official courtesy. Joseph Fielding Smith, Jr., son of one of the Mormon presidents, became a steadfast friend who guided the Smith family through the historical and scenic attractions of the state, including a stormy excursion on Lake Utah.[48] On Sunday, February 14, he was invited to address the Mormons assembled in their famed tabernacle. Unwilling to offend his hosts at this juncture, he intoned some platitudes about the "great worth" of the truth contained in the Bible, the Book of Mormon, and the Doctrine and Covenants, and urged all to seek these "precious jewels." He could not ascertain whether the breaches between the two churches would ever be bridged, but he expressed confidence in the divinity of the work instituted by his grandfather and pledged to advance its cause.[49]

By the summer of 1905, the beginning of his mission of reconnaissance and kerygma for his own church, he had formed stronger conclusions and had internalized the rather attenuated arguments of his father and the Saints of the early Reorganization that his grandfather had never taught or practiced polygamy and that Brigham Young had usurped the leadership of the church from its rightful heir, Joseph Smith III. Further, he proclaimed in the *Salt Lake Tribune* that

> The mission work of my life will be, as has been the mission work of my father before me, to save the good Mormonism, to eradicate what has crept in because of the lusts of the flesh and the weaknesses of mankind, and to make the name of Joseph Smith honorable.[50]

He noted to his brother that this mission was undertaken in the face of tremendous odds, especially the "superstition" of the Mormon people. Members of his own faith were also superstitious, but he cursorily and inaccurately limited their indulgences only to the extent that they "recognized an eternal Father and a martyred Christ."[51]

His initial sortie in the battle against "apostasy" was an open letter from "the Seed of Joseph the Seer" to the people of the Mormon church. Accusations to the effect that the Mormon hierarchy had broken the laws of the country and transgressed the revelations of God filled the document. Mormon bishops, for instance, collected tithes and rendered no accounting to their people; the law of "common consent" was nullified by "high-handed" practices; and, oddly in light of his own protestations of presidential authority, he condemned the president of the church for his exercise of supreme power over the quorums. He warned that the Mormons stood on dangerous ground and, "Unless they shall heed the warning voice calling them to repentance, woe shall come upon them and they shall be scourged," for "The gathering place is appointed, and the Reorganized church is established there."[52] To President Joseph Fielding Smith he wrote a letter of warning and at the same time requested that his distant relative open the churches of Utah to him as the chosen instrument of the Lord, to deliver a message "which is made a duty upon me." Refusal to respond would ensure "dire consequences" to follow; "beware how you reject the call."[53] Joseph Fielding Smith was singularly unimpressed with his Independence cousin's fulminations and refused his demand for Mormon meeting houses in which one of the leaders of the Reorganized church could "misrepresent, abuse, insult, and malign our people and the Church." The ancestry of an "apostate" meant little to the Mormon president, and he, in turn, called on Smith to repent for misrepresenting and betraying the faith of his grandfather by his own refusal to unite with the true church in Utah.[54]

Rankled and self-righteously indignant because of this rejection, and either unconscious of or unconcerned by his own self-contradiction; or momentarily repelled by the absolutism he observed in the Utah hierarchy, the seeds of which he ignored in himself; or, in recognition that absolute power must have its absolute limits, Fred M. proceeded to flail the Utah leaders for their undemocratic and theocratic practices. He found it inconceivable that the Mormon people could bow to domination and accept the excommunication of dissidents or those who candidly expressed an opinion contrary to leadership. Mormon leaders

> have for years been assiduously drilling their people into a state of complete submission to the priesthood of the church, a submission that penetrates into every phase of the lives of their people.[55]

Forced to justify his own authoritarian utterances while simultaneously anathematizing those of the Utah church, Fred M. qualified his concept of "obedience" for his *Herald* readers. The Reorganized church under his father's leadership, he explained, had never demanded "unquestioning obedience" to any directive coming through human agents with purportedly divine unction. Through common consent the Saints possessed the inherent right to weigh, evaluate, or measure against past revelations any priestly statement that might become binding upon them, and accept or reject it through the voice of the people in conference action. He found none of these rights practiced in the Mormon church, but they were very much a part of his own. As a member and leader of the Reorganized church, he affirmed he had never sworn away the right to question anything or anyone who presumed to act or speak in the name of God;[56] God, not man, was sovereign:

> Obedience to God always; but "unquestioning" obedience to men, even though they hold the priesthood, never. Obedience to God and his commands always; but obedience to commands or purported

commands which came through human agencies (agencies in which human liability to error is always present) without first determining them to be in harmony with God's law, never.[57]

And, as Thomas Jefferson would ostensibly find qualitative value in the multitudes of people, Fred M. found in the "multitude of council there is wisdom, and perhaps safety. . . in awaiting for the impulse which must necessarily come from the weight of unanimous opinion."[58] As he matured, however, his appreciation of the "unanimous opinion" lessened while the substantive and procedural temper of his administration became more akin to that of his Mormon rivals than he would ever care to admit.

Before he succeeded to his father's office, the major outlines of his future administration were already clear. He was an authoritarian personality who adhered to the *führer* principle, who valued respectful, obsequent followers, and who wished to centralize the governing structures of his church in himself and his office. Ten years before becoming president he exerted the power of that office over the Quorum of Twelve, a bureaucracy "second" in authority that carefully guarded its autonomy and prerogative. When he initiated his reporting system, he was at the same time declaring that the Presidency oversaw all administrative activities of the church, including that of the Twelve. Moreover, his exercise of the Presidency's right to nominate local officials without the concurrence of the Twelve adumbrated the larger contests between him and that quorum from 1917 to 1922.

Cognizant of his son's talents, abilities, authoritarian proclivities, and the possibly insuperable tasks that were before him, Joseph III imparted to him what would be his last words of counsel from his deathbed on Sunday, November 29, 1915. He praised his son's strength and said he was thankful that God had provided for the church "one whose hands will not slip on the rein, nor tremble in the emergency."[59] But at the same time he urged him to exercise patience and restraint in his relationship with members and fellow workers:

> If the people are heady, if the church is heady, the eldership are heady and take the reins in their hands as they have done a little, especially on the rules and regulations . . . don't worry . . . let it pass, let the church take the consequences and they will after a while grow out of it. . . . It's better that way than to undertake to force them and coerce. That would bring bad trouble.[60]

Fred M. listened to his father but did not hear; to "let it pass" was to acknowledge defeat, lose the initiative, and dissipate his vision of the kingdom. Great men, after all, imposed their personalities and will on their political, social, or economic environments with an indelible stamp and redirected them into newer, perhaps improved, channels. Never a personality given to self-abnegation or defeatism, in the ensuing years he created circumstances in which he would put himself and the church to the test: would the church accept the centralized, authoritarian, bureaucratic system he envisioned, or would it be content to flounder while his mutinous crew haggled over direction? For him the answer was clear, and for the next eleven years the "bad trouble" foreseen by his father plagued his administration, fragmented, while it also streamlined the institution, and confirmed his anticipation that duty was a "relentless taskmaster."[61]

Whether it was civil or ecclesiastical, obedience to law was the filter of progress through which Fred M. viewed his nation and his religious institution. Fundamentally, law was the accumulation of rights and regulations derived from nature, God, or human traditions and embodied in statutory form.[62] To support his view he often referred to the statement on civil governance adopted by the early Restoration and reaffirmed in the Reorganization:

> We believe that governments were instituted of God for the benefit of man, and that he holds men accountable for their acts in relation to them, either in making laws or administering them, for the good and safety of society.
>
> We believe that no government can exist, in peace, except such laws are framed and held inviolate as will secure to each individual the free exercise of conscience, the right and control of property, and the protection of life.[63]

Government was the instrument of law that God had bestowed on humans for their own edification, and when its structure, spirit, and necessary leaders were acceded due respect, order, peace, and progress followed, all of which were Fred M.'s highest values for civil society. In the area of religion, that "parallel institution of divinity," obedience to laws and officers were no less required of loyal followers.[64] Disobedience to law and disrespect for duly constituted authority were the twin companions of decadence and social disorganization he saw in the first third of the twentieth century, especially in the twenties. In the context of that decade he again enjoined his followers to learn the lessons of obedience.[65]

If we have learned the lesson in the past and forgotten it, let us learn it anew. Obedience to law, natural; it will preserve our health. Obedience to law, divine; it will lead us onward and upward to the goal of our high calling in Jesus Christ. Obedience to law, statutory; it has been placed on the statute books by conscientious men in the interests of religion, in the interests of morality, in the interests of safety of the Government. Give obedience, knowing that therein alone has the fulfillment of the will of God and the coming of his Kingdom on earth.[66]

He pled, however, for compliance not motivated by fear of coercion but more by the "intellectual solidarity" of an informed, responsible citizenry.[67]

His sermons were heavily laced with denunciations of those "would-be leaders" who promulgated "dangerous doctrines" of license hidden under the guise of democracy, freedom, or "personal liberty."[68] Even George Washington, he wrote, feared for the welfare of his country when he considered the dangers of "so-called" democratic elements to society.[69] Those he questioned most were the ones whose lawlessness was ensconced in the "glamour of glorified rebellion," and "the so-called principle of 'consent of the governed,' or 'common consent.'"[70] Among the results of uncontrolled democracy were

governments in turmoil, breaking overnight, changing with a frequency and rapidity which is baffling to . . . students. . . . The forces of political dissolution seem everywhere at work . . . through the avenues of discontent. Established leaderships are overturned or struggling against untoward forces. Would-be leaders are augmenting the spirit of restlessness by denouncing present orders. They would ride to power on the wave of discontent, failing to recognize that any institution established on disloyalty is a house built on sand.[71]

Moral, social, industrial, and political "safety" was firmly based in respect for authority and that implied restriction on some degrees of personal liberty; otherwise, "dire consequences" were sure to ensue, for "law is based on authority, and disrespect for authority breeds disobedience to law, and disobedience to law spells social dissolution."[72]

Furthermore, his own understanding of church government led him to the conclusion that attacks on its legitimately "called" and ordained superior officers in the name of free speech and democracy were utterly wrong. Once laws or regulations were accepted by the Conference "every honest-hearted, well-intentioned, and whole-souled Latter Day Saint ought to . . . distinguish between the right to oppose a thing before it has become a law and to protest against it after it has become law."[73] Democracy in the church could function successfully only when the people were in agreement on the fundamentals and could present a "solid front" to the much broader and more insidious enemies of humanity.[74]

One particular barrier to that solid front was rooted in what he thought was a misconception of the role of democracy in the church which resulted in the "over-organization" or diffusion of authority in unclear bureaucratic lines in its hierarchy. As he told G. Stanley Hall:

> In my experience as an executive (not a wide one, I admit) I have learned to appreciate the great hindrance to progress which lies in over-organization with its concomitant of "red tape", and the remedy, as I see it, is found only in the autocratization of authority with fundamentality of "constitution" and simplicity of by-laws . . . My experience of being held back in the development of our work by the "democracy" of our annual conferences has aroused an alertness on the question of over-organization.[75]

What he meant by the "autocratization" of authority was centralization of power in the executive for greater efficiency in passing from the "selfishness" of the present to the altruistic kingdom of the future. "If Zion is to be established," he said, "it is going to demand a strongly centralized government. . . . I would like to burn that into the heart of every Latter Day Saint. It is going to take a strongly centralized government."[76]

He cautioned members to justly distinguish between that centralization and what they were quick to label as "despotism." It was a Latter Day Saint tradition for the executive to allocate power through various agents under his jurisdiction subject to their approval in conference action. As long as the people themselves decided what laws they were compelled to obey and could veto any arbitrary act of the president by a simple majority vote not to sustain said officer in his calling, despotism seemed an impossibility to him. The people always had the final word. This "recall" power of the conference was much more effective than that functioning on the state level in the political world. No petition was necessary to remove a general officer, nor was he allowed to appeal to a court for "just cause." Simply, Fred M. said, he would be required to yield to the will of the body, and "you would not need to suffer very long until off would come his official head."[77] Thus, he advised his followers:

> If you cannot trust your President, silence him. You can do it without filing charges and he has no recourse. . . . It is your privilege and duty not to sustain . . . if you think the interests of the work are jeopardized. But so long as they remain in office, the supreme rights of the executive arm of the church lie in the Presidency.[78]

He could safely advise members of their recall prerogatives because he knew that in all probability they would never successfully exercise them against him. More than anyone, he was acutely aware that the traditions of the institution were centered in the "prophetic" office which he occupied. To the *majority* of its people, he was God's mouthpiece, grandson of the founder of the faith, "called" by revelation to guide the church and the faithful to the kingdom, and for those reasons alone he received their basic loyalty and support, dissenters notwithstanding.

Smith conceived of his role as president of the church as an authoritarian one, the power of which was derived from the very fact of its acceptance by the membership, and the efficacy of which was determined by their recognition and loyalty. Reciprocally, this "philosopher-king" was the visionary for the direction of the institution, the teacher who educated his people toward the kingdom and the chief executive—not simply the administrator—of the laws that could produce that desired effect.[79] From the perspective of a recent student of his administration, Smith considered himself to be an altruistic "statesman of the Reorganization," a "selfless man who had been given the authority to speak with the understanding as leader, prophet, and seer."[80]

One of the vehicles for authoritarian expression of which he availed himself while leader of the church was the concept and practice of plenary revelation. Originating in the early church and institutionalized by the Reorganization, the acceptance of official presidential statements as the epiphanous voice of God to the people by their majority vote was a persisting tradition throughout the history of the movement. His father had presented seventeen instructional briefs treating doctrine or changes in the personnel of the higher bureaucracies before the Conferences of the church, and Fred M. was called to the Presidency as his father's successor by this very process.[81] In his own institutional leadership career he used revelatory documents and other sacrosanct procedural and substantive traditions of the church to guide it in the directions he thought proper. He attempted to imbue the experience of revelation with a modicum of intellectual sophistication by treating it as an aspect of the ecstatic and erethetic states which were the foundational themes of his Ph.D. dissertation,[82] and he chose not to limit the means by which that enlightenment would be received or expressed. As he proclaimed before a Conference:

> If thou, O God, art desirous of revealing thy will to us, or to me, be it far from me to say how. If it be that thou desirest to write across the arch of thy heaven those words that thou shalt see fit to transmit to thy people, then give me the wisdom to read. Or if thou dost choose to manifest thy power in the thunderous tones that thou art capable of giving, so that they will ring through all the arch of heaven, let my ears be open. Or if, in the still, small voice that comes from within, thou shalt choose to reveal thy will to me, then let thy Spirit attune my spiritual ear to the reception of thy word. Or if thou dost choose to utilize those powers with which thou hast by nature endowed me, quickened by thine own processes of development, to transmit through them the message that thou hast to give to thy people, then my pen shall be ready. Or if thou dost choose to bathe my soul in thy Spirit until my spiritual vision shall behold what thou dost desire thy people to accomplish, even then shall I endeavor as thy instrument to transmit the message to the people.[83]

Like his father, he also expected that a "pervasive inspiration" would attest to the validity of his message as it was scrutinized by the duly constituted councils and conferences of the church and compel the cooperation of disparate interest groups or individuals.[84]

On April 5, 1916, he presented the first of what would be several "revelatory" statements of his career, assuaging some of the latent fears of his colleagues and followers at the Conference that "our President was too much given to education."[85] Similar to most of his subsequent directives, this one was contextual, instructing the church to release Presiding Bishop E. L. Kelley, its aging financial officer, and replace him with Benjamin R. McGuire,[86] a New York lawyer and financier whose name had titillated his mind as an obvious choice because of his successful business career.[87] Further, he entreated the members to have confidence in their leaders, for the "hastening time" now demanded "great activity" and the consecration of "talents, abilities and substance."[88]

He consistently importuned the conferences, councils, and quorums in this manner throughout his administrative career. When the support he desired was not immediately forthcoming, he assumed a position of extreme distance and uneasy silence while the "prophetic voice" was subjected to the democratic scrutiny of those he felt could make elephantine the most embryonic of issues.[89] He bristled inwardly and resented the omnipresent "carping critics" who were quick to accuse him of usurpation when he led, or of neglect when he withdrew from confrontation. Equally disturbing to him were those who assailed his programs from conference floors, in church periodicals or by the virulence of rumor.[90] To him, rumormongers were guilty of the sin of "false witness" and in dire need of repentance for their destructive acts.[91] He did not understand, chose to ignore, or wanted to rescind the longstanding tradition of dissent in the Reorganized church. That institution had been built by those who were sensitive to abuses of power they saw in the early Restoration and in Utah, and who were determined to avoid those circumstances in the new church. His father accommodated and encouraged their "guardianship," but Fred M. did not. When heavily pressed, he often equated the "heady" spirit of the Saints against which his father had warned him as one of dissent and disloyalty directed against himself and his programs for the church,[92] and in frustrated lamentation prayed, "How long, oh Lord, how long before your people will wake up. . . . Have we yet learned obedience by the things we have suffered?"[93] In less pressured instances he realized that all leaders lived perpetually in the "white light of publicity,"[94] and the concomitant dilemmas of that exposure were the "whip for the back" of those who sought to exercise power responsibly.[95] One such dilemma for him appeared in his "jottings" in this fashion:

> If as an officer I mix freely with the people, then there appears the danger of the adage. . . familiarity breeds contempt. If on the other hand I hold myself aloof, the danger confronts me that people, because they do not know me, will give credence to the rumors and tales started without ground.[96]

In sermon, treatise, and revelation, Fred M. propounded an official resolution for this condition: "Let contention cease."[97]

It was a rare moment when he broke his official silence and responded directly to the critics of his alleged noisome and oracular tendencies. Exasperated by the invective and innuendo that permeated the Conference of 1922, on December 3 he vented his frustrations in a sermon treating the "essentiality of loyalty" at the Stone Church in Independence. In this gambit he expressed wonder that such a faction-ridden institution so pervasively skeptical of its leadership could serve the kingdom-producing purposes for which it had been established. To him there was no more effective weapon in "Satan's hand" than the "self-appointed leaders"[98] who, reminiscent of the elephant in Aesop's *Fables*, strained at a gnat, broke its leg, and was eaten by a lion.

Fred M. agreed with his adversaries that the church would survive without the presence of his own "royal family," but he steadfastly maintained his position that strong executive leadership was necessary for direction and effective labor. Fealty to the cause and to those who were made responsible for it was mandatory if the church was to approximate its mission, and "that loyalty can consistently and justly be demanded by those who are carrying the burden of standing as representatives of Christ and taking the responsibility of working in this organization." He asked when Christ returns, "will he find on the earth a body of people loyal to his ideals and organization, following those leaders that have been placed in a position of responsibility?"[99] He reiterated his theme of obedient loyalty:

> There are times when people must follow a leader not blindly, but with a faith so sublime that they will be able to say, "I do not see all the steps that are required of me according to the plans of this leader, but from the exercise of all the powers of observation God has given me, from the exercise of all the degrees of spirituality that I

can call to my command, I, in analyzing the program, can reach no other conclusion than that the leader is leading us toward our goal; therefore I will follow." That takes loyalty; that takes courage. . . . That does not mean that you are placing blind faith or confidence in me. That simply is. . . your own exercise of faith.[100]

He concluded the sermon by affirming that his authority was derived from the fact of his acceptance by the people of the church. A prophet leader was accepted by the common consent of his constituents in response to the investive revelation of God, and the inspiration thus provided the leader by the prayerful support of the people conditioned the quality of his leadership, often enabling him to transcend their own limited vision: "And if your leaders are supposed to know the way a little bit better than you do. . . can you trust them? There is your application of practical loyalty."[101]

In April, 1924, he made his position on church governance quite clear in a document drafted for a Joint Council of the Presidency, the Twelve, and the Bishopric. He restated that the church created by Joseph Smith was indeed a "theocratic-democracy" and that its government was carried out by "divine authority through priesthood." Its beneficent purpose of bettering human conditions was achieved with the "common consent" of the people, and as such it was a "divine government among the people, for the people, and for the glory of God. . . ." Moreover, God directed the church through the "clearly indicated channels" of leadership to which the assenting voice of the people must be appended.[102] But, to

effect the purposes of the church, effective administration is imperative, and organic solidarity is maintained only by effective discipline. . . strongly enough administered to prevent the purposes of the organization from being frustrated by individual caprice and rebellion. Authority to be effective must be respected.[103]

Lastly, he noted that there existed "grades of official prerogative and responsibility" in the organization, but the court of last resort, the *supreme directional control* of the church rested in the "chief and first quorum" of the Presidency.[104] Although this was poor wording to describe his theory of governance, supreme directional control was his way of depicting the locus of authority necessary to efficient administration. He believed that this power was lodged by church law in his office for quick dispatch of prophetic and legislative fiat in harmony with "divine command" and for smooth coordination of all its departments, programs, and policies.[105]

After nearly a decade of struggle with quorums and conferences, he would ask the Conference of 1925 to decide which was more important to them: the democracy and autonomy of the early Reorganization, or the authority and centralization of the longer-standing Restoration tradition that he wished to reassert. The opposite of his father, Fred M. consciously chose to operate from the more theocratic side of theocratic democracy, labeled that choice as a forward-looking reform within his institution, and made *himself* the real issue before his people and the quorums. He could have continued his father's policy of accommodation with the more democratic elements in the church, but in his view of the nature of the institution— and of society at large—democracy was equated with inertia and inefficiency, while centralized power was dynamic, based in expertise, and efficient. If power was "autocratized" in his office, he sincerely believed he could then lead his people and priesthood into more orderly ranks for a march to the kingdom.

The Presidency and the Quorum of Twelve, 1917-1922

In December, 1916, firmly in the seat of the Presidency, his formal preparation terminated by his Ph.D. degree, Fred M. embarked on a course to make his institution functionally efficient. He asked the church to prepare for readjustments necessary to meet new conditions that might be disturbing.[106] His initial confrontation to set in order what he conceived to be the ragged bureaucracy of the institution came with the Quorum of Twelve and represented a continuity of his earlier attempts to exert the authority of the Presidency over their traditions and prerogatives.

To the Twelve who were assembling for their pre-Conference meetings in March, he forwarded a letter in which he requested them to channel all information regarding administrative or personnel changes to his office for suggestions before acting.[107] What he essentially required was that all general officers of the church serve under the administrative direction of his office. As the presiding body of the institution before Joseph III became its first president in 1860, and his special watchdog until the revelation and council of 1894, the Twelve had long accustomed themselves to bureaucratic semiautonomy. Although they acceded to the Presidency as counselor and leader, their basic concern centered in the question in the magnitude and the detail of his direction.[108]

By tradition and practice, the apostles considered their individual authority to encompass both missionary and administrative leadership of the geographic areas over which they presided. Fred M. did not concur with their interpretation of apostolic responsibility. Instead, in order to insure more efficient use of their proselytizing potential he wanted them to confine their efforts to the missionary fields only—and that under his own executive guidance. "Out of respect to custom I have been slow to make changes in their work," he claimed, but by the Conference of 1917, he sensed a need to intensify and accelerate the release of creative institutional energy. Thus, the quorum must be "left free to functionalize . . . in carrying into effect the executive policies of the Presidency upon whom is cast the responsibility of the work in all the world."[109] He also sketched before the Conference his plans to reorganize the entire mission field of the church by changing boundaries, extending the demarcation between local administration and missionary work, stressing competency and specialization, and reducing the number of stipendaries. In all, *"the standard of efficiency will be raised."*[110] For him, the energies and resources of the church could be both conserved and systematically maximized through

> compactness of organization with increase of labor, if there is consecration of talent and energy with the coordination of effort found in unity of purpose. And this means that somewhere there shall be a well-recognized directional force.[111]

The Twelve temporarily acquiesced to his "directional force," but not without questioning his administrative wisdom for the next two years. In their preconference quorum meetings in the winter and spring of 1919, their questions changed to expressions of dissatisfaction with their new status and open protest against his administrative reorganization. They agreed that some modifications in the old system were urgently needed, but they preferred that they originate in joint discussion between themselves and the Presidency,[112] not by executive fiat or in the declarations of the Standing High Council. On February 11 they began a series of meetings to consider their reservations regarding President Smith's desire for hegemony over their missionary organization and administrative procedures. They agreed that their deference to him was experimental only and not even that had been ratified by a written document. Furthermore, they judged the experiment a failure and forwarded a resolution to him stating their opinion that the entire missionary field should function under their own supervision administratively. Citing appropriate scriptural authority, they argued that under the concurrent interaction of the Twelve and the Presidency the mission field should be divided into sections over which an apostle presided, and that officer's authority should extend to both the administrative and missionary work of the church, whether local or general. As well, each officer had the power to appoint and direct the missionary corps of his area, region, or district.[113] Essentially, they argued that these prerogatives were theirs by right and not derived from the Presidency.

Not to be gainsaid, Fred M. expressed his consternation with the independent action of the Twelve in this matter and declared that their conclusions and recommendations had lost sight of the "proper perspective of the provisions of the law" that placed on him the burden of responsibility for the direction of church work.[114] In late February he summoned a Joint Council of the Presidency, Twelve, and Presiding Bishopric to treat these issues and settle their differences. The council resolved little, however; in fact, it widened the rift between the emerging antagonists. Among other questions considered was one dealing with foreign missions generally and a Palestinian mission specifically. President Smith had earlier suggested the formulation of a mission of select, educated, and dedicated Saints to that area, and the apostles' criticism of this proposition at the council caused him no little irritation. They considered the move ill-advised until the disruptive effects of World War I in that geopolitical area were allayed by the Versailles Peace Conference and its "political, economic and social composition" secured by the British government. They also challenged his allegation of inspirational "light" for this program in the absence of any revelatory document prepared by him to be considerd by the usual process of "common consent" in councils, quorums, and General Conference. Indignant and hurt by evident lack of trust and what he styled as insubordination, he dismissed the council.[115]

The apostles continued their traditional quorum sessions, however, and turned their attention to financial questions, especially to those expenditures the president incurred which they considered to be possibly excessive. From figures provided by the bishop, they summarized the expenditures of fifteen church leaders, those of the Presidency included, and found President

Smith's to be substantially higher than any other.[116] Thereupon they requested that he provide a proper accounting to them by the first of March. He flatly refused, and informed them that they were exceeding the bounds of their authority and propriety. Such examinations, he believed, could be requested and received only by members of the Presiding Bishopric, and to them only would he respond.[117]

President Smith was not inclined to solve his outstanding differences with the Twelve in a special council composed of what they described as quorums of "concurrent jurisdiction" whose findings would be submitted to the Conference. The apostles, then, recognizing that he was "disinclined to take a reasonable course," decided to take the issues directly to the Conference for legislative action. On March 15 he relented and called another Joint Council to try again to deal with their outstanding differences and conduct business as usual. One of the business items that surfaced there concerned the marital difficulties of a church appointee that President Smith brought before the council for action. Since the evidence in question was "ex parte" only, the council declined action and referred the case to the Presidency for further investigation and report. Late in the session, Fred M. accused one of the council members of betraying the confidential nature of this "family trouble," and the accused rejoined with a charge of undignified domestic interference against the president. As a result of this altercation he told the council and the Twelve that he would no longer meet with either of them as long as the offender remained in that body.[118] In such an instance, "disorder" in its higher ranks, church law required that special joint councils of the Presidency, the Twelve, and the Seventy be called to deal with the "emergency,"[119] but Fred M. refused to comply.

By the time the Conference of 1919 convened, members of the Twelve had affirmed willingness to "do our part...but we decline to permit the power and responsibility of the calling we have received to be neutralized by any autocratic or dictatorial conduct of any one man." Further,

> Inasmuch as the sources of power in the Christian Church are reason and conscience, we advise respectfully that our consent to such policies, no matter from whom originating can have our endorsement only when they meet with the approval of such reason and conscience we possess. We indignantly protest against reflections upon the members of the Quorum...as to create doubt about their integrity and honor.[120]

While the Twelve thus formulated and stated their position, President Smith secluded himself in a small, central Missouri town to meditate and prepare for the battle he anticipated to continue in early April.[121]

On April 6, 1919, he addressed the delegates of the General Conference who had assembled in the Brick Church of Lamoni, Iowa. There he outlined the problems between himself and the Twelve and expressed his acute awareness of what he considered to be the paradox of his leadership:

> We are loud in proclaiming the identity of our organization with that of the Master, but reluctant in furnishing the working confidence necessary for the personnel of official organization to properly function. To lustily and even feelingly sing, "We thank thee O God for a prophet to guide us in these latter days," is easy, but to furnish the warm, living flesh and blood of confidence and support to the skeleton of our organization is more than a matter of music.

To hail the leader in glad acclaim is somewhat at variance with the process of fettering him for fear he will lead astray.[122]

He went on to describe his major points of contention with the Twelve. It was an "open secret" that an *entente cordiale* no longer permeated relations between those quorums and that a series of insults from the Twelve had terminated all possibilities of accommodation. The apostles' "distinctly reactionary attitude" had turned their faces toward "old conditions" wherein they trusted their own judgment rather than that of their leader and his broader vision. He protested no qualms with the legislative functions of the Twelve and even acknowledged their equality to the Presidency in that function; but, in the line of administration he considered them subordinate to himself or his counselors in all respects, including missionary and local organizational endeavors.[123] In addition, he categorically declared himself to be

opposed to the old system of dividing the world up into fields, each to be presided over by an apostle. This policy, pursued up to two years ago, has made of the Twelve a body of individualists, without a unified policy either in local or missionary work, and some of our present difficulties are due to this wrong system.

The work of the Twelve is immediately under the direction of the First Presidency without field appointment as of old, to go as sent . . . into foreign and new domestic fields to open up and organize the work, and with frequent change and shifting, until out of their common experience in harmony with the First Presidency, a common unified missionary policy, domestic and foreign, can be developed—something the Quorum of Twelve has not had in my memory.[124]

To be adequate to the missionary tasks that he had planned for Europe, the Near East, the South Pacific, and Latin America he further asserted that "systematic, scientific and rational preparation" was uniformly necessary. He believed that "a man's education should not be held against him," and in order to develop a "broader mental culture . . . especially among the ministry" he urged that "select" missionaries be brought together at Graceland College for training in the languages, history, and social political institutions of the peoples to whom they would be sent, and in the doctrines of the church. And all this required centralized direction and policy.[125]

Change toward this more centralized, efficient administration, he continued, was vital to the progress of the church and violated none of its sacrosanct principles or dogma. While many well-intended adversaries had hastily branded him a heretic or a reckless reformer,[126] he disavowed the titles, placed himself thoroughly and completely in the Restoration tradition of leadership and put the question to his followers: "Is your leader, your president, to be a real executive or a mere receiver of reports?"[127] He cited his years of preparation to qualify for the office of president and his zealous service in that position as evidence of his loyalty and dedication. Along with other Saints he was required to meet external opposition, "sneers, and even ridicule," but the particularly withering criticism coming from alleged friends and supporters *within* the institution for the last year was "to ask too much." Compromise seemingly impossible and accommodation with "reaction" unthinkable, he concluded with a recommendation that the Conference select another leader in whom it could have implicit and explicit confidence. He then presented his resignation to shocked delegates.[128]

As secretary for the Twelve, John Rushton read a brief prepared by his quorum restating the issues as they understood them,[129] and then the entire matter was referred by Conference action to a Joint Council of the Presidency, the Twelve, and the Seventy. Having tendered his resignation, Fred M. had no inclination to participate in these sessions that could possibly exacerbate the pain of existing wounds, but his counselor Elbert A. Smith agreed to be his representative and present his statement to the Twelve alone for their consideration.[130] This statement, with a few minor modifications, became the "working agreement" between these contending units in the church hierarchy and was basically a victory for Fred M. In the facedown his resignation caused the apostles to blink first. What they regarded as unwarranted interference in their affairs was the lesser burden when compared to the rootlessness and insecurity that would be the concomitants of a leaderless institution while they waited for another to succeed Fred M.

The agreement that the quorums ratified and presented to the delegates for action on April 15 categorically stated, "The work of the Twelve is under the direction of the Presidency in the administrative or executive work of the church both in missionary and local lines." No longer were they to be appointed to specific fields as individuals; the Presidency decided where and to whom they were sent, for what purposes, and the length of appointment. Once local organization was effected by the missionary corps of the church, local leaders, not the missionaries or the Twelve, were in charge of their operations. Also, some of the Twelve were to be "near if not at the seat of the Presidency" for consultation and advice at all times, and candidates for missions were to be cleared by the interaction of the Presidency, Twelve, and Bishopric, either through "concurrence" or "joint council."[131] The delegates approved the document unanimously and moved on to an item of greater concern to them: the resignation of their president.

In spite of the fact that some of the Saints were quick to criticize Fred M. for his ideas, his personality, or his obstinacy, he was still of "the seed of the prophet" Joseph Smith, Jr., chosen by revelation; thus his words or wishes were not taken lightly. Most of his followers were truly aggrieved by his resignation—a fact of which he could not have been unaware—but he did not consciously avail himself of its influence simply to manipulate or coerce them, even though that was its ultimate effect. His exasperation with the lack of cooperation of his subordinates and what he considered as their misguided, myopic tendencies for democracy and decentralized power had finally triumphed over his patience, and he was determined to extricate himself from his discomfort.[132] After he left its chamber, the Conference voted not to accept his resignation and further declared in a resolution that "by this vote we express our confidence in him as prophet, seer, and revelator to the church and as the President thereof."[133]

To comfort those whose faith had been shaken by the "forensic encounter" in which alleged servants of God had bitterly assailed each other, President Smith again addressed the Conference. For this purpose he asserted "it is not without design that God intends that these hours of trial to our faith shall come, for faith, like everything else that is genuine, is enhanced by the processes of refinement." Furthermore, "those whose faith is disturbed by seeing the man beneath the cloak of the servant are those who perhaps will be continuously subjected to this trial of faith." He begged their indulgence for his own humanity and voiced a hope that the "directional influence of God and his peace" would characterize the future of the Saints in their mission.[134]

Peace with the Twelve proved to be a chimeric truce that dissipated under fire. While the Conference of 1920 passed with very few volleys of quorum dissent as President Smith replaced two of the Twelve and advised that "contention cease,"[135] the interquorum quarrels over jurisdiction, programs, and administration emerged again shortly afterward. He determined to settle this standing dispute, and on October 2, 1922, presented to the Conference a revelation which provided for the release of four members of that quorum and the selection of six others he hoped would be more amenable to his program to succeed them and fill the vacancy of two.[136] After protracted debate and discussion, the final tally of 656 to 452[137] gave him the majority support he sought, but it also reflected significant dissatisfaction with the temper of his administration among both membership and priesthood. Not merely the expression of a few erratic cranks, the 40 percent negative vote represented the official dissent of the many who read church laws differently and voiced their opinion from conscience rather than pique. Some of these accepted the Conference decision with resolute dignity. John Rushton, the most articulate of the Twelve, accepted its new members magnanimously and justified his earlier opposition to President Smith as "a matter of conscience, the deepest kind." But now, he said, "the battle is over. This people has spoken. *Vox Populi, vox Dei* is the essential principle of our parliamentary rule of the government of common consent."[138]

Others, however, were not content with the results of the Conference and continued to attempt to circumscribe what they considered to be a much too centralized ecclesiastical structure. The Quorums of Seventy, for example, as allies of the Twelve, asked the delegates and ex-officios to postpone the expenditure of any funds for projects other than those of a specifically missionary nature and even those to be allocated under the close scrutiny of a Joint Council of the Presidency, Bishopric, and Seventy. His voice edged with iron, President Smith answered that "not even if this Conference orders it and I am directed to present to the body first will I obey such an order." The Conference could not tread on his executive prerogatives. After a short period of discussion the resolution was tabled as that legislative body again acquiesced to the president.[139]

At the conclusion of this long and particularly demanding Conference, Fred M. confessed:

> My hopes in the accomplishment of the goal of the church are not so bright as they were, but perhaps with the passing of the clouds the sun may shine on that goal once more. I frankly confess that my zeal has been greatly dampened, but even that may be warmed up. But if it be warmed up it will be necessary for me to feel that I have the united support of the ministry of this church. I plead for it. I think I am entitled to it.[140]

With this statement the Conference ended, but questions regarding his directional authority over the other quorums of the church were not resolved, and the "united support" for which he pleaded was not forthcoming.

Like a corporate director, President Smith was repelled by the inertia and dysfunction he detected in the church. From his perspective the business of the institution was to save individual souls and to build the kingdom of God, and he resolved to make it functionally efficient to meet the demands of that mission. Even though the church recognized its president/prophet as head of the organization and its priesthood, the powers of that office were limited in practice by hierarchialized, semiautonomous bureaucracies. Fred M. was extremely frustrated by these circumstances, and he found the Twelve especially provincial—more concerned with prerogative than mission. By tradition, apostles exercised administrative and missionary powers in the areas they assigned themselves in consultation with the Presidency, but he believed that combination of responsibilities diluted their expertise in mission—the prime reason for which they had been called into service—wasting their talents and using manpower inefficiently.

From his purview of church history and his confidence in scientific management as a key to progress, President Smith was convinced that he was right; therefore he initiated moves to "subordinate" the apostles. He wanted them to concentrate solely on the art of spreading the gospel and developing missions, leaving the administration of established areas to the local, unpaid ministers who would fall under his own administrative umbrella. In connection with more direct attention to their "office and calling," he wanted them to expand their work into the broader world and develop a trained, modern, missionary corps through the use of the educational facilities of Graceland College. Most significant, he said it was urgent for them to accede to a "well recognized directional force." That force, similar to the corporate executive, had broader vision, transcended petty interests, and wisely allocated resources and manpower.

While he viewed this "autocratization" of power in his office as a positive reform, the apostles considered it the germinal point of tyranny, destructive of their freedoms and long-standing traditions. Furthermore, they considered his plans for world mission not only too extravagant for the meager resources of the church but injudicious in timing and scope. The mission he contemplated for Palestine, for example, they found inpropitious in the years immediately following World War I. They were also aware that he knew less about local problems than they, and they reacted negatively to his desire for a "college trained" missionary corps. For them, ministry was a product of the "spirit," not the intellect. When they opposed him in council and conference, an adversarial relationship between the quorums ensued, and he defeated them by resorting to the existing leverage of his office: his willingness to step down as president/prophet in 1919, and his use of revelation to release and replace members of the offending quorum in 1922.

Although he won the battles, perhaps he lost more than he gained in achieving his goals. The fear of presidential tyranny became less hypothetical to the 40 percent of the delegates who voted not to ratify his revelation at the Conference of 1922, the Twelve were acquiescent but not obsequent, and what was worse for the president, his institution was no more efficient than before the contest. The issue of his directional authority over the Twelve and other quorums, cojoined with growing antipathy for his centralized social, economic, and organizational programs, smoldered for the next three years.

Administrative Centralization, 1916 to 1920

While the power struggles between the Presidency and the other leading quorums of the church were the most spectacular of his efforts to centralize the administrative structure of his institution, Fred M. found that his attempts to organize the Center Place into stakes and departmentalize the "general auxiliaries" of the larger church organization were equally significant. Because Independence was the showcase for the church and the nucleus of Zion, he wanted it directly under his administrative control in order to personally oversee the education of its priesthood, select its key officers, and formulate cohesive plans for mission and stewardship. Beyond this, the special church-wide organizations for women, youth, and religious education were uncoordinated, acted independently of each other and the Presidency, and often overlapped in their jurisdiction or duplicated services. From his perspective this situation was an example of the gross inefficiency he wished to eliminate in the church, and he proposed to centralize their policies, coordinate their efforts, and integrate their programs through his own indirect managerial powers.

As per his request in 1916, the Conference divided the Center Place into three separate administrative stakes for the areas of Independence, Kansas City, and Holden, Missouri. The nucleus of the Independence Stake was to be the First Independence Branch, and the stake president would be its chief presiding officer, appointed by Fred M. to supervise all other stakes and congregation work and forward copiously detailed reports of all its functions, activities, and programs. Each congregation in the stake was required to call monthly priesthood meetings calculated to systematically improve the caliber of local ministry and to contribute to *Unity*, the stake publication initiated for the same purpose. Later, in order to continue to upgrade their ministry, he insisted that all ordained men attend the Presidency's weekly instruction on Sunday afternoons. By 1920 he ascertained that the Independence Stake had qualitatively evolved to the point at which it could be declared the official church headquarters, over which he and the Presiding Bishopric could assume outright control.[141]

He had long believed that the various bureaucracies and departments of the church should be "clustered around the Presidency's office" in order to insure proper interrelationship and efficient operation.[142] At the onset of his administration the church auxiliaries such as the General Sunday School Association, Zion's Religio for the youth, and the Women's Auxiliary for Social Service functioned semiautonomously, and with the exception of annual activity reports, chose their own officers and managed their own affairs external to the Presidency and the Conference.[143] The Women's Auxiliary, for example, reported to the Conference of 1916 the meetings and accomplishments of its ancillary departments of Home and Child Welfare, Literature and Education, Domestic Science, Eugenics and Social Hygiene, listed sixty-four locals and an enrollment of 1,111, and stressed the importance of moral education of the children of the church.[144] He applauded their "fine efforts," but he found that the duplication of their program by the Religio and the Sunday School Association a wasteful dissipation of energy. From his angle of vision this independent status and diffusion of power smacked of inefficiency and cried aloud for the coordination that could be realized only by "closer executive supervision of their work by the Presidency."[145] Basically, he postulated:

> When we outline the aim of each department and then gather them up into an ensemble, we have a fulfillment of the subject which has been given to us showing the unifications of our various aims. . . . This pronouncement or thesis of the unity of our purposes presages a belief in divine telesis, the existence of a creative plan, well formulated and well conceived from the beginning and the activities of mankind and the universe directed towards consummation of that great plan in the end. It is the efficacy of the gospel to save mankind.[146]

In other words, God liked cohesiveness, unity, coordination, order, and centralization . . . and so should they.

He was pleased when the Conference of 1917 approved the petition of the Religio to organize a "coordination committee" to promote cooperation with the other auxiliaries and the church organization itself. This committee, chaired by Fred M., was composed of his wife Ruth, for the Women's Auxiliary; George N.

Briggs, President of Graceland College, for the Department of Education; Granville S. Trowbridge for the Religio; and Daniel Macgregor for the Sunday School Association.[147] The ensuing Conference heard and adopted the report and recommendations of the committee. First of all, it divided the existing auxiliaries into six departments: Sunday School, Religio, Women's Auxiliary, Education, Publication, and Remedial and Corrective Agencies. The executive head of each of these departments was to be nominated by the Presidency and ratified by Conference action, and all subordinate officers would be nominated by the now permanent coordination committee. Each department was further directed to confine its annual convention to the time allotted to General Conference, and each head was required to report its activities directly to the Presidency and to clear all financial expenditures with that office and the Bishopric. Acceptance of the guidelines of this document was "a mere beginning of a full coordination of the interests of the church and its auxiliaries."[148]

Some of the department heads were appointed in 1919 as the Conference directed, and the committee made suggestions as to how its work could become more effective and efficient.[149] But the transition to the new system was slow indeed, encumbered by resistance from the ranks of the membership as well as priesthood. For instance, the new Religio was opposed by some because its stress on recreational and social activity for the young was repugnant to their pietism, nurturing "lovers of pleasure more than lovers of God." The group previously featured class study of the Book of Mormon and other Latter Day Saint literature; that responsibility, now transferred to the Sunday school, was reluctantly abandoned by many local administrators of the youth organization.[150]

Compared to the longer and more rancorous battle with the Twelve, President Smith achieved control over these departments and auxiliaries with ease. The personnel of the latter organizations did not view themselves as competitors with him; they possessed no cherished governing powers or traditions they felt compelled to defend, and they agreed with him that their services could be improved by proper direction and coordination. As chairman of the permanent coordination committee and officer who nominated its members and the heads of departments, Fred M. was securely in charge. When he attempted to extend that nominating power into the ecclesiastical structure of the stakes, districts, and congregations of the church after 1922, however, he discovered it could not be accomplished as easily.

The Common Consent and Nomination Controversy of 1923

President Smith was persuaded, as were other efficiency advocates, that all elements within an organization's structure had to work harmoniously in the same harness. Among other things, this meant to him that all department heads and subordinates must be willing to work with "the chief" locally as well as generally. To achieve this end he declared that church appointee officials, stake, district, and local presidents should exercisc thc right to nominate persons to fill offices during elections on those levels. In part, he hoped that this process would prevent "warring factions" from gaining positions of responsibility from which they could "ride hobbies" and dissipate the creative energies of the institution.[151]

While most of the members of the conferences and the church at large accepted his premise that effective administration necessitated a legitimate exercise of authority and a measure of centralized power, his nomination policy put into relief the question of the degree to which both could be employed and still guarantee that their own wishes could be expressed and noted. From one extreme, he and those who unreservedly supported him believed that the movement toward the kingdom depended on a highly structured, centralized government in which obedience was the measure of success and that undisciplined democracy, departmental autonomy, or individual independence were its salient impediments. Obedience to those who were in authority was the key to the kingdom. At the other extreme were those who were accustomed to self-governance and believed that centralization was simply Fred M.'s guise for autocracy. They thought that individual independence and democratic rights were essential for them to nurture the higher qualities of character needed in the kingdom. For the former, administrators possessed the sole right to nominate potential officers; the people's function was to accept or reject the candidates through their "common consent." In the event of rejection, administrators could present another name for consideration. For the latter, however, administrative officers possessed no inherent right to nomination; that power rested solely with those who were the governed, and it was especially cherished in the smaller branches as a prime legislative right. These people heeded the warnings of Joseph III against the "one man rule," and they jealously guarded their right to choose those who would minister to them locally.[152] Both sides drew from the democratic or theocratic traditions of Restorationism to bolster their particular contentions, and Fred M., as much an elitist mugwump as a Saint and disdainful of democracy, opted for the latter.

The most intense controversy over common consent and nomination had its genesis in late 1922 and early 1923 with the publication of several *Herald* articles on departmental work in Independence Stake.[153] President Smith responded to what he discerned as favorable opinion among the ministry and in January 1923 stated to the stake conference that "the time has come for a more definite coordination of the departments in Zion and a more uniform method of procedure in selecting officers."[154] He then proffered the following as a basis for reorganizing those processes:

1. The heads of the general departments of the church and the pastor in Zion [Independence Stake] in consultation with the First Presidency shall nominate the heads of departments in Zion, subject to ratification by the conference in Zion.
2. The four department heads in Zion shall then in consultation with the pastor in Zion select the heads of the departments in the various congregations, the pastor in each congregation to be duly consulted. These selections shall be presented to the conference for approval.
3. In each local congregation the four local heads of departments together with the pastor shall appoint all subordinate officers and teachers.[155]

Action on the document was postponed until the spring Conference, but discussion pertinent to the issue of "centralization of power" continued unbridled until then, especially on the third point: appointment of "all subordinate officers and teachers." When the Conference assembled, a substitute to the original motion was passed in which the conferees asserted, "The right of nomination lies primarily with the body because of membership, and not . . . by virtue of office." The First Presidency and the stake departments and presidency were also extended the privilege to submit nominations for stake offices, but local congregations would continue to elect their own officers and department heads without external suggestions.[156] Questions raised by the debate over the resolution did not disappear after the local conference ended; rather, the heat they generated proceeded to warm the General Conference of 1923.

On Thursday, October 4, 1923, Apostles J. F. Curtis and T. W. Williams stood among the 3,500 Saints attending the General Conference in Independence and sponsored a resolution that reaffirmed the principle and practice of common consent:

> We, the officers and delegates in General Conference assembled, hereby reaffirm our belief in, and adherence to, the principle of "common consent . . ." and further,
>
> We affirm that the right of nomination is inherent in membership in the church, and further,
>
> We express disapproval of any centralization of power in the hands of any administrative officer, or officers, whereby the expression of free choice and the deliberate will of the body may be invaded or abridged.[157]

The lengthy preamble to their resolution was buttressed by selected statements and directives from the Doctrine and Covenants,[158] Book of Mormon,[159] and writings of Joseph Smith III.[160]

When the motion came to debate on October 6, two other members of the Twelve—J. A. Gillen and M. A. McConley—offered a substitute motion in which they presented the other perspective of common consent and nomination in a "theocratic democracy" and declared the "concurrent nominations" from members were always in order:

Inasmuch as question has arisen in the church over the meaning and application of the law of common consent; and

Inasmuch as the church of Christ is a theocratic democracy, in which the will of God is executed by divinely-appointed ministers, with the consent of the members; therefore be it

Resolved That we, the officers and delegates of the Reorganized Church of Jesus Christ of Latter Day Saints in General Conference assembled, reaffirm our belief in and our adherence to the principle of common consent as set forth in the Doctrine and Covenants, the Book of Mormon, and the Holy Scriptures; and be it further

Resolved, That this conference affirms the right of the presiding officers of the general church, and of stake, district, and branch organizations, to nominate, in filling elective offices under their jurisdiction; and, be it further

Resolved, That this action shall in no way be interpreted as prohibiting concurrent nominations coming from the membership of the church, in the various conferences and business meetings, general and local.[161]

Thus stated, the original motion and the substitute were not substantially different except for the magnitude of centralization that the former wished to decrease in the name of democracy and the latter wanted to increase for the sake of efficiency. Both motions applauded the idea of common consent from church tradition and its concomitant expression in the nomination rights of members and officers alike. Nevertheless, the debate raged for the next three days over the *potential* consequences of each if carried to extremes. Apostle J. F. Curtis, for instance, spoke against the substitute because he found in it no rights of the people to originate nominations; they merely ratified the slate prepared for them by members of the hierarchy. Such practices, he declared, were common to the Utah brand of Mormonism, but foreign, indeed, to the democracy of the Reorganization.[162] In response, Daniel T. Williams, a Smith appointee to the Twelve, praised democracy generally but found it not endangered by the priestly prerogatives of theocratic democracy because the people could always decide to vote "no" on any issue. Moreover, he continued, pure democracy as best represented by ancient Greece was impossible in mass, contemporary society or in the church. Delegation of authority was mandatory in order to function with any degree of effectiveness.[163] Myron A. McConley also pled the case for the substitute.[164]

But T. W. Williams, a former secretary to the conservative wing of the California Socialist Party and another of Smith's appointees to the Twelve in 1920, weighed the substitute motion in the balances of democracy and found it wanting. In a speech that lasted one and one-half days and reached both sublime rhetorical heights as well as the banal depths of the same, he protested that the church was "nurtured in the lap of liberty, in the very seat of democracy," and that President Smith possessed no ecclesiastical rights to stifle its expression or inhibit its development by "rigging" elections with nominations of those who agreed with his policy. Common consent, he said, was more than plebescitarian; it had an initiatory function as well and should diffuse, rather than centralize, power. No single person could "have the right to execute for God without the consent of the people." There was no "Gaussian curve" in the kingdom of God with the idiots, morons, and imbeciles at one end and those born to lead at the other. The church was not Fred M.'s "organized army" with superiors and subordinates to give and to follow orders without question or to punish those who were nonconformists. Loyalty and devotion from followers must be earned, not demanded, by leaders, and the life and ministry of Christ was the example that the president—and all—should follow. If the substitute passed, he feared that nominations would pass more and more into the hands of existing officers, to the exclusion of the people.[165] Therefore, he implored the delegates to

> Vote for the substitute if you want to and thus lodge the power of the administering and executing entirely in the ministry, then good-by liberty! good-by freedom! good-by common consent![166]

More than anyone, it was Apostle Williams who impeded Fred M.'s nomination policy, and at this point the president must have seriously wondered if he had been mistaken by calling him to the Twelve.

The debate was over when Elbert A. Smith took the floor to defend the substitute against Williams' polemical assault and to find the "common ground" that would reunite the people of the church and Conference. He addressed himself to the problem of centralized power and concluded that it was part and parcel of the early Christian church, that without it the church would evolve ecclesiastical "locomotor ataxia" and have no direction for its efforts. Too, he found it odd that Williams could so vigorously deplore and denounce the nominating privilege of church officials when he had advocated and used the same power himself as head of the Religio in 1920. If the president has erred, he said, "let him be scourged"; but, "let no man who went farther. . . lay the lash." In light of this contradiction, Counselor Smith asked Williams to join with him to find the common ground for which Joseph Smith III had labored so diligently for years.[167] After this verbal "thrashing" Apostle Williams was further embarrassed when Fred M.'s wife confronted him for his "tactless" and "pointless" arguments against centralization.[168] (Tactless he may have been, but never pointless.) If possible, President Smith did wish to appoint those in whom he had confidence to office; and the nomination process, if abused, was a means of stifling dissent. Furthermore, Apostle Williams was aware of the basic philosophical contradictions of theocratic democracy, and he did not wish to see it resolved in favor of theocracy. He would remain a Smith opponent for the rest of his career in the institution.

Although other exercises of more stentorian quality illuminated the pages of the *Conference Minutes* devoted to these issues, the key speeches had been presented, and finally Apostle F. Henry Edwards, Smith's son-in-law, offered an amendment to the substitute motion that ended the debate. His amendment deleted the last two paragraphs of the substitute and made its intent clearer by adding a resolution that

> this Conference affirms the right of the membership to nominate in filling all elective offices in church, stake, district, and branch organizations in the various conferences and business meetings, general and local; and be it further
>
> Resolved, That this action shall in no way be interpreted as denying the right of presiding officers to present to the appropriate

conferences or business meetings concurrent nominations for the filling of such elective offices.[169]

This amendment assured both argumentative poles—at least temporarily—that they had nothing to fear from each other, and when the previous question was ordered on the entire matter, the Conference adopted the substitute motion as amended.[170] The practice of nomination by officialdom and concurrent ratification or nomination by the membership continued much as it had before the Conference; the only real change was an increase in suspicion and bitterness from both camps.

President Smith had missed the earlier parts of the Conference because of illness, and when he did attend to hear the debates he was vocally as responsive as a Trappist monk. He broke his official, acerbic silence only to caution T. W. Williams not to misrepresent their private conversations and to advise the apostle that he would speak for himself if the occasion demanded.[171] He and his supporters were sure that what most of his critics really wanted was a personal attack on him, and the common consent controversay was merely a tactic to implement that strategy.[172] They were offended by the innuendo and invective of the debates but they were wrong in consigning the democratic sentiments of their opponents to mere pique or personal vendetta. The first generation of the Reorganization was created by Saints who conceived of themselves as the guardians of autonomy, congregationalism, and democracy in the church—people who feared the autocratic excesses of the early Restoration church and sought to avoid them in the new institution. The first generation provided a legacy for the second, and in this context it was the president—not they—who was the radical seeking to tip the balances of power in the opposite direction. Even T. W. Williams, Fred M.'s own appointee to the Twelve, fought him hard for the principles he saw inherent in the nomination crisis.

At best, the Conference of 1923 closed with another uneasy truce between the protagonists of centralization, the president in particular, and the defenders of local, ecclesiastical democracy. Ultimately, neither wished to entirely exclude the other, but the vigor and tenacity with which Fred M. pursued his rationalized kingdom created and perpetuated apprehension for long-cherished democratic rights and practices in quorum and congregation alike. By the time the long Conference ground to a halt, however, both delegates and quorums hoped that what appeared to be a truce might eventually develop into a lasting peace.[173] Within three months, however, another issue surfaced in which the president's opponents took the offensive.

The Herald Controversy, 1924

When the Conference of 1920 adopted the recommendation of the Presidency to transfer legal headquarters of the institution from Lamoni, Iowa, to Independence, Missouri, it seemed only logical to the Bishopric that the Herald Publishing House should also shift its plant to the new locale. *Zion's Ensign*, the missionary paper of the church, had been published in Independence since 1891; the *Saints' Herald* and most of the periodical literature originated in Lamoni. By late May 1921, the merger of these two institutions created the Herald Publishing House of Independence, and both the Presidency and Bishopric were satisfied with the potential business efficiency of the new printing establishment.[174] The actualization of that potential, however, was questioned by the new Board of Publication in its annual meeting in January, 1924. The results of that meeting precipitated controversy between Fred M. and the board, now chaired by Presiding Bishop McGuire. For the board, the narrower issue inhered in its prerogative to choose the editors and policies for church publications; the broader ones centered in guaranteeing the principle of freedom of speech and in limiting the president's potential for autocratic control of the church. For Fred M. editorial charge of church publications by the Presidency was a necessary ingredient in educating the Saints for the kingdom, and he felt this goal was threatened when the board excluded him from that position.

This board was composed of five people nominated by Presiding Bishop McGuire, ratified by the Conference of 1923, and empowered to establish and execute both managerial and editorial policy.[175] Although the history of the Reorganized church revealed that Fred M. and his father very often functioned in the capacities of editor, associate editor, or corresponding editor of the *Herald* while members of the Presidency of the institution, the power to appoint these positions resided in the board.[176] In 1891 the General Conference passed Resolution 361, officially declaring that the editorship of the *Herald* was not inherent in the powers of any office or responsibility, that of the Presidency included.[177] The elder Smith, who was editor of that publication for most of his official life, concurred and after the Conference was over remarked that the board controlled the *Herald* and must be left at liberty to choose an appropriate and qualified editorial staff. The Presidency participated only at their request. If the time came, he continued, when they were no longer needed or acceptable in that capacity, then "it would be an act of egotism to hold further."[178]

In its January sessions the board and its president, B. R. McGuire, were dominated by concern for declining *Herald* subscriptions over the past ten years. Determined to ascertain the reasons for this diminution of interest in the official church publication and to balance income with expenditures, the board appointed a committee of three of its own members to investigate the problem and make suggestions for a solution. The committee decided to use the polling technique to gather relevant data from all church appointees and local, self-sustaining officers. They drafted and forwarded a questionnaire to each, requesting their frank and candid opinion regarding the decline of the periodical.[179]

On the basis of approximately six hundred responses the committee prepared its report and submitted it to the board. First of all, the committee read the responses to indicate that the *Herald* was a "class paper" interested in education and departmental machinery; it appealed over the heads of the masses to the elite who were not interested in "spiritual quality" or representative of the "plain gospel" that was distinctively Latter Day Saint. In this sense, the church population rejected the *Herald* because it contained too much of President Smith and his ideas. Moreover, internecine struggles among the quorums and leaders of the church depressed the people, eroded their confidence, and generated indifference that was reflected in their unwillingness to purchase the periodical. It was a "partisan" paper, favoring views espoused by the Presidency and anathematizing contrary opinions. Finally, economic depression in rural areas limited the purchasing power of many potential readers, while poor, inefficient management offended other subscribers.[180]

A copy of this report was forwarded to President Smith on May 9, along with a request for any suggestions that he would care to make to the forthcoming board meeting of May 23. No reply was received by that date, so the board proceeded to establish future editorial policy of the *Herald*. This policy was to guarantee its columns open to "all general officials" equally and impartially for "free and frank discussion" of problems related to the church. This liberality would be qualified only by their concerted effort to limit "destructive or altogether negative criticism." The board also wanted the paper to be broad enough in its doctrinal, educational, departmental, "spiritual," and news content to appeal to the membership as a whole. To help rally the support of the church for all its publications, the board resolved to place the *Herald*, *Ensign* and *Autumn Leaves* (the church publication for youth and young adults) under one managing editor with contributing staffs for each.[181]

Board members then forwarded their resolutions to President Smith who met with them on May 29 to register his objections to the changes. He had been editor of the *Herald* since 1917, and the action of the board now transferred him to a contributing editorship only.[182] To him this was an act of exclusion and autonomization at the very time he was trying to centralize the church resources and ancillary institutions. They did not consider his dissatisfaction as sufficient justification to change their plans and appointed R. J. Lambert as managing editor. On June 18 Fred M. made his protest official with a message to the church:

> I regret to find it necessary to denounce the action of the Board of Publication. . . . The Board. . . has assumed unwarranted powers in the matter, and the church must now be informed that the Presidency has not only disapproved the action of the board but has made formal protest. . . .
>
> For the first time since 1865 the editorial columns of the *Herald* do not represent the Presidency. It will be clear that the "official" character of the *Herald* has thus been changed.
>
> The action of the board is not alone unwarranted but greatly to be deplored at this time.[183]

On June 25 Board President McGuire and Secretary Arthur E. McKim answered his denunciation for the board and correctly defended its action as one totally comprehended in the traditional and legal precedents of the church. They reminded Fred M. of his father's supportive statements for their view during and following the Conference of 1891 and noted that the "official" status of the *Herald* was established in the 1850s before there was a Presidency of the Reorganization. Therefore, they reasoned, the official nature of the paper was in no way dependent on its relationship to the executive, and they were not guilty of seizing "unwarranted power." Indeed, that power had always reposed in the board.[184]

Unconvinced and unmoved by the McGuire argument, and ignoring the inconsistency of his own vis-à-vis his bids for extending powers of the Presidency, Fred M. wrote each of the board's editorial appointees and restated his opinion. Editorial control of the *Herald* and all church literature should be directly under the Presidency, he declared, and that power had been unreasonably usurped by the board.[185] He also unsubtly warned each member "you should know the disadvantage you will be under by undertaking the work with the disapproval of the Presidency."[186] Several of those to whom he sent these lines wrote public statements of acceptance to the *Herald* to justify their position. T. W. Williams accepted a contributing editorship to that periodical and argued for "Freedom of the Press":

> The rights of the President of the church have not been invaded or abridged by the action of the board. The pages of the *Herald* are as accessible to him as to all others. The President will not be permitted to exercise censorship. The *Herald* will not be the personal organ of President Smith or anyone else. It will be what it was always intended to be, the official organ of the entire church, the Presidency included.[187]

The argument in this instance was clear and correct; neither Fred M. nor anyone else was excluded from the columns of the *Herald*. What he resented was his lack of total control over the publication.

Asked to be a contributing editor to *Zion's Ensign*, Joseph Luff supported the board's position and noted that he had served as editor of the *Herald* for three years during the 1890s in lieu of Joseph Smith as per legal board appointment.[188] Paul M. Hanson detected a ploy in the president's moves to force the *Herald* to fail and devolve to his control until Conference would again convene. Furthermore, he could not anticipate circumstances that would force the president away from the columns of church publications to voice his own views. More interesting yet, recognizing the inconsistency, Hanson said that he was puzzled by Fred M.'s appeal to precedent for support of his contention that the Presidency should control official church literature. After all, precedent had not been considered at all sacrosanct by him in his conflict with the Twelve or in his program to reorganize the governing structures of the instituton.[189] Fred M. was never swayed by precedent unless it supported his existing view. The "foolish traditions" of the elders constituted reaction; they were the enemy in his crusade to centralize and modernize his institution. Yet in the case of the *Herald* editorship he found a tradition he thought worthy to uphold because it provided a tool to build the efficient organization he knew the church could be with proper direction and leadership. What appeared inconsistent to others was harmonious and rational to him.

The new editors were not intimidated by his warning, and pledged themselves to the board's free and open editorial policy that permitted fair representation in print to all sides of controverted issues.[190] According to a Conference resolution of 1885, however, in the event that very "radical" differences of opinion occurred between prominent leaders, all discussion relative to the points of contention would not take place on the pages of the *Herald* but rather in quorum or committee sessions.[191] Nevertheless, from midsummer 1924 through April 1925 the new editors helped to make possible an intense debate among factions of church leaders as they rose in protest—or in support—of the governing philosophy of their leader. During what became a crucial Joint Council meeting in April 1924, quorum representatives adopted the president's "Document on Church Government" by a narrow margin. The phrase, "supreme directional control," that he used to describe his centralized philosophy of governance sparked a debate in the pages of the *Herald* and in tracts that did not end until the Conference of 1925.

The April 1924 Joint Council and the Debate Over Supreme Directional Control

In late January and early February 1924 Presiding Bishop McGuire responded to what he sensed as an "acute financial condition" of the church and asked President Smith to convene a Joint Council of the Presidency, the Order of Bishops, and the Twelve to develop strategies to remedy the situation. The participating quorums all agreed that a uniform approach on administrative matters might rekindle the confidence of the members and increase needed revenue for church coffers.[192] The council that began on April 14 was initially characterized by congeniality which was aptly demonstrated by President Smith's serving the Communion to its members.[193] That accommodating élan continued while the council agreed to sell unused or unneeded properties to replenish the depleted general and Auditorium funds, to proceed with the construction of latter building, to adopt a uniform stewardship program, and to explore the possibilities of the president's bureau of research to survey church resources.[194] When he presented his "Document on Church Government" for consideration, however, the tension it produced caused this temporary cooperative solidarity of the council to degenerate. The issues of centralization versus bureaucratic autonomy, authority versus democracy, and modernity versus tradition were again brought to the surface.

His document was a concise restatement of the themes that had dominated his official life and administration since its beginning: the government of the church was a theocratic democracy in which divine authority was exercised by priesthood with the assent of the people; its priestly hierarchy was graded into levels of authority and prerogative with the "supreme directional control" of the function of all lodged in the Presidency; and efficient administration and "organic solidarity" could be maintained only by effective discipline wielded by strong hands.[195] Simply stated, the executive could carry out policies determined by "prophetic" insight and legislative enactment as he deemed appropriate in interconference periods, but only in the executive line was he supreme.[196] Nothing in the document was new except the appellation, "supreme directional control," and that alone was sufficient to conjure visions of future autocracy in the minds of both clerical and lay constituents. However, his correlative insistence that Presiding Bishop McGuire was also subordinate to the Presidency as he guided the "temporal" or financial affairs of the church made their fears substantive.

Relations between Smith and Bishop McGuire in previous years had been marked by cordiality as the two men exercised the responsibilities of their separate offices, even though the president resented the bishop's reticence to follow his recommendations for stewardship development.[197] Basically, the president's responsibilities were to preside over the spiritual welfare of the "whole church" and its priesthood and to teach its doctrine,[198] but he was not to be burdened with the temporal affairs of the organization which were left for the bishop. The latter was trustee-in-trust for the church, custodian of its properties, and was empowered to receive and disburse its funds "subject to the general direction of the church and higher church authorities." Originally stated in the Articles of Incorporation of the church, clarified by a "Basis of Agreement" between the Twelve and the Bishopric in 1878 and reaffirmed by the General Conference in 1881, each of the succeeding presiding bishops—Israel L. Rogers, George Blakeslee, and Edmund L. Kelley—had employed these powers of the purse, and Bishop McGuire stood firm for the principles advocated and practiced by his predecessors.[199] What was now at issue, President Smith maintained, was not that as one of the "higher church authorities" he was supreme in financial matters, but that the bishop was not supreme, and that the Presidency had the right to contract debts, allocate funds, and override his decisions should circumstances dictate the necessity to so act.[200] As early as the spring of 1923, he wrote Bishop McGuire requesting a conference regarding the "subordination" of the Bishopric in these matters, but no accommodation or understanding satisfactory to either had been reached by the following spring,[201] and that lack of a modus vivendi between them was later exacerbated by the bishop's acts as president of the Board of Publication to exclude Fred M. from editorial responsibility.

President Smith told the council that he was willing to abide by its decision regarding his document, and that the time had come to see whether he or the bishop was the head of the church: the church could not have two leaders. If the decision went against him, he said, "I hope I will have the manhood to get out of the way," and others should do the same.[202] When the council of the Presidency, Twelve, and fifteen bishops voted in the majority for the document, President Smith then turned to Bishop McGuire and declared:

> Brother McGuire, I am going to say something to you and I will carefully weigh my words. Before this council closes I want you to tell this body whether you are going to abide by the decisions of this group of men. If you are not I want to know it so that I may take some official action.[203]

Although he insisted that resignation was not one of the options he anticipated from Bishop McGuire,[204] he never specifically stated what he did expect. But the bishop had only three alternatives: acquiescence, resignation, or stalemate.

For the next week that office was in effect on trial, with President Smith in the role of both prosecuting attorney and judge. The bishop protested the whole procedure as an attempt to legislate the relationship between him and the president without the approval of the Conference.[205] Before he submitted his answer, he drafted his own list of questions treating the extent of supreme directional control, which he submitted to the president on April 21.[206] Fred M. responded to each the following day. After informing the bishop that his questions were "hypothetical" he candidly formulated his answers. He affirmed that it was the duty of all departments and officers to keep their superiors informed on all matters; he acknowledged what he believed to be his right to censor all articles for publication from any department, that of the Bishopric included; he denied that he would force members of the Bishopric to make what they deemed to be unwarranted or undesirable expenditures; he noted that the Presidency could request and receive any correspondence or orders given by the bishop to his subordinates; he advanced the argument that the "discretionary" powers over the finances and property of the church given to the bishop were limited; he asserted his own right to contract debts for the church without the consultation or approval of the bishop, "should the occasion demand"; he declared that he could select and obtain bishops and other subordinate officers without McGuire's specific approval; and he insisted that the General Conference functioned legislatively for the church, but orders to its officers came only through the executive or administrative line.[207]

On April 25, Bishop McGuire declined to accept or abide by President Smith's interpretation of church governance and stated his intention to exercise his authority as the trustee-in-trust for the temporal affairs of the organization. Since the Conference had sustained him for the purpose, he stated, "I feel it my duty to God and to the church to discharge the functions of my office in accordance with the law and usages that have obtained in the Reorganization for over half a century,"[208] Moreover, he said,

> Deep conviction to principle, therefore, will not permit me to comply with your demand which, for the first time in the history of

the church, seeks to place "supreme directional control" of the temporal affairs in the hands of the Presidency.

To my mind, compliance with this demand should be tantamount to a betrayal of the confidence and trust reposed in me by the people of the church and a violation of the law.[209]

Until the next Conference had spoken, Bishop McGuire opted for stalemate and refused to budge. From the perspective of church traditions and practices, he was correct; President Smith was the aggressor who sought to change the balance of these two quorums into hegemony for himself.

In spite of Fred M.'s incredible public assessment that the council had taken a "long step . . . towards a restoration of complete unity and confidence so essential to the success of the work of the church,"[210] to those who entertained intense convictions regarding supreme directional control—or "SDC" as it came to be known in the diminutive—battle lines had been drawn. On June 2, only a few days after Bishop McGuire's Board of Publication had appointed the new editors for church publications, an "Open Letter to the President, Ministry, and Membership of Church" appeared over the signatures of seventeen erstwhile members of the April Joint Council who sought a resolution to the crisis. Among those who signed it were John Rushton and T. W. Williams of the Twelve, and B. R. McGuire and Israel A. Smith (the president's brother) from the Presiding Bishopric. They expressed their faith that the Conference and its enactments combining the "inspiration of God and the will of the people" constituted the highest authority in the church, and that all programs and policies, in order to be binding on all, must be submitted to its scrutiny. The two divisions of the administrative work of the institution were the temporal and the spiritual; the temporalities were under the charge of the bishop as trustee-in-trust. He was directly responsible to the General Conference alone to account for his use of that power and to none other. Furthermore, he could limit the expenditure of all departments to the figure appropriated by the Conference, even that of the Presidency.[211]

Until the release of this open letter, President Smith had preferred that the dialogue over SDC, if any, be confined to the quorums. With its publication in the *Herald* and the "leak" of some of the council discussions, he wrote T. W. Williams that he was guilty of a breach of courtesy and professional code. T. W. countered this charge by asserting that the information was the property of the whole church and that proceedings of the council should be known:[212]

> I have the utmost contempt for anything which savors of star chamber methods. . . . I believe in acting out in the open where all men can see and know. The time has come when we should run up the blinds and let the sunlight in. We must open the doors and drag the sick things into the open air. We need to clean house.[213]

Bishop McGuire believed that it was President Smith who was trying to divide the church into two camps, and he made no apology for his attempts to inform the membership regarding his own view of the controversy.[214] By early July, Fred M. was exasperated and felt put upon by those who did not share his concepts of what were the true, ineluctable principles of the Latter Day Saint gospel and scientific management, and in the context of a sermon he warned,

I cannot yield to the voice of the opposition, so I am in the fight, and it will undoubtedly be a finish fight. Either the opposition which has asserted itself is going to become supreme and the rest of us eliminated, or vice versa.[215]

His official response to the open letter was printed in the July 6 issue of the *Herald* along with the supportive signatures of Elbert A. Smith, F. M. McDowell, President J. A. Gillen and five others of the Quorum of Twelve, and sixteen bishops. This rejoinder reprinted the Smith "Document of Church Government" with an addendum that implored the Saints not to discredit their president as he sought to exercise his lawful prerogatives, but to support him while studying the law, carefully weighing the matters under consideration, and "reserving their final judgement until the conference meets to hear the cause."[216] The Bishopric believed, however, that the issues were clearly drawn between a theocratic-democracy and a "theo-autocracy," and they prepared to match their rhetorical wits with that of their leader to educate the membership toward the truth as they understood it.[217]

The *Herald* was the most significant forum for the ensuing debate. Although that periodical was in the control of those against the administration view, Editor Richard J. Lambert pledged himself to be a fair referee, to employ the "higher methods of spiritual warfare," and to honor the Conference directive to minimize rancorous conflict, innuendo, or invective in its columns.[218] During the months in which literary dialogue regarding SDC filled the *Herald* before the Conference of April 1925, about fourteen of its columns provided official statements elaborating President

Smith's ideas; seventy-eight advocated its approval, one hundred and twelve argued for its defeat, and forty-five took the middle ground.[219] In conjunction with attracting debate that accompanied these *Herald* articles, President Smith and his ideas were boiled in a cauldron of printer's ink while the readers reacted with hostility, dismay, and, after several months, fatigue.

Most of the writers were the general officers of the church who disagreed over the location of final authority in the institution of their allegiance. Those who supported Fred M. had the advantage in that they were defending the Presidency under attack, were consistent with each other in their arguments, demonstrated that their leader did not adhere to the extreme versions SDC attributed to him, and enlisted some of the more respective leaders and writers such as Elbert A. Smith in their cause. Even with the cooperation of the Presiding Bishopric, the opponents of SDC were very individualistic and less consistent in their approach, argued from precedent in the early Reorganization, and were more emotional and polemical in their crusade to protect the church from an autocrat.[220] Except for President Smith who argued from the additional premise of scientific management, those who engaged in the debate resorted to church law, tradition, and theology as their sources. They never really understood President Smith's efficiency principle, and they assumed that any rhetoric of that genre he employed in defense of his position was mere subterfuge.

Elbert A. Smith's *The True Philosophy of Church Government* was the best stated case for the administration. Speaking for Fred M. he defended SDC as a longstanding church tradition that his superior wished to clarify for the sake of administrative order. He cited Joseph Smith III and historian Herman C. Smith as primary advocates of SDC when they commented on the scriptural injunction to the Presidency to "preside in council and set in order all the affairs of the Church and Kingdom."[221] If any others were appointed to these duties, they were empowered only in a "secondary" sense, guided by the counsel of the First Presidency.[222] But the controls exercised by the Presidency were supreme in the executive sphere only, and the power of the people in conference to discipline his possible abuses was absolute. They could initiate or reject legislation and accept or reject prophetic messages or the messenger himself. To both Smiths, "No autocrat ever existed who depended on the vote of the people for office, and on their support for his measures, and whose people were free legislators."[223] Yet any attempt to make theocratic democracy akin to civil democracy was a "new and dangerous doctrine" that would result in "disaster"; the voice of the people was not always the voice of God: "I affirm that . . . the voice of the people is a big thing in the church, but the voice of God is *the big thing*" to which their "diffusive inspiration" attests.[224] And the voice of God to the church came only through the priestly authority of the prophet who could "advise, direct and set in order" the house of God on earth.[225]

In Elbert's estimation Fred M.'s leadership was not the epitome of "wild, free handling of power" by a demagogue, and he regretted that some of the church officials attempted to "trim principles to fit personalities" in maligning him.[226] The bishop was misinformed, for example, when he argued that his control of church temporalities was subject only to the president's "counsel." In reality, the president was the "higher" church authority that the Articles of Incorporation invested with the power for the general direction of the institution. As well, total control of finances would give the bishop executive power over missions and programs that were deeply interrelated with "spiritual" direction or goals.[227]

From the opposition's perspective, the most direct response to this "true philosophy" came from the pen of Israel A. Smith, the president's brother, an attorney, and one of the three bishops who constituted the Presiding Bishopric. For him, Fred M. did not understand "division of labor" or checks and balances, and his attempt to combine the temporal and spiritual domains of the institution into one that he could dominate was a violation of tradition of their father and the legal structure of the church. The "attack" on the Bishopric was unwarranted in law, premeditated, and aggressively prosecuted. The April council was not a legally constituted legislative session or court, and Fred M. had tried to use it as both to deprive the bishop of his "primary" temporal rights. He also found Elbert Smith's attempt to cite his father and Herman C. Smith as supporters of SDC a "travesty" perpetrated at the expense of these two men of the people who spent their lives "unmasking" centralization and autocracy in Utah. Furthermore, the writer noted that the history of the Nauvoo experience illustrated that consolidation of power to the hands of one individual led to mischief and confusion. When Joseph Smith, Jr., assumed the position of trustee-in-trust in lieu of the bishop, the financial affairs of the church quickly moved toward chaos and the original church disintegrated; he feared that history might repeat itself.[228]

In *The Unbroken Chain: A Treatise on the Law of the Lord Relating to the Work of the Bishopric*, Benjamin McGuire and his colleagues elaborated the continuity of their temporal prerogatives from the beginning of the church and found them "indelibly written in the law, practice, and history of the Reorganization. As an unbroken chain they have endured, notwithstanding changes in personnel."[229] In anticipation of future autocracy they concluded with the rhetorical question:

> Will the latter-day Israel continue in the old paths of governmental procedure, commanded by God and established by our forefathers, or
>
> Will the church, after all these years, abolish the divine system of checks and counterchecks in church government and make one quorum *supreme* in both spiritual and temporal affairs?[230]

McGuire also wrote in the *Herald* that the government of the church inhered in "God and the people," and the priesthood was the adjunctive servant of both, to perform divinely ordained functions of both temporal and spiritual nature.[231]

Other writers were not as temperate as they critiqued Fred M.'s policies. B. L. McKim assailed his rule of the Independence Stake as one too affected by "university teachings" and devoid of real common consent.[232] James F. Keir leveled a charge of attempted "infallibility" at the Presidency.[233] Daniel Macgregor found SDC a "euphonious phrase of foreign importation" that was "un-American and strikes at the root of representative government."[234] C. B. Hartshorn wrote that SDC and centralized power were historical atavisms "wrong in principle, unscientific in practice, un-American in character, and unwarranted in the law of God."[235] Paul M. Hanson compared President Smith's proposal to his grandfather's version of theodemocracy at Nauvoo.[236] F. M. Sheehy concluded "we have heard... 'follow leaders' in Independence until it has become obnoxious....If the blind lead the blind, they both fall in the ditch."[237] And T. W. Williams again pilloried the president attempting to implement an elitist theory of governance based in caste, privilege and obedience to "superiors."[238]

T. W. Williams' reproach endured longer and was more severe than that of most detractors. What President Smith wanted, he postulated, was to establish and maintain a "church machine like unto the army of Moses" wherein chosen ones could prevent free discussion and "railroad" measures through legislative sessions. In support of this allegation he cited Fred M.'s manipulation of the Northern California District Conference at Irvington in the fall of 1924. He said the president had assumed the presiding chair, abolished the spring conference, selected and instructed seventeen General Conference delegates to vote for adoption of his document on governance, appointed a nominating committee and explained to all that this was appropriate legislative procedure. To J. W. this "priestcraft" was hardly common consent in action, and he questioned the seating of the delegation at the coming General Conference.[239]

The president of Northern California District, his two

vice-presidents and secretaries, and the local missionaries replied to the Williams articles to rectify what they considered to be a case for despotism that was too tightly woven. President Smith occupied the chair, they wrote, only because the conference requested it by their unanimous vote and chose to ignore his publicly expressed desire to be excused. As chairman he was asked to appoint a nominating committee for General Conference delegates, but it was also he who noted that the conference had the right to make additional nominations. While the committee was in session outside the conference, two members of the body proposed that the delegates be instructed to vote for the SDC document, and their motion passed with a substantial majority. As well, the writers noted that Williams overlooked the fact that it was the San Jose, California, branch that first instructed delegates how to vote because they were charged by their local business session to vote for the "Open Letter" and against SDC.[240] While President Smith chaired the conference, they concluded,

> he did not attempt to influence or participate in any manner in the matters coming before the body, other than as a *servant* and not a *master* of the conference. He did only those things which he was asked by the body to do.[241]

They did not deny, however, that he was pleased at that which had occurred.

Most of the moderate commentators on the SDC controversy preferred that the matter be settled as soon as possible by the quorums of the Presidency, Twelve, and Bishopric in council or by the General Conference of 1925. They stressed the importance of coordination and cooperation among the two quorums that claimed control over the finances and properties of the church and maintained that no single person had the right to obligate the organization or spend its money without due authorization from its legislative body. Anticipating compromise and extolling the virtues of patience, kindness, and brotherly love, they looked forward to the impending Conference.[242]

The General Conference of 1925: The Formal Triumph of Supreme Directional Control

The Conference, convened at the Stone Church in Independence on April 6, was tensely politicized and opened with a brief but abortive delegate seating challenge by those who were disgruntled with the nominating process.[243] The basic issue, however, was President Smith's statement on church governance that had been narrowly passed by the April 1924 council and had been vigorously debated for the remainder of that year. He had already presented that document to the quorums on April 2 and on the opening day of the Conference laid it before the delegates with the suggestion that the matter be given the undivided attention of the body until the issue was resolved.[244]

Printed and available to the body was a "Proposed Basis of Agreement" prepared by the leaders of the Quorums of Seventy and offered by Apostles J. F. Curtis and John Rushton as a substitute for the document prepared by Fred M. Their proposal supported his statement that government of the church was a theocratic democracy expressed through divine authority and the common consent of the people and administered through a hierarchialized priesthood.

The Presidency of the church was recognized as the quorum with the general responsibility for the direction of the institution and its high priesthood subject to previous canon law, Conference resolutions, and the "concurrent jurisdiction" of the three leading quorums.[245] Omitted from this substitute was the original motion's emphasis on government through priesthood, its stress on "effective discipline," and the words "supreme directional control"; accented were the consenting power of the people and circumscription of theocratic prerogative by checks and balances.[246] Administration forces were amenable to changing the objectionable phrase "supreme directional control" to one less offensive to its opponents if its intent could be preserved without giving the appearance of abandoning an untenable precept,[247] but this one did not fit the model. On the following day the quorum reports from the Twelve, High Priests, and Elders supported the original document by a ratio of two to one in each,[248] but discussion on the Conference floor continued unabated.

The stridency of the controversy was augmented by several factors. One of these was a legislative change in the structure of the Board of Publication that instructed Bishop McGuire that the board would hereafter consist of one member of the Presidency, one member of the Twelve, one member of the Bishopric, and two members elected by the Conference. Moreover, the Presidency would be recognized as the editors-in-chief of all church publications.[249] When this measure was approved by the Conference on April 6, President Smith's opponents were quick to discern in his victory the malignancy of autocracy and opposed him yet more vehemently.

Interspersed between the Conference sessions and official argumentation were "spontaneous" meetings on the Temple Lot immediately across from the Stone Church on Lexington Street in Independence. Attending these meetings were approximately three-hundred dissidents—basically from the Independence area—who experienced the president and administration most directly, and who represented the most disturbed partisans of the opposition. Numbered among these were T. W. Williams, John Rushton, and Benjamin McGuire.[250] At one of their meetings before the Conference session of April 8, some members of this group circulated "A Protest" against SDC drafted by Apostle Williams and twenty-four others. In it they deplored SDC and its baneful concomitants: threats to eliminate opposition, illegal selection and instruction of delegates, limitation of the legislative function of Conference to mere assent to executive fiat, and centralization of power in the hands of one man. The president was excoriated by the protesters for instigating the controversy and disrupting sacrosanct procedures of the past; and, they stated, if his document was adopted, it would be "tantamount to apostacy—a departure from the accepted principles and practices of this Reorganized Church. . . ." They concluded with a pledge to "protect the constitutional rights of the officers and members of the church against this insidious departure from the faith."[251]

This statement and its three hundred signatures was read into the Conference minutes and explained by

Bishop McGuire. To the applause of many in the delegate audience, he warned that the adoption of the SDC document might result in "divorce" within the church.[252] As a rejoinder, President Smith insisted that all of the signatories remove their names from the document or "forfeit the right to represent us."[253] At this point he was alleged to have also waved his clenched fist and growled, "Bishop McGuire, you take your name off that paper before sundown or suffer the consequences."[254] He decried the action of the protesters as the unjust result of propaganda by pulpiteers and publicists calculated to undermine his presidency, and he resoundingly condemned the Presiding Bishop's conduct as "treasonable," infecting the quorums and paralyzing the whole church. The plans offered by the two were mutually exclusive—as different as oil and water—and no compromise was possible between them.[255] Bishop McGuire replied to the treason charge as "slanderous" and demanded that it be retracted. None of the protesters struck their signatures from the paper. President Smith ignored the demand and declared that the Saints must choose whom they would follow—the legitimate authorities of the institution or the "self-appointed" leaders.[256]

Advocates of harmony and conciliation were numerous, however, and they plied their talents to assuage the damaged egos and harried consciences of the adversaries. Apostle F. Henry Edwards of the Twelve was assigned to deliver a sermon at the height of the debate, and he centered his message on the necessity of repentance, forbearance, and fraternal love.[257]

There were lighter moments that brought comic relief

to the mounting tensions produced by the intensity of the legislative battle. When Daniel Macgregor concluded a tirade against the president by exclaiming that the SDC meant "Smith Don't Care," Elbert Smith rejoined that it really connoted "Smith Does Care." Another speaker arose and stated that the initials really expressed the sentiment, "Shucks, Dan, Cease," and Daniel Macgregor returned to his seat.[258] After a particularly blistering attack on administration forces in which the critic made reference to the Biblical text, "The dumb ass speaking with man's voice forbade the madness of the prophet," the chairman concluded, "This day is this scripture fulfilled in your ears."[259] Even Fred M. could laugh at himself as he penned a limerick for his own therapy:

There once was a preacher erratic,
Who had some queer things in his attic;
Said he, "I sure see in this moot S.D.C.
A gesture of rule autocratic."[260]

In his official statement to the Conference before the vote on April 10, he tendered his most systematic defense of his document on governance. He resolutely stuck to his premise that the institution was founded and perpetuated by divine authority, and any efforts to ignore that foundation and "democratize" the church would sweep away its claim to uniqueness. Further, "I have reached the conclusion that when I yield the question of divine authority and say that religion is democratic I shall cease to be a member of any church."[261] Such authority was not bestowed on the church or its priesthood by the people, but the people could decide whether or not that priestly power would be exercised on their behalf. In Latter Day Saint tradition and scripture he found that authority came from God, and men who became priesthood members were called through revelation and ordained through the "Holy Spirit." The people through common consent could decide whether or not to accept the services of that minister. He observed further that the legislative body of the church was not democratic, but representative, excluding nondelegates from its midst.[262]

Supreme directional control was merely the expression he chose to illustrate that the executive department of the institution was to implement the will of the people as per the decisions of the Conference in its interim. He told the Conference that it was not an executive "board of directors" but a legislative body that required "executive machinery" to implement its will while it was not in session. The executive provided by the constitutional law of the church could be eternally frustrated by the contention that its two heads—temporal and spiritual—were equal. Resorting to the idiom of business efficiency he explained to the Conference that executive authority in any corporation was usually arranged so "there is one person or one place where responsibility can be fixed and an accounting called for."[263] As a word of comfort to his critics who had appointed themselves the guardians of the liberty of the church, he again explained that SDC had reference only to the "administrative line of work" not to the legislative. Too, he explained that his phrase, "effective discipline," had been misconstrued to be solely punitive, an excuse for "laying the cat of nine tails." In actuality, he protested, that discipline was positive, constructive, and directive in its nature, calculated to assist all administrators to develop efficient means and methods to achieve goals the church had established. In conclusion, he alluded to the proposed base of agreement that was offered as a substitute to his own document as one that affirmed the "rights of the President over the high priesthood," but it relegated to the trash heap the important principles he had just elaborated.[264]

When the chairman called for the vote on April 11, the Smith forces carried the day. The substitute lost 942 to 394 and the "Document on Church Government" passed 919 to 405. Most of the delegates to the Conference recognized and accepted the authoritarian and centralized Restoration tradition of governance that President Smith clothed in the garb of managerial efficiency. Cognizant of his overwhelming victory and in recognition that the Conference had spoken, the erstwhile crusaders for democracy submitted to defeat and acknowledged that Frederick M. Smith should continue to direct the church; but they did not remove their signatures from the protest nor acquiesce in his charge of treason.[265]

The Presiding Bishopric—B. R. McGuire, J. F. Keir, and I. A. Smith—conceded defeat, however, and on April 16 asked the Conference to release them.[266] Instead of complying with their request, the Conference voted to defer and "seek the Lord through the prophet . . . for direction"[267] regarding the matter. President Smith agreed and secluded himself in an upstairs room of his Kansas City home, remaining there until Elbert Smith, Floyd McDowell, and John Garver arrived to carry his message to the assembly.[268] In the draft read to the General Conference he said "through the voice of inspiration" that it was "wisdom" to release Bishop McGuire and appoint "for a time" Albert Carmichael of Lamoni, Iowa, to act in his stead with the freedom to choose his own two counselors. Additionally, the church was commended for approving the recommendations of the April Joint Council and enjoined to unify its ranks and end bitter contention.[269] The Quorum of High Priests and two-thirds of the Council of Twelve voted to accept the message as a manifestation of divine guidance for the church, but the content was warmly debated on the Conference floor to the accompaniment of such aspersions as "snap judgment," "convenient subterfuge," and "mistake." Notwithstanding, a final vote of 351 to 97 ratified the document, and Carmichael proceeded to select as his first counselor Mark Siegfried, president of the Jackson County Bank.[270]

One more skirmish remained between administration and the outnumbered opposition forces. At the end of each Conference the delegates and ex officios voted whether or not to sustain the general authorities of the church in their special callings and responsibilities. There were several fiery speeches directed against sustaining Fred M. in his calling as "President, Prophet, Seer and Revelator," and among the most vehement of these was that of James E. Yates in the closing session, April 21, 1925. First, he bemoaned the fact that President Smith now controlled the administrative and editorial organs of the church and could stultify the exercise of the freedoms of speech and press. Second, he deplored that the future missionary work would be controlled by the president's pet ideas, and any who differed and wanted to keep their jobs must "keep a padlock on their mouths." For the last decade, he expostulated, the basic problems of the church were centered in one man and his policies, and, "In the calm assurance that eternity will reveal the truth of my words, I say to President Frederick M. Smith: *Thou art the man!*" Therefore, he continued, as his last official act before resigning as a missionary under the control of such a "grinding, crushing, and eliminating machine as has entranced itself here," he would cast his vote against President Smith:[271]

I vote against sustaining the President, and will wholly disavow and repudiate his monarchial claims to supremacy of control of the Church of Jesus Christ even though the audacious claim be supported by this *illegally constituted*. . . *conference.*[272]

Fred M. again survived the onslaughts of such in-house adversaries as the delegates voted to sustain his ministry. On the other hand, members of the Quorum of Twelve who had opposed SDC and the revelation that dropped Bishop McGuire did not fare as well. The Conference opted to vote on its members individually rather than consider the whole quorum generally. Apostle Rushton conferred with President Smith the day previously, recounted his twenty-four years of loyal service, and declared that he must follow his conscience and not sacrifice his integrity. At the conclusion of their discussions, Fred M. asked the apostle for his resignation, the latter tendered it immediately, and the Conference accepted it. Although his resignation was also requested by the administration, T. W. Williams did not comply because he believed that he owed his apostleship to the Conference and not to the president. The Conference then responded with a vote of "no confidence," and he was not sustained in his "office and calling." J. F. Curtis and Paul M. Hanson had also opposed the president's stand on SDC and did not recant, but they declared their willingness to continue to serve the body and the church under the present condition of his leadership. They and the remaining eight of the Twelve were then sustained by the delegates.[273]

At this juncture President Smith denied that he desired to purge any and all opponents from the ranks of the hierarchy, but he had no qualms in demanding that all official representatives of the church loyally support its policies as legislated in General Conference.[274] Those whose beliefs would not allow compromise with principles they considered both sacred and undeniable were therefore forced by their own consciences to the periphery of the institution, if not beyond it, but most of its leaders and constituents at the Conference readily accepted the president's rationalized system as a prominent feature of their shared tradition and maintained their allegiance to the church and his leadership.

And why did the Conference vote to approve SDC, sustain Smith, express "no confidence" in T. W. Williams, and accept the resignation of John Rushton—one of the most respected members of the Twelve? In part, the answer lies in the geographic complexion of the Conference itself. Forty percent of the delegates and ex-officios came from the areas in or around the Center Place: the stakes of Independence, Kansas City, and Holden, Missouri, and Lamoni, Iowa. These were the stronger centers of the anti-Smith factions in which the issues of centralization and SDC were discussed with intensity and vehemence. The remaining 60 percent of the voters hailed from distant missions, Canada, and scattered districts and areas in the United States.[275] With notable exceptions such as the De Kalb, Illinois, branch,[276] delegates from these areas were less acquainted with SDC as an issue, distance increased their reverence and respect for the president and prophet of the church, and they viewed the dissenters as erratic, disrespectful cranks. In addition, the larger majority of his followers were as zealous as he for the kingdom of God, separated their religious and political lives, and were willing to accept the democratic deficiencies of their religion.

On the other hand, the protestors reacted to the deeply established Restoration tradition of centralized power in a prophet/president that the early Reorganized church fathers wanted to avoid and which Joseph Smith III chose to reassert only on rare occasions. Frederick M. Smith, a more demanding personality, influenced not only by the Mormon tradition but by an ideal of institutional efficiency, opted to refurbish the past in order to equip the church to meet the demands for the future. He wished to put into relief the clear lines of authority that led directly to his office as the center point of a rationalized, modern organization, and with the Conference of 1925 that yearning was formally fulfilled. At the close of the Conference he occupied a position of power that was almost unequaled. Administratively, he controlled all quorums, councils, and territories; he appointed missionaries, department heads, stake and district presidents, and pastors in the Independence

Stake. He "called" or released by revelation individuals in the church hierarchy including those in the Twelve or Bishopric. He could allocate or withhold finances during the interconference period. And he was the editor-in-chief of all church publications. He exercised profound legislative strength by initiating legislation through his dominance of the joint councils, presenting revelations in which the prophetic voice so revered by Mormon custom was required to be accepted or rejected by a majority of true believers, and chairing Conference meetings in which he was empowered to control debate. And judicially, he presided over the Standing High Council, the court of highest appeal in the church.[277]

President Smith's approach to institutional reform was not foreign to the mainstream crusaders of the progressive era. Even the most effective of these individuals on the leadership level succumbed to messianism, judging their own success at the polls as the most significant issue. In the case of Wisconsin, Governor Robert LaFollette decided what the people needed and expected them to ratify his choices.[278] Similarly, the most literary exponent of the social gospelers surrendered to the mesmerizing, elitist thrust of his own rhetoric. Walter Rauschenbusch and his clerical alter-egos gathered yearly in their "Brotherhood of the Kingdom" to perform a "Holy Chivalry for Christ" through prayer and testimony on behalf of the people, but not with the people. As well, he presumed to speak for labor while actually addressing the upper classes to educate them for reform as disinterested idealists and as mediators between capital and labor. The rank and file members of labor organizations were thus required to trust the judgment of their preachers for the strategy and tactics of industrial war.[279] This same elitism was also an important feature in G. Stanley Hall, [280] Smith's most direct contact with academic mugwumpery, and it fit well into the existing fabric of his more primarly religious sources of authoritarian, priestly leadership.

Fred M. believed that he possessed insight into what the people of his institution needed. He could have easily followed the example of his father who resorted to patience and persuasion as techniques to move the institution toward the kingdom of God, but from his own perspective of theocratic democracy, the people owed their allegiance to those whom God had selected to guide them. Infinitely less patient than his predecessor, Smith was not content to allow the rank and file or competitive quorums to obstruct his vision of the future. In "supreme directional control" Smith asked his followers to trust him to select the roads leading to fulfillment of their utopian dreams, and most of them did exactly that. He valued obedience more than intelligent dissent and conformity more than individuality; to "fall in line" with his leadership was his test of true discipleship, and LaFollette asked no less of his own political constituency.

"Centralization" as a philosophy of governance and a means of reform antipathetic to mass democracy also suffused the historical era that nurtured Smith and it, too, fit well into the Restoration traditions he tried to clarify for his church. Progressive intellectuals such as Herbert Croly in his *Promise of American Life* (1909) tendered centralization of power in high-placed bureaucracies and persons as the best means to achieve and maintain social and economic justice in the United States. Precisely because of collectivity in every phase of American life Croly believed that the Jeffersonian vintage of individual, provincial, and "anti-nationalist" democracy was incapable of finding appropriate solutions to modern problems. These "old fashioned Democrats" wasted their energies professing "the approaching extinction of American democracy in what they call the drift towards centralization," and he relegated their fears to the domain of the "absurd":[281]

There comes a time in the history of every nation, when its independency of spirit vanishes, unless it emancipates itself in some measure from its traditional illusions; and that time is fast approaching for the American people. They must either seize the chance of a better future, or else become a nation which is satisfied in spirit merely to repeat indefinitely the monotonous measures of its own past.[282]

For Fred M. as well as Croly, centralization was the best means to progress and the fulfillment of institutional goals. The theocratic traditions of the early church provided a direct, centralized backbone upon which he could build a strong and well coordinated structure. Only a "strongly centralized government" could lead the church to fulfill its mission. Like the founding fathers of his century he did not trust the diffusion of authority and power that decentralized democracy entailed, nor did he have confidence in the ability of the common people to be above what he deemed "selfish interest" or the manipulation of institutional demagogues. A clearly defined locus of administrative authority and direction was necessary in all institutions if they were operated successfully, and he repeatedly implored his people to recognize that authority in their own. He also insisted that the bureaucracies in the hierarchy of the church forsake their traditional claims to autonomy and recognize his central management over their activities or specific functions. When they resisted, he put them to the test before the General Conference—e.g., the Twelve in 1919 and 1922, and the Bishopric in 1925—and received votes of confidence from the people of the church at large. His centralized authority was constantly supported by the broader constituency of the institution who acceded to the "Lord's Anointed" as one who was sent by Deity to lead them. Pardoxically, the common people he so distrusted were the very ones who sustained his elitist leadership. His democratic opponents, using all the rhetoric and influence at their command could not overcome this faith in the prophet-leader that was the deeper, more abiding aspect of the Restoration tradition.

A final thread running through his larger religious fabric was the "gospel of efficiency," a message that precipitated a veritable "secular Great Awakening" among reformers in businesses, industry, government, and social institutions in the late nineteenth and early twentieth centuries. The efficiency movement stressed the "natural laws" of industrial efficiency, the personal qualities of honesty, hard work, and discipline, the application of economies of scale to governmental procedures and institutions, and capable, centralized leadership.[283] Professional expertise and honesty were two sides of the same coin that some of these reformers spent lavishly in developing the city-commissioner and city-manager forms of local government so popular between 1901 and 1914. Throughout his life, Smith supported his faith in centralized government not only from his basic Mormon background, but also with the rhetoric of efficiency and sound management. For Smith, efficient government was the ideal for his institution, and centralized leadership and management was the means to that end. Firm in what he believed to be the cardinal principles of his faith, Smith ignored his father's advice to allow the people to continue in "error" until they saw the light for themselves. He preferred to bring the issue of centralized authority versus democratic decentralization to a resolution that would result in the movement of his church toward the kingdom of God. It was Smith himself who made the issue a viable one and it was Smith who won the battles, but what had he gained? Mere defeat of his opponents and elimination of nay-sayers did not constitute reform or make his institution "efficient." The actual changes resulting from his victory made the war seem meaningless.

NOTES

1. "Recorder's Report," *GCM* (July 28, 1915), pp. 19, 39, 123; *History of the RLDS*, vol. 7, p. 626.
2. Ruth Lyman Smith, *Concerning the Prophet: Frederick Madison Smith* (Kansas City: Burton Publishing Company, 1924), p. 32.
3. Albert E. Bergh, ed., *The Writings of Thomas Jefferson* 20 vols., Definitive ed. sponsored by Thomas Jefferson Memorial Association (Washington, D.C., 1907), vol. 12, p. 282; vol. 15, pp. 23, 214.
4. Elmer T. Clark, *The Small Sects in America* (Nashville,

Tennessee: Cokesbury Press, 1937), p. 13; Warner, p. 4.

5. Thomas F. O'Dea, *The Mormons* (Chicago: University of Chicago Press, 1957), pp. 21, 116-17.
6. Edward A. Warner, "Mormon Theodemocracy: Theocratic and Democratic Elements in Early Latter-day Saint Ideology, 1827-1846" (Ph.D. dissertation, University of Iowa, 1973), p. 36.
7. Joseph Smith, Jr., "The Globe," *Times and Seasons* 5 (April 19, 1844): 510.
8. Warner, pp. 42-43; Doctrine and Covenants 42:42a.
9. Warner, pp. 42-43. The hierarchy was not a trained, professional clergy. Most males in the church were given priesthood status and a title to office at a time when lay responsibility in church government was a widespread phenomenon. The priesthoods were divided into two basic levels, the lower, or "Aaronic (deacons, teachers, and priests)," and the higher, or "Melchisedec." The basic office of this higher priesthood was that of "high priest." "High priests" were those from which most of the leading administrative officers of the church were chosen. A high priest could be a "patriarch" or spiritual father to the church, one of twelve "apostles," and executive and missionary high council, or a bishop in charge of the temporal affairs of the church. The high priest could also serve as a president of the administrative bureaucracy of the church in "stakes" or "wards." A more common responsibility of adults was the office of elder with other offices of a more special nature evolving by 1835. A "seventy," for instance, was a traveling elder or missionary. All of the "General Authorities" of the church were subject to the ultimate authority of the First Presidency, a quorum composed of the "Prophet, Seer, and Revelator," to the church, who was also President of the High Priesthood of the church, and his two counselors. When these priesthood members acted in their specialized offices in concert at General Conferences they were designated at "quorums." (For further information on this topic see O'Dea, *The Mormons*, pp. 160-61, 174-85; Reorganized Church of Jesus Christ of Latter Day Saints, *The Priesthood Manual* [Independence, Missouri: Herald Publishing House, 1964], pp. 8-77; Doctrine and Covenants 83:104.)
10. Ibid., pp. 42-43.
11. Ibid., pp. 42-44.

12. Smith, "Interview in the Salt Lake Tribune," 949-50.
13. Robert B. Flanders, "The Mormons Who Did Not Go West: A Study of the Emergence of the Reorganized Church of Jesus Christ of Latter Day Saints" (Master's thesis, University of Wisconsin, 1954), pp. 48-49.
14. Joseph Smith, "Voice of the People Should Rule," *SH* 20 (October 15, 1873): 650; Joseph Smith, "Supreme Authority," *SH* 52 (April 16, 1905): 416.
15. Joseph Smith, "Authority—Its Use and Abuse," *SH* 42 (March 20, 1895): 179.
16. Doctrine and Covenants 114:16; "Joint Epistle of the Bishopric and the Twelve," as cited in *History of the RLDS*, vol. 4, pp. 603-04.
17. Robert D. Hutchins, "Joseph Smith III: Moderate Mormon" (Master's thesis, Brigham Young University, 1977), pp. 88-91. See also Clare D. Vlahos, "The Challenge to Centralized Power: Zenas H. Gurley, Jr., and the Prophetic Office," *Courage: A Journal of History, Thought and Action*, 1 (March, 1971): 148-54.
18. Vlahos, "The Challenge to Centralized Power," 145, 154.
19. Joseph Smith III, "Editorial," *SH* 26-27 (May 1, 1880): 143; Joseph Smith, ibid. (September 1, 1880): 268; Joseph Smith, "Editorial," *SH* 40 (July 8, 1893): 422; Joseph Smith, "Consecration," *SH* 48 (May 29, 1901): 433; Joseph Smith, "Power and Finance," *SH* 50 (May 13, 1903): 425; Joseph Smith, "Report for the First Presidency," *GCM* (April 6, 1903), p. 567.
20. General Conference Resolution 386, as cited in Reorganized Church of Jesus Christ of Latter Day Saints, *Rules and Resolutions* (Independence, Missouri: Herald Publishing House, 1964), p. 49.
21. Ibid., p. 50.
22. Doctrine and Covenants 122:2a.
23. Ibid., 122:5; 123:24.
24. Joseph Smith, "Common Consent," *SH* 42 (December 25, 1895): 821.
25. Joseph Smith, "People's Part in the Church," *SH* 46 (June 28, 1899): 409.
26. Smith, *Concerning the Prophet*. . ., p. 140; Editorial, "General Conference," *SH* 50 (April 15, 1903): 331; Paul Edwards, "Theocratic Democracy: Philosopher-King in the

Reorganization," in F. Mark McKiernan, Alma Blair, and Paul M. Edwards, eds., *The Restoration Movement: Essays in Mormon History* (Lawrence, Kansas: Coronado Press, 1973), pp. 344-45; Mary Audentia Smith Anderson, ed., "The Memoirs of Joseph Smith, 1832-1914"; *SH* 84 (January 30, 1937): 143-44.

27. FMS to Israel A. Smith, December 27, 1911, RLDS Archives, letter file.
28. FMS, "First Presidency," *GCM* (April 7, 1909), pp. 1177-79; *History of the RLDS*, vol. 6, p. 167; Edwards, ". . . Philosopher-King . . . ," pp. 344-55.
29. Anderson, ed., "The Memoirs of Joseph Smith" 143-44; Edwards, ". . . Philosopher-King . . . ," p. 349.
30. Joseph Smith, "Obedience to Counsel," *SH* 39 (February 20, 1892): 113-14; Smith, "Voice of the People Should Rule," 650; Smith, "Supreme Authority," 416; Smith, "Authority—Its Use and Abuse," 179.
31. That Smith was a more forceful personality than his father was clear to some by 1896. See Orren Dudley, "Phrenograph of Frederick M. Smith," *Autumn Leaves* 9 (January, 1896): 21.
32. For an example, see Vlahos, 141-58, passim.
33. FMS, "Obedience," *SH* 50 (February 11, 1903): 128-30.
34. Ibid.
35. Ibid.
36. FMS, "Reports," *GCM* (April 6, 1914), p. 1801.
37. FMS to William H. Kelley, December 26, 1896, William H. Kelley Papers, RLDS Archives.
38. FMS to William H. Kelley, February 4, 1903, ibid.
39. FMS to William H. Kelley, June 20, 1907, ibid.
40. FMS to Quorum Presidents, July 10, 1913, RLDS Archives, letter file.
41. FMS, "Reports," p. 1801.
42. FMS to the Quorum of Twelve, April 8, 1909, William H. Kelley Papers, RLDS Archives; FMS to Quorum Presidents, September 10, 1912, RLDS Archives, letter file.
43. Ibid.
44. A summary of the *Herald* articles to this effect may be found in *History of the RLDS*, vol. 6, pp. 107-09; See also FMS to Miss V. A. L. Jones of the *St. Louis Post Dispatch*, February 27, 1907, RLDS Archives, letter file.
45. Joseph Smith, "Men and Things," *SH* 50 (November 4, 1903): 1026.

46. Statement of FMS from Salt Lake City, Utah, December 16, 1905, RLDS Archives, letter files.
47. FMS, "Report from the First Presidency," *GCM* (April 9, 1906), pp. 874-75; Smith, *Concerning the Prophet. . .*, p. 159; *History of the RLDS*, vol. 6, p. 109.
48. FMS, "Our Utah Trip," *SH* 51 (April 6, 1904): 315; Smith, *Concerning the Prophet. . .*, pp. 158, 167-71.
49. FMS, "Editorial—In the Tabernacle, Salt Lake City" (A reprint from *The Deseret News*, February 15, 1904), *SH* 51 (February 24, 1904): 169, 177.
50. FMS, "President Frederick M. Smith Protests" (Reprint from *The Salt Lake Tribune*, July 1, 1905), *SH* 52 (July 19, 1905): 699-700.
51. FMS to Israel A. Smith, November 25, 1905, RLDS Archives, letter file. This statement is strange in light of Smith's own lapses into superstition. While in Utah, for instance, he attempted to cure his "appendicitis" by drinking olive oil consecrated by the elders of his church. See Smith, *Concerning the Prophet. . .*, pp. 162-63.
52. FMS, *A Message from the Seed of Joseph the Seer to the People of the Church of Jesus Christ of Latter Day Saints* (Independence, Missouri: Herald Publishing House, ca. 1905), unnumbered; see also FMS, "President F. M. Smith Sounds a Note of Warning" (Reprint from *The Salt Lake Tribune*, July 28, 1905), *SH* 52 (August 9, 1905): 772.
53. FMS to Joseph Fielding Smith, August 21, 1905, RLDS Archives, letter file.
54. Joseph Fielding Smith to FMS, as cited in Church of Jesus Christ of Latter-day Saints, *Appeal of Frederick M. Smith to President Joseph F. Smith for Unlimited Use of the Meeting Houses of the Latter-Day Saints and His Reply* (Salt Lake City: Deseret Publishing Company, 1905), unnumbered.
55. Statement of FMS from Salt Lake City, Utah, December 16, 1905, RLDS Archives, letter file.
56. FMS, "Unquestioning Obedience," *SH* 53 (August 22, 1906): 796.
57. Ibid.
58. FMS, "United Order of Enoch," *SH* 57 (August 17, 1910): 800.
59. "Statement of President Joseph Smith to His Son Frederick M. Smith, Sunday, November 29, 1914," *Zion's Ensign* 26 (February 11, 1915): 1.

60. Ibid.
61. FMS to the Church, January 21, 1915, as cited in *History of the RLDS*, vol. 6, p. 585.
62. FMS, "Obedience to Law," *SH* 71 (June 24, 1924): 533-36.
63. Doctrine and Covenants 112:1-2. This statement was quoted by Smith in a June 23, 1929 sermon. See FMS, "Sanctity of the Law," *SH* 76 (October 9, 1929): 1224; also FMS, Notes for a sermon on government, n.d., FMS Papers.
64. FMS, "Sanctity of the Law," 1224; FMS, Notes for a sermon on government, n.d., FMS Papers.
65. FMS, "Obedience to Law," 533-36; FMS, "Safety in Law, and Liberty in Respect," *SH* 74 (November 9, 1927): 1305; FMS, "The Sanctity of the Law," 1227.
66. Ibid.
67. Ibid.
68. FMS, "Safety in Law, and Liberty in Respect," 1305; FMS, Notes for a Masonic Lecture, n.d., FMS Papers, Masonic file; FMS, Statement by FMS for the First Presidency, *GCM* (April 7, 1909), p. 1179.
69. FMS, Notes for a Masonic Lecture, ca. 1929, FMS Papers, Masonic file.
70. FMS, "Sanctity of the Law," 1225-26.
71. FMS, "Looking Forward to the Redemption of Zion," *SH* 72 (May 13, 1925): 527.
72. Ibid., FMS, "Safety in Law and Liberty in Respect," 1305; FMS, "Respect for Law," *SH* 74 (June 29, 1927): 737-38; "Letter to Herbert Hoover," *GCM* (April 10, 1930), pp. 49-50.
73. "President Smith's Views on Democracy in Church Government: Extracts from an Address of Frederick M. Smith at the Stone Church, January 4, 1920," *SH* 67 (March 3, 1920): 193-94.
74. Ibid.; FMS, Sermon notes, n.d., FMS Papers.
75. FMS to G. Stanley Hall, February 8, 1917, CULP, FMS student file.
76. "President Smith's Views on Democracy in Church Government. . . ," 193-94.
77. Ibid.
78. FMS, "Lectures to the Priesthood," *SH* 64 (April 25, 1917): 392.
79. Edwards, ". . . Philosopher-King . . . ," pp. 345-47; Underlinings and notes by FMS in Nicholas Murray Butler, *The Responsibility of Youth* (n.p., 1944), FMS Papers.

80. Edwards, "...Philosopher-King...," p. 347; FMS, Notes on leadership, n.d., FMS Papers.
81. Doctrine and Covenants, sections 114 to 122 and 124 to 131.
82. FMS, *The Higher Powers of Man*, (Lamoni, Iowa: Herald Publishing House, 1918), pp. 55, 66-70.
83. FMS, "Some Church Ideals," *Zion's Ensign* 29 (November 7, 1918): 5-7.
84. Ibid., 8.
85. Elbert A. Smith, "Notes on the Last Conference," *SH* 63 (April 26, 1916): 393.
86. Doctrine and Covenants 133:1-2.
87. Ruth Lyman Smith to G. Stanley Hall, late April, 1916, CULP, FMS student file.
88. Doctrine and Covenants 133:3-4.
89. Edwards, "...Philosopher-King...," p. 354.
90. FMS, "Conference Address [April 6, 1927]," p. 4128; FMS to J. M. Stubbart, May 5, 1927, RLDS Archives, letter file; FMS, "Am I Lazy?" *SH* 85 (July 9, 1938): 868.
91. FMS, "False Witness," *Priesthood Journal* 9 (January, 1923): 8; FMS, "With Whom Should We Discuss a Brother's Faults?" *SH* 75 (May 23, 1928): 609.
92. FMS, "Address to the Conference [April 6, 1920]," p. 2865; Mrs. B. M. Anderson to FMS, July 22, 1921, Edwards Collection; Alice M. Edwards Questionnaire, 1972.
93. FMS to Mrs. B. M. Anderson, July 10, 1932, Edwards Collection.
94. FMS underlinings on clipping, "The Penalty of Leadership," *The Saturday Evening Post* (January 2, 1915), FMS Papers.
95. FMS, "The Lord's Supper," *SH* 76 (April 3, 1929): 385.
96. Random notes, n.d., FMS Papers.
97. Doctrine and Covenants 133:2b; 134:7; 136:3b.
98. FMS, "The Essentiality of Loyalty in the Development of Zion," *SH* 70 (January 10, 1923): 26.
99. Ibid., 27-28.
100. Ibid., 28.
101. Ibid., 29-30. See also FMS, Notes for talk to the Order of the Eastern Star, "The Lesson of Esther," n.d., FMS Papers, Masonic File; FMS, "Safety in Law, and Liberty in Respect," 1305; FMS, "Obedience to Law," 533-36.
102. FMS, et al., "Concerning Church Government," *SH* 71 (July 6, 1924): 651-52; FMS, "Document on Church Government," *GCM* (April 6, 1925), pp. 3803-04.

103. Ibid.
104. Ibid.
105. FMS to M. H. Siegfried, July 21, 1924, RLDS Archives, letter file.
106. *History of the RLDS*, vol. 7, p. 166.
107. Quorum of Twelve Minutes, 1916, pp. 16, 49, as cited in ibid., p. 114. These minutes are not open to historical research.
108. *History of the RLDS*, vol. 7, p. 113. Conflict over the administrative authority of the Twelve and the Presidency had surfaced earlier in 1908. See ibid., p. 266.
109. FMS, "President's Address to the Conference," *SH* 64 (April 11, 1917): 341.
110. Ibid.
111. FMS, "Report of the First Presidency," *GCM* (April 6, 1917), p. 2282.
112. *History of the RLDS*, vol. 7, p. 326; Quorum of Twelve Minutes (1919), p. 11, as cited in ibid., pp. 324-25.
113. *Brief Submitted by the Quorum of Twelve* (n.p., 1919), pp. 1-2, RLDS Archives. (See also Doctrine and Covenants 104:12; 105:12; 122:9; 123:23.)
114. FMS to the Quorum of Twelve, February 24, 1919, as cited in ibid.
115. *Brief Submitted by the Quorum of Twelve*, pp. 3-5; Quorum of Twelve Minutes (1919), p. 11, as cited in *History of the RLDS*, vol. 7, pp. 324-25, 328.
116. The records showed that Smith received the following amounts from the church treasury for these respective years: 1916, $3,978.07; 1917, $5,652.19; and 1918, $5,995.84. These figures represented personal and family expenditures only, and did not include those for transportation, office, or library expenses, and in 1917 alone were $4,063.27 higher than the average stipend for the other fourteen men. See ibid., p. 4.
117. Ibid., p. 4.
118. Ibid., p. 6.
119. Ibid., p. 7, Doctrine and Covenants 122:10.
120. *Brief Submitted by the Quorum of Twelve*, p. 8.
121. FMS, "Message of the President," *GCM* (April 6, 1919), p. 2693.
122. Ibid., p. 2692.
123. FMS, *The President's Message to Conference, 1919, Lamoni, Iowa* (Lamoni, Iowa: Herald Publishing House, 1919), pp. 5-6.

124. Ibid., pp. 7, 9.
125. Ibid., pp. 7-8; FMS, "Message of the President [April 6, 1919]," pp. 2694, 2969-97. See also FMS, "The President's Call," *Zion's Ensign*, 30 (May 8, 1919): 289, and clipping from *Central Christian Advocate* (April 30, 1919): 4; FMS Papers, wherein Smith is described as an educated, "modern man" compared to his people whose "faith rests on gulping down . . . preposterous claims," and in resisting modernization.
126. FMS, *The President's Message to Conference*, 1919, p. 6.
127. Ibid.
128. Ibid., pp. 5, 9.
129. See *Brief Submitted by Quorum of Twelve.*
130. *GCM* (April 7, 1919), pp. 2273-74; ibid. (April 10, 1919), p. 2784, ibid. (April 11, 1919), p. 2785.
131. Elbert A. Smith and John Rushton, "Ministerial Policy," *GCM* (April 15, 1919), pp. 2295-96.
132. Elbert A. Smith, "Some Memories of President Frederick M. Smith," *SH* 104 (May 13, 1957): p. 440; FMS, *The President's Message to Conference, 1919, Lamoni, Iowa*, p. 5.
133. *GCM* (April 17, 1919), pp. 2800-01.
134. FMS, "Address by President Frederick M. Smith," *GCM* (April 18, 1919), pp. 2834, 2836.
135. Doctrine and Covenants 133.
136. Ibid., 134; FMS, "Statements by President Frederick M. Smith," *GCM* (October 2, 1922), pp. 3199-200.
137. *GCM* (October 12, 1922), pp. 3241-44; Walter W. Smith, "The General Conference of 1922," *Journal of History* 16:137; Elbert A. Smith, *On Memory's Beam* (Independence, Missouri: Herald Publishing House, 1946), pp. 233-34.
138. Speech by John Rushton, *GCM* (October 13, 1922), p. 3248.
139. *GCM* (October 15, 1922), pp. 3279-80.
140. Ibid. (October 18, 1922), 3307. His outlook for the future was not quite as bleak as this statement indicated, however, and during an evening of this Conference he penned the words of the hymn, "Zion the Beautiful Beckons Us On," and Mrs. Silsbee Smith put the words with the Stephen Foster "Beautiful Dreamer." See Carlyle F. Keuffer ed., *Stories of Our Hymns: Latter Day Saint Hymns and their Composers* (Independence, Missouri: Herald Publishing House, 1938), p. 142; *The Hymnal*, pp. 452-453.
141. FMS, "Address to the Conference [April 6, 1920]," pp.

2870-71; *History of the RLDS*, vol. 7, pp. 131, 145; FMS, "Notes and Queries," *Unity* 3 (June, 1917): 7-8; FMS, "A General Pastoral," *Zion's Ensign* 28 (May 24, 1917): 1-2; FMS to "Dear Brother," October 14, 1918, RLDS Archives, letter file.

142. FMS, "President's Address to the Conference [April 11, 1917]," p. 341.
143. Smith, "Some Memories of President Frederick M. Smith," p. 442.
144. "Report of the Women's Auxiliary for Social Service," *GCM* (August 9, 1916), p. 2155.
145. FMS, "Message of the President [April 6, 1919]," 2696; Herman C. Smith, "The Conference of 1918," *Journal of History* 12 (July 18, 1919): 259-78.
146. FMS, "Our Aims Are One," *SH* 70 (June 17, 1923): 725. See also Daniel Macgregor to FMS, n.d., FMS Papers.
147. *History of the RLDS*, vol. 7, pp. 187-88.
148. FMS, George N. Briggs, Daniel Macgregor, G. S. Trowbridge and Mrs. F. M. Smith, Report of the Coordinating Committee (Lamoni, Iowa: Herald Publishing House, 1918), pp. 1-4.
149. *GCM* (1919), pp. 2811-12.
150. Thomas W. Williams, "Report of T. W. Williams, General Superintendent, Religio Department," *GCM* (April 7, 1920), p. 2975; FMS, "Report of the Department of Recreation and Expression," ibid. (September 8, 1923), p. 3366.
151. FMS, "Notes and Queries," pp. 7-8; FMS, "Coordination," *Priesthood Journal*, vol. 8 (November, 1922), pp. 163-64.
152. Samuel A. Burgess, "The General Conference of 1923," *Journal of History* 17 (January, 1924): 23, 25; Smith, *On Memory's Beam*, p. 236; *History of the RLDS*, vol. 7, pp. 558-59; Speech by Daniel T. Williams, *GCM* (October 6, 1923), pp. 3539-49.
153. For example, see A. Max Carmichael, "How to Change Forms of Organization in Local Department Work," *SH* 70 (January 10, 1923): 36; A. Max Carmichael, "The Departments," *SH* 70 (May 2, 1923): 413; and *History of the RLDS*, vol. 7, pp. 531-32.
154. FMS, "Independence," *SH* 70 (April 25, 1923): 405.
155. Ibid. The Kansas City Stake would soon pass a resolution to the same effect. Speech by Daniel T. Williams, *GCM* (October 6, 1923), p. 3546.
156. Speech by J. F. Curtis, *GCM* (October 6, 1923), pp. 3522-24;

History of the RLDS, vol. 7, pp. 532-33; Burgess, "The General Conference of 1923," 23.

157. *GCM* (October 4, 1923), p. 3452.
158. Doctrine and Covenants 25:1 "All things shall be done by common consent in the church," ibid., 27:4 "All things must be done in order and by common consent in the church, by the prayer of faith."
159. Mosiah 13:35: "Make it your law to do your business by the voice of the people."
160. Joseph Smith III, "Nominations to Office," *SH* 39 (July 16, 1892): 454, 455; Smith, "Voice of the People Should Rule," p. 650. Herein Joseph Smith expressed his antipathy for autocracy and upheld the right of the people to voice and vote in the selection of their leaders. Limitations in the right of choice through nomination was "gross abuse of the liberties of the people."
161. *GCM* (October 6, 1923), p. 3457.
162. Speech of J. F. Curtis, ibid., pp. 3524, 3533.
163. Speech of Daniel T. Williams, ibid., pp. 3538-49.
164. Speech of Myron A. McConley, *GCM* (October 6, 1923), p. 3518.
165. Speech of T. W. Williams, ibid. (October 8 and 9, 1923), pp. 3562-67, 3572-74, 3582-84. In 1896, however, Williams argued that the power of the quorums in matters of "doctrine, rule and order" of the church were anterior to that of the people. (See T. W. Williams, "General Conference," *SH* 43 [February 12, 1896]: 108.)
166. Ibid., p. 3567.
167. Speech by Elbert A. Smith, ibid. (October 9, 1923), pp. 3586-91, passim.
168. F. Henry Edwards to Alice M. Edwards, October 4 and 10, 1923, Edwards Collection.
169. *GCM* (October 9, 1923), p. 3464.
170. Ibid.
171. Ibid., pp. 3555, 3565.
172. F. Henry Edwards to Alice M. Edwards, October 20, 1923, Edwards Collection.
173. *History of the RLDS*, vol. 7, pp. 570-71.
174. "Report of the Board of Publication," *GCM* (April 7, 1925), pp. 3710-13.
175. Ibid., p. 3704.

176. *History of the RLDS*, vol. 6, pp. 114, 199, 291, 504; vol. 7, p. 202.
177. As cited in "Report of the Board of Publication," p. 3709.
178. Joseph Smith, "To the Saints," *SH* 38 (May 9, 1891): 289; Elbert A. Smith, "Statement of Acceptance," *SH* 71 (July 2, 1924): 626.
179. "Report of the Board of Publication," p. 3704; R. J. Lambert, "Editorial Policy of the Herald," *SH* 71 (June 4, 1924): 529. No sources reviewed by this writer give any reason why the questionnaire was not sent to the membership at large. Perhaps some of the reasons revolved around the expense of such a project in an institution already strained by increasing costs and decreasing subscriptions, or the belief by the Board that better intelligence could be ascertained from leaders rather than followers.
180. "Report of the Board of Publication," pp. 3704-05.
181. Ibid., pp. 3706-07; Lambert, "Editorial Policy of the Herald" 529-30.
182. "Report of the Board of Publication," p. 3706; Lambert, "Editorial Policy of the Herald" 529-30.
183. FMS, "Official," *SH* 71 (June 18, 1924): 578-79.
184. Benjamin R. McGuire and Arthur E. McKim, "The Facts of the Case," ibid. (June 25, 1924): 604-05, "Report of the Board of Publication," pp. 3707-10.
185. As cited in Paul M. Hanson, "Statements of Acceptance," *SH* 71 (August 13, 1924): 771-72.
186. Ibid.
187. T. W. Williams, "Freedom of the Press," ibid., (July 16, 1924): 674-76.
188. Joseph Luff, "Know All Men By These Presents, Etc.," ibid., (July 23, 1924): 698-99.
189. Hanson, 771-72.
190. R. S. Salyards, "Freedom of the Press and Free Discussion," *SH* 71 (August 6, 1924): 756-58; Luff, 698-99; Williams, "Freedom of the Press," 674-76.
191. General Conference Resolution 298, April 10, 1885, as cited in *Rules and Resolutions*, pp. 44-45.
192. Benjamin R. McGuire, James F. Keir and Israel A. Smith, *The Unbroken Chain: A Treatise on the Law of the Lord as Relating to the Work of the Bishopric* (Independence, Missouri: n.d.), pp. 1-8; Benjamin R. McGuire, James F. Keir,

Israel A. Smith, John W. Rushton, T. W. Williams, A. V. Karlstrom and Roderick May, *Protest Against Supreme Directional Control* (Independence, Missouri: n.d.), p. 3; Elbert A. Smith, *The True Philosophy of Church Government* (Independence, Missouri: Herald Publishing House, 1924), p. 8; Elbert A. Smith, *On Memory's Beam*, p. 238; *History of the RLDS*, vol. 7, pp. 592, 598.

193. Smith, *On Memory's Beam*, p. 238; Elbert A. Smith, *The True Philosophy of Church Government*, p. 8.
194. FMS, "The April Council of the First Presidency, Members of the Council of Twelve in America, and the Order of Bishops," *SH* 71 (June 18, 1924): 578-79, Smith, *The True Philosophy of Church Government*, pp. 9-10.
195. FMS, "Document on Church Government," pp. 3803-3804.
196. FMS to M. H. Siegfried, July 26, 1924, RLDS Archives, letter file.
197. *GCM* (March 17, 1917), p. 2401; ibid. (April 6, 1918), pp. 2492, 2496-2498.
198. Doctrine and Covenants 87:5; 104:42; 122:2; General Conference Resolution 386, as cited in *Rules and Resolutions*, p. 49.
199. Doctrine and Covenants 38:8c; 122:5, 6; 123:24; 126:10; 128:2, 3, 8, 9; "Basis of Adjustment," as cited in *History of the RLDS*, vol. 4, pp. 223-225; "Articles of Incorporation of the Reorganized Church of Jesus Christ of Latter Day Saints" (1872), preamble and articles 2 and 7, as cited in *Rules and Resolutions*, app. A, pp. 194-198; McGuire, Keir, and Smith, pp. 1-10; Edmund L. Kelley, "Statement by Former Presiding Bishop," *SH* 71 (July 30, 1924): 724.
200. McGuire, et al., *Protest Against "Supreme Directional Control,"* pp. 8-11; T. W. Williams, "Aftermath of the Advisory Council," *SH* 71 (November 5, 1924): 1068.
201. Israel A. Smith, "For Justice, and in the Interest of Peace," *SH* 71 (August 6, 1924): 754; Israel A. Smith, *Let the Facts Be Known* (Independence, Missouri: n.p., n.d.), pp. 18-19.
202. Williams, "Aftermath of the Advisory Council," 1066, McGuire, et al., *The Protest Against "Supreme Directional Control,"* pp. 8-10.
203. As cited in Smith, *The True Philosophy of Church Government*, p. 8.
204. FMS to Elbert A. Smith, September 14, 1924, RLDS Archives, letter file.

205. Smith, "For Justice, and in the Interests of Peace," 755-56; Smith, *Let the Facts Be Known*, pp. 24-25.
206. B. R. McGuire to FMS, April 21, 1924, as cited in McGuire, et al., *Protest Against "Supreme Directional Control,"* pp. 8-11.
207. FMS to B. R. McGuire, April 22, 1924, as cited in ibid.
208. B. R. McGuire to FMS, April 25, 1924, as cited in McGuire, Keir and Smith, *The Unbroken Chain*. . ., pp. 12-13.
209. Ibid.
210. FMS, "Joint Council Sessions," *SH* 71 (April 30, 1924): 409.
211. John Rushton, T. W. Williams, B. R. McGuire, et al., "Open Letter to the President, Ministry and Membership of the Church," *SH* 71 (June 4, 1924): 531.
212. FMS to T. W. Williams, June 18, 1924, as cited in Williams "Aftermath of the Advisory Council," 1068.
213. T. W. Williams to FMS, June 23, 1924, as cited in ibid., 1069.
214. McGuire, et al., *Protest Against "Supreme Directional Control,"* p. 11.
215. Ibid., p. 13; Israel A. Smith, *Let the Facts Be Known*, p. 29.
216. FMS, Elbert A. Smith, J. A. Gillen, et al., "Concerning Church Government," *SH* 71 (July 6, 1924): 651-52.
217. McGuire, et al., *Protest Against "Supreme Directional Control,"* pp. 15-16.
218. Richard J. Lambert, "Anent the Herald Controversy," *SH* 71 (August 13, 1924): 769-70; Richard J. Lambert, "A United People," ibid. (June 11, 1924): 554-55.
219. These figures represent the assessment of F. Henry Edwards, the official RLDS historian of the period. See *History of the RLDS*, vol. 7, p. 599.
220. Ibid., pp. 599-601.
221. Doctrine and Covenants 87:5, as cited in Smith, *The True Philosophy of Church Government*, pp. 12-13; 40-50.
222. *History of the RLDS*, vol. 1, p. 281, as cited in Smith, *The True Philosophy of Church Government*, pp. 13-14.
223. Smith, *The True Philosophy of Church Government*, pp. 14-15, 28; (See also Smith, *On Memory's Beam*, pp. 240-41.)
224. Ibid., p. 18, 35.
225. Ibid., p. 50f.
226. Ibid., p. 35.
227. Ibid., pp. 37-41. For other articles supportive of Smith's policy see E. R. Davies, "Leadership and Church Government," *SH* 71 (October 1, 1924): 940-41; Ralph W. Farrell, "Glimpse at Government," ibid. (August 27, 1924): 820-24; J. A. Koehler,

"Settling the Controversy," ibid. (September 17, 1924): 895-99; A. B. Phillips, "Leadership and Orthodoxy," ibid. (August, 1924): 746-47; A. B. Phillips, "Authority in Church Government," Part III, ibid. (December 24, 1924): 1232-34; Garland E. Tickemyer, "The Philosophy of Ecclesiastical Government in the Reorganized Church," ibid., 113 (February 15, 1966): 117, 131-32.

228. Israel A. Smith, "Know the Law," *SH* 71 (November 12, 1924): 1087-92; Israel A. Smith, "Know the Law: Supreme Directional Control," ibid. (November 26, 1924): 1135; Smith, "For Justice, and in the Interest of Peace," 750-51; Smith, *Let the Facts Be Known*, pp. 8-9, 24-25. For elaboration of the latter point, see Arthur E. McKim, "Joseph Smith as Trustee-in-Trust: Some Unhappy Items of History Have Bearing on Present Problems," *SH* 71 (November 26, 1924): 1131-32.
229. McGuire, Keir, and Smith, *The Unbroken Chain*. . . , pp. 1-10, 19.
230. Ibid., p. 19. Essentially the same reasoning is presented in McGuire, et al., *Protest Against "Supreme Directional Control,"* pp. 1-16, also printed in *SH* 71 (August 20, 1924): 796-800.
231. Benjamin R. McGuire, "Let Us Carry On," *SH* 71 (August 13, 1924): 773-74. (For another example of a moderate critic, see John W. Rushton, "Let the Church Decide," ibid., 774-78.)
232. B. L. McKim, "Is It a Change" and What Does It Mean?" ibid. (October 29, 1924): 1042-45; McKim, *Has the Church a Prophet at Its Head?* (n.p., n.d.), pp. 9-10.
233. James F. Keir, "Infallibility," *SH* 71 (July 9, 1924): 663-64.
234. Daniel Macgregor, "Supreme Directional Control," ibid. (December 31, 1924): 1261-62.
235. C. B. Hartshorn, "Is 'a Strongly Centralized Government' Desirable?" ibid. (December 24, 1924): 1235-39.
236. Paul M. Hanson, "Prove All Things," ibid. (October 1, 1924): 941-42.
237. F. M. Sheehy, *Nothing Done Until Done Right* (Independence, Missouri: n.p., 1924), pp. 1-2.
238. T. W. Williams, "Can the Common People Be Trusted?" *SH* 71 (July 9, 1924): 649-50; Williams, "Aftermath of the Advisory Council," 1068-70.
239. T. W. Williams, "Supreme Directional Control in Operation," *SH* 71 (August 20, 1924): 793-96; T. W. Williams, "Further Examination of Northern California Action," ibid. (October

29, 1924): 1038-42; T. W. Williams, "Instructing Delegates," ibid. (December 10, 1924): 1188-89.

240. J. D. White, W. H. Dawson, J. T. Smith, Jr., Cecil Hawley, Bernice Christopher, J. B. Carmichael, Virgil Etzenhouser, and E. B. Hull, "The Facts About the Northern California District," ibid. (October 22, 1924): 1013-16.

241. Ibid., 1016.

242. Samuel A. Burgess, "Concerning an Open Letter," ibid. (July 30, 1924): 722-23, 741; J. A. Gillen, F. Henry Edwards, J. F. Garver, R. S. Budd, E. J. Gleazer and D. T. Williams, "The Case from Another Standpoint," ibid. (August 27, 1924): 823-24; Edward Rannie, "The Lord's Way," ibid. (July 16, 1924): 678; E. L. Kelley, "Statement by the Former Presiding Bishop," ibid., 724.

243. Edwards, ". . . Philosopher-King . . .," p. 353; *History of the RLDS*, vol. 7, p. 629.

244. *GCM* (April 6, 1925), pp. 3803-04.

245. Ibid.

246. T. C. Kelley, E. E. Long, J. T. Riley, E. A. Curtis, R. L. Fulk, and J. W. Davis, "Proposed Basis of Agreement," ibid. (April 3, 1925), pp. 3805-06; Independence *Examiner* (April 6, 125), p. 1.

247. *History of the RLDS*, vol. 7, p. 630.

248. *GCM* (April 7, 1925), pp. 3808-09. In the Quorum of Twelve, those supporting the original motion were J. A. Gillen, M. A. McConley, J. F. Garver, R. S. Budd, C. F. Ellis, D. T. Williams, E. J. Gleazer, and F. H. Edwards; those opposed were J. W. Rushton, J. F. Curtis, P. M. Hanson and T. W. Williams.

249. Ibid. (April 6, 1925), pp. 3843-44; Independence *Examiner* (April 8, 1925), p. 1.

250. Independence *Examiner* (April 8, 1925), p. 1.

251. Ibid., "A Protest," *GCM* (April 8, 1925), pp. 3809-10. See also E. E. Long, *Minority Rights or in the Footsteps of the Fathers: The Protesting Saints Declare Themselves* (Independence, Missouri: n.d.), pp. 10-14; T. W. Williams, "History of the Protest Movement in Independence," *Messenger*, 1 (October 1, 1925): 1-2.

252. Independence *Examiner* (April 8, 1925), p. 1; GCM (April 8, 1925), p. 3809.

253. Independence *Examiner* (April 10, 1925), p. 1.

254. R. M. Maloney to FMS, n.d., as cited in *Messenger*, 2 (March, 1927).

255. Independence *Examiner* (April 10, 1925), p. 1.
256. Ibid. (April 11, 1925), p. 1; *Kansas City Star Magazine* (April 5, 1925), p. 13; Williams, "A History of the Protest Movement in Independence," 1-4.
257. F. Henry Edwards to Alice M. Edwards, April, 1925, Edwards Collection.
258. C. Ed. Miller, "Memories of C. Ed. Miller," Part XI, *SH* 104 (October 14, 1957): 978-79.
259. Random notes, 1925, FMS Papers. The scripture in reference was II Peter 2:16.
260. Ibid.
261. *GCM* (April 11, 1925), p. 3815.
262. Ibid., pp. 3815-17.
263. *GCM* (April 11, 1925), p. 3818.
264. Ibid., pp. 3819-21.
265. Ibid., pp. 3822-31; Independence *Examiner* (April 13, 1925), p. 1.
266. *GCM* (April 16, 1925), pp. 3855-56; Independence *Examiner* (April 17, 1925), p. 1.
267. *GCM* (April 17, 1925), p. 3858; Independence *Examiner* (April 17, 1925), p. 1.
268. Smith, "Some Memories of President Frederick M. Smith," pp. 465-67.
269. "Statement and Revelation," *GCM* (April 17, 1925), p. 3836; Doctrine and Covenants 135; Independence *Examiner* (April 18, 1925), p. 1.
270. *GCM* (April 17, 1925), p. 3865; Independence *Examiner* (April 20, 1925), p. 1.
271. James E. Yates, *Refusal to Sustain Doctrine of Supremacy of Church President* (Independence, Missouri: n.p., 1925), pp. 1-3.
272. Ibid., p. 4.
273. *GCM* (April 22, 1925), p. 3822; "Stormy to the Last," Independence *Examiner* (April 22, 1925), p. 1.
274. Ibid.
275. Figures supporting these conclusions may be found in *History of the RLDS*, vol. 7, pp. 624, 639.
276. E. E. Long, *The De Kalb Agreement* (n.p., n.d.), pp. 1-3.
277. Paul M. Hanson, "Statement, Protest, and Notification," *Messenger*, 2 (October 1, 1926): 1; T. W. Williams, E. D. Moore, and Vida E. Smith, "Under Supreme Directional Control," ibid., 1 (April, 1926): 83; Edwards, ". . . Philosopher-

King. . . ," pp. 355-56; Daniel T. Williams, Oral History Memoir, pp. 39-41, 62-63, RLDS Archives.

278. David P. Thelen, "Robert LaFollette's Leadership, 1891-1896: The Old and New Politics and the Dilemma of the Progressive Tradition," *Pacific Northwest Quarterly*, 62 (July, 1971): 105-06; David P. Thelen, "Progressivism as a Radical Movement," in Howard H. Quint, Milton Cantor and Dean Albertson eds., *Main Problems in American History*, II (3rd ed., Homewood, Illinois: The Dorsey Press, 1972), p. 157.

279. Aiken and McDonnell, pp. 133-34, 140-43; Walter Rauschenbusch, *Christianity and Social Crisis*, ed., Robert D. Cross (New York: Harper and Row, 1964), pp. 409-11.

280. Dorothy G. Ross, *G. Stanley Hall: Psychologist as Prophet* (Chicago: University of Chicago Press, 1972), pp. 311-12, 318; FMS to G. Stanley Hall, February 8, 1917, CULP, FMS Student file.

281. Herbert Croly, *The Promise of American Life* (New York: E. P. Dutton and Company, Inc., 1963), pp. 265-79.

282. Croly, p. 279.

283. Samuel Haber, *Efficiency and Uplift: Scientific Management in the Progressive Era, 1890-1920* (Chicago: University of Chicago Press, 1964), pp. x-ix, xii; Holli, pp. 141-143.

284. Melvin G. Holli, "Urban Reform in the Progressive Era," as cited in Lewis L. Gould, ed., *The Progressive Era* (New York: Syracuse University Press, 1974), pp. 146-48, 150-51.

Chapter VI

SUPREME DIRECTIONAL CONTROL, 1925 THROUGH 1946: FORM WITHOUT SUBSTANCE

The excesses of supreme directional control that protesters feared would lead to total autocratization of the church never materialized to any significant degree. Only in Independence and its environs did President Smith attempt to personally direct the political and economic affairs of the church for spiritual purposes, and even there the system functioned in an unwieldy, cumbersome manner far removed from his goal of efficiency and was ignored by many. In the face of the schisms following the Conference of 1925, continued resistance from vocal opponents, financial retrenchment necessitated by the depression of the next decade, and his declining vigor, he came to recognize that power alone did not guarantee efficiency or progress toward Zion. While still maintaining the ideal of governing efficiently through supreme directional control, he learned patience through the years. He directed his presidential energies more toward professionalizing the ministry of the church and formalizing its religious ceremonies and services.

For the twenty-one years between 1925 and 1946 his supreme directional control of the ecclesiastical structure of the larger church was uneven and sporadic, but in Independence he made a prodigious effort to create a prototype for the kingdom of God and implored his faithful retinue to "fall in line." While the Independence Zion did not fulfill his hopes for its future, it did represent the most he could achieve under a governing philosophy in which most of its resident Saints acquiesced but did not savor.

The Continuity of Dissent

Following the General Conference of 1925, ripples from the SDC controversy continued to disturb the surface of Independence and its surrounding stakes. To the protesters who were serious about their democratic rights in the context of the church, SDC was the equivalent of autocracy and "popery." Some of these dissenters continued to oppose President Smith as "loyal opposition" within the institution; others, unable to reconcile theocracy and democracy, left it. Fearing for the future, they kept the issue of autocracy alive for the rest of his administration and frustrated the development of his showcase for Zion.

During the latter part of the Conference of 1925 the unorganized protest against his leadership began to formalize. Some of the former RLDS clerics who had been placed under ministerial silence chose to transfer their institutional allegiance to the Church of Christ, another small faction headquartered across Lexington Street from the Stone Church.[1] One of the attractions of this church to them was the absence of a First Presidency and the preeminence of the Twelve as its collective leadership. On the last Sunday of April, while still maintaining their fealty to the Reorganized church, John Rushton, T. W. Williams, and B. R. McGuire attended the Church of Christ and addressed the congregation of 200 on the topic of "spiritual degeneracy," declared their allegiance to Christ as the only absolute head of the church, and pleaded for divine "light" for their future course of action.[2]

Those who could not support SDC continued to meet there during the month of June and drafted a letter to President Smith in which they—600 strong—attested to their desire not to withdraw from the Reorganized church. In response to their request to worship separately, Fred M. countered with a "working agreement" to the effect that they would continue to meet with all other Saints in services that emphasized their areas of concurrence.[3] The protesters held out for their own meeting, and in October they convened their own conference with T. W. Williams as chairman. At this meeting they elected him editor of *The Messenger*, declared their support for the principles of free thought and expression and, with the exception of "errors" in the Doctrine and Covenants, accepted that canon along with the Book of Mormon and the Bible as scriptural authorities.[4] Among the errors they saw in the Doctrine and Covenants were its provisions for an independent presidency, centrality in administrative and judicial affairs, and power to control succession.[5]

Fred M. widened the gap between the official church and the protesters by denying them the privileges of assembly in institutional houses and the use of its trust funds. T. W. responded with his own "Declaration of Rights" in which he denounced the "radical changes" imposed on the church by its president and resolved to continue to hold public meetings, publish *The Messenger*, and raise funds. Fred M. then revoked the ministerial licenses of T. W. Williams, E. D. Moore, and B. L.

McKim as a means of coercing them.[6] Williams followers decried this act as the "silencing" of "men whose integrity has never been questioned and who . . . have been guilty of no crime."[7] They were "brutally stricken down, prejudged and condemned by an implicated judge" determined to "eliminate" all dissent.[8] Hardly intimidated, they organized their own small "Protestant Group of Independence" under the pastorate of T. W.,[9] and continued to excoriate Fred M. as an unconscionable religious despot. His stewardship program was a mere "tax collection agency for the church" to underwrite his spendthrift ideas,[10] and religious education for priesthood at Graceland College and Independence was calculated to create trained ministerial automatons.[11] Furthermore, he had "wrested" away their church buildings and treasuries,[12] and combined legislative, executive, and judicial authority to an extent repugnant to American and English citizens; "even kings" controlled less than President Smith as "divine-right" monarch.[13] Finally, President Calvin Coolidge was cited as relegating centralized, bureaucratic power to a tyrannical, reactionary past that the United States had outgrown.[14]

Restraint characterized Fred M's reaction to these frontal assaults. By the Conference of 1926, approximately 600 Saints were associated in varying degrees with the protest movement and he wished to reconcile them. He confessed to the Conference his mixed feelings of sorrow for the disaffection among the ranks and his gratitude for the deeper devotion of those who remained.[15] Beyond this, he sanguinely ascertained that the last Conference had "definitized" the direction of the church and terminated years of bitter contest.[16]

One attempt to heal the breach between the Saints was a motion from the floor to amend his "Document on Church Government" by replacing the word "supreme" with "general" in the phrase "supreme directional control."[17] He acknowledged that SDC had been represented as "implying autocracy, papacy, infallability, monarchy, and invasion of the legislative rights of the people," but these charges misrepresented his intent. Rather than admit to error and accede to the change of "supreme" to "general," he and his advisers presented resolutions to the effect that only God was supreme in the church; that the General Conference was the legislative arm of the church through which its people might speak or "approve, disapprove or initiate legislation"; that the president was the first executive of the church to administer laws approved by General Conference, and that office disclaimed any and all "offensive applications" of supreme directional control; and that all the "honest in heart" should heed their invitation to return to the fold. The report was adopted by a vote of 463 to 28 and was forwarded to all protesters.[18]

Along with this "olive branch," President Smith and his colleagues in the Presidency wrote a series of open letters in specific reply to some of the Williams indictments. They commented that recognition of earthly leaders in no way denied the ultimate leadership of Christ, and noted that even Williams had been chosen as a pastor for a large group of the protesters.[19] Furthermore, he had demonstrated through his actions that he was unable to abide by democratically secured decisions. He had pledged himself in the "Open Letter" of June 4, 1924, to accept the Conference decision regarding SDC and, after a year of debate in the *Herald* and on the Conference floor, all viewpoints had been aired and that body had decided in favor of the president. Why, they asked, would this democratic champion of the Saints "flout" such an overwhelming verdict and encourage others to destroy the church? Was his wisdom greater than that of the majority whose common consent he had so long defended?[20] As well, they concluded, who was the real defender of tradition against innovation and change—T. W. Williams, who wanted to severely edit the Doctrine and Covenants as a scriptural canon and eliminate the Presidency, or Smith, who stood firmly for each?[21] From the perspective of the Presidency, T. W. was the iconoclast, and they were right. It was Fred M. who represented the deeper, authoritarian tradition of Restorationism.

While some of the protesters were persuaded by the president to return to the Reorganized church, as many were not convinced of the sincerity of his invitation or the cogency of his rebuttals. To the latter, the most egregious error was the ministerial silence he arbitrarily imposed on those clerics who could not accommodate his system. Apostle Paul M. Hanson published a list of these "fine leaders" who had already fallen before his headman's axe and now were estranged from the church. He also wrote President Smith in October warning that ripples of the protest were radiating outward from the Center Place.[22]

The most well-known of the protest groups beyond Independence centered in the De Kalb, Illinois, branch. Its president had been silenced for "insubordination," but fifty-three members of the congregation signed a petition indicating that they continued to sustain him as their elected leader.[23] Fred M. did not address the issue until late April, when the group voted to refuse SDC. To pressure conformity he then sent Apostle John Garver to possess the church property, disorganize the branch, and enforce the order of silence. Because the protesters considered Garver simply a "hatchet man" for the "illegal" doctrine of SDC, they ignored him. When suit was brought by the church in March, 1927, both parties agreed to settle their differences out of court when the defendants indicated that they were willing to pursue the case to the legal question of "true" succession to the original church, a Pandora's Box that Fred M. did not wish to open at that point.[24] Also mitigating their feud was his hope to minimize the rancor and bitterness of such altercations and to peacefully mend broken fences. In the settlement between the church and the dissenters the silence imposed on the pastor was lifted and the espousal of SDC was recognized as optional to local congregations.[25]

Although President Smith often directed his associates to take the hard line in coping with the problems of dissent and disaffection, he was the first to make the road easy for all but the most recalcitrant to return by permitting quiet, procedural and substantive disagreement with his leadership as long as they eventually acceded to majority will.[26] The most prominent of individuals to take that road were John Rushton, who served the church as a high priest until he returned to the Twelve in 1932; Benjamin McGuire, who continued in local ministry while he practiced law in New York; and James F. Keir, who functioned as business manager of Herald Publishing House from 1936 to 1942 and as a member of the Standing High Council. T. W. Williams returned to politics and held a seat on the Los Angeles City Council until his death in 1931.[27]

Nevertheless, throughout his administration after 1925, President Smith was considered by his Independence constituency to be an autocrat. In the 1930s he was an "ecclesiastical Hitler"[28] or Mussolini to his critics, who never forgot their defeat in 1925, and his defenders were mere conniving sycophants. To those who denigrated his ministry to the machinations of a dictator, he consistently replied as he did to the Saints of Walnut Park Church on January 12, 1942: "I don't want to be like Hitler. I don't give orders in my work. I make a suggestion and sometimes wait for years to have the suggestion fulfilled."[29] Or, as he complained to auditor Richard Trowbridge in early April, 1927, "Dick, some folks think under Supreme Directional Control I have absolutely my own way, but I want to tell you there are some men in that council [pointing to the Joint Council chamber] who do their own thinking yet."[30]

For him, "Moses' seat always appears comfortable and attractive except to the one whose right it is to occupy,"[31] and being the "Big Chief" or "B.C."—as he was called by various officials of the church hierarchy[32]—was to be circumscribed more with liabilities than freed by advantages. Not only did he believe that he was required to watch over the whole church "like unto Moses," but also he had the self-appointed task of administering the Independence "Zion" that numbered 7,500 Saints among its inhabitants in the latter 1930s. This core of the church was more than a cluster of branches or congregations to him; it was his prime example to the organization and to the external world of how its anatomy should operate under the Presidency. It was crucial to him that it function smoothly under his direct attention without disruption from a "somewhat distorted democracy" who resented the appointive, nominative directive powers of his office.[33] He had opposed that incohesive force throughout his administration, and hoped that out of the struggle would

> grow the city of Zion, that cooperation, that sense of sacredness, that loyalty to the church that will make this the outstanding organization of the whole church and be an example in spirit, in loyalty, in organization, in efficiency, to the whole church. Let's not go backward, Saints. Let's go forward.[34]

The "endowment" of spiritual power he expected for the future would never be experienced by a divided people.[35]

His semblance of control over the institution diminished with distance. Most of the Twelve complied with his request for detailed reports of their ministerial activities in the areas of their assignment, for example, but they did not consider themselves his traveling representatives. From their own respect for authority they perfunctorily deferred to his demands. As official representatives of the church, they found themselves at other times forced to justify his misconceptions and complete lack of real information about local situations. When he visited the Detroit area Board of Stewards in early December, 1939, he was unaware that the board was just beginning to recover from the financial strain of a building program that he had sponsored there three years ago, and now posed questions regarding a new, $300,000 physical expansion for the beleaguered group in lieu of a renewed missionary program. Board members were too respectful to contradict the president, but they took the matter to D. Blair Jensen, F. Henry Edwards, and Bishop G. Leslie DeLapp who confronted him with the facts he had either neglected to read, forgotten, or misunderstood before his trip. Mediating between their chief and the irate board they were able to encourage the latter to overlook his mistakes and reestablish the missionary program.[36]

Internecine quarrels, perfunctory compliance with his requests, dissent, and near-schisms plagued Fred M's administration for its duration, absorbing significant quantities of his time, energy, and enthusiasm. While he always resented democratic or bureaucratic dissenters, he developed a degree of tolerance for "in-house" critics as the years passed. He repeatedly pledged himself to execute any law or directive passed by the people in General Conference because he knew there would be no instances when that body would enact legislation contrary to his will or decline to ratify what he thought necessary. Critics had ceremonial value to him, and by their very existence they contradicted the charges of autocracy they leveled at him. Moreover, he knew that their exaggeration of the democratic aspect of their Restoration heritage would force them to accept the majority rule that democracy extolled and which usually decided in his favor. They were, however, a block in the machinery of efficiency for which he had fought and which still eluded him. Throughout the church in the late twenties and thirties, he learned to ignore dissenters and bureaucratic stagnation. He turned more toward professionalizing its ministry, formalizing its religious services, and developing its youth organizations.

Supreme Directional Control Through the Mid-1930s

In the years after 1926 President Smith was consistent in his demand for excellence and cooperation from all clerical levels and departments of the institution. What he wanted most was uniform policy systematically executed by willing and uncoerced ministers[37] who recognized that they could multiply their effectiveness and respectability through the efficiency provided by better organization. At the onset of the depression he encouraged the Twelve and the Seventy to delegate authority to local, unpaid ministers who were able and in whom they had confidence, instruct them in order to ameliorate their deficiencies, and then supervise their activities from a distance they deemed appropriate.[38] One bit of interesting advice he offered his clerics was to cease plagiarizing their sermons and give credit to those authors to whom they resorted as sources for homiletic exposition.[39]

His penchant for a trained, more professional ministry did not necessarily demand that his appointees be academically prepared, although he preferred those with some educational background. D. T. Williams had only four years of formal schooling, yet he was selected to serve with the Quorum of Twelve.[40] Often embarrassed by the incompetence of a lay ministry called from among peers, President Smith insisted that all ordained clerics upgrade the quality of their service by giving systematic attention to self-improvement through formal courses and/or careful reading and disciplined study. While the quorums were not professional "associations" he urged their members to use that structure to standardize their approaches to specific duties, to discuss grievances or problems, and to engage in organized classwork. Such serious attention would liberate them from ignorance and enhance their natural abilities as they integrated faith, intellect, and duty.[41] Among other things they should learn to know themselves, become acquainted with the history of the Christian church and its theology, know the structure of civil and ecclesiastical government, employ the basics of clear speech and writing in their ministry, and become aware of what was required for appropriate and meaningful ceremony.[42]

He also demanded that all ministers who represented the church be morally above reproach in order to decrease their vulnerability to the ravages of "dame gossip."[43] For those who were "believed" to be guilty of "immoral or unChristianlike conduct" or were persistently inactive, he insisted on imposing ministerial silence administratively, allowing the accused sixty days to appeal to the Standing High Council to challenge the action.[44]

Just as important to him were dignity, poise, and decorum. Priesthood members needed to be in complete control of themselves as they conducted or presided over the various worship services and sacraments of the institution. He directed those with such responsibilities to avoid manifestations of nervousness such as moving their hands, scratching about the face or head, or acquiescing in passionate or emotional expression. They were also advised not to cross their legs, shrug their shoulders, or slouch in pulpit chairs. Most importantly, they must "win the confidence of the masses, yet remain above the foibles of the hoipolloi," be alert to the church program, give loyal support to superior officials, or keep silent.[45]

Furthermore, President Smith had always wanted the church and its priesthood to organize and offer a systematic program for its youth. Since "Our youth are largely what we make them,"[46] he hoped that the ministry under his knowledgeable guidance could create a positive, wholesome, nurturant experience that would provide for them a viable alternative to the baneful influences of secular culture.[47] In the Independence area he encouraged youth discussion clubs to treat religion, philosophy, morality, citizenship, and myriad other topics, and he was especially flattered when they named themselves the "Fredericks" in his honor.[48] At the Conference of 1930 he and concerned departmental leaders placed the youth activities of the church under the general authority of the Department of Religious Education, a move that satisfied his urge for organized bureaucracies. Between this date and 1936 he encouraged young people to hold conventions in Lamoni and Independence to discuss their role in the church and to develop projects that would assist to pay its debts, provide scholarship funds, and initiate programs of study.[49]

Parallel to these organizations were independent youth groups scattered throughout the church and known by various names such as "Our Brother's Keeper" in Kansas City, the "Onward to Zion" movement of Far West Stake, and "Zion's Christian Legion" of the Great Lakes area. The latter was organized by Apostle D. T. Williams as "Commander" of the "Supreme Council" and was regimented into companies and sections on a military model. As an honorary colonel in the Missouri Militia, Fred M. found this nomenclature appealing and its activities satisfied him even more. By May 1937 the Legion had collected $7,737 in local work projects, all of which it dedicated toward the retirement of the Auditorium debt. In the same year, however, it was disorganized because the Conference recommendation for centralizing the youth activities of the institution was close to implementation. It also resembled a "Hitler Youth"[50] that proved embarrassing to President Smith. The Conference of 1936 approved the formation of a young people's advisory council of five members to be appointed by Fred M. The advisory council's responsibilities were to conduct research and surveys, constitute a clearing house for ideas, promote activities, and develop materials for enrichment of the younger members of the faith. Planned by the council, the Youth Conference of 1937 adopted the name "Zion's League" to fit those who volunteered to participate in this church-wide organization.[51]

As he studied and observed the religious practices of his heritage, he evinced a distinct preference for worship services and sacramental ordinances that were solemn and dignified events characterized by beauty, order, and reverential awe on the part of the participants.[52] In this element of his religious perspective he departed from the largely pietistic nature of his sect. Members of the Reorganized church rejected the ritualistic practices and ceremonies of the Mormon church and opted for the more emotional, informal services of evangelical protestantism. Because of taste, education, and his thirst for order and predictability in all phases of personal and institutional life, President Smith eschewed emotion, perceived his faith through intellect, and preferred formality rather than spontaneity in worship. As well, he believed that emotionally oriented services tended to accentuate individualism, while those that were more austere and formal involved the worshipers in a conscious, cognitive process that enhanced their corporate character. Essentially, he was a semiritualist who presided over a pietistic church,[53] and his liturgical "reforms," while opposed by most of the Saints, were generally respected by the social, economic, and educated elite members of his Independence constituency.

Particularly, he appreciated the symbolic ritualism in baptism, confirmation, ordination, marriage, blessing of children, and Communion and wished to sensitize his people to its value for them. Furthermore, he believed that meditation was a primal factor in religious life that increased the susceptibility of the individual to the presence of God in the "thought stream, or stream of consciousness," and it demanded silence, concentration and "inobtrusive" music to enhance its efficacy as a part of public worship.[54] Essentially,

> The attitude of the audience is a large factor in church services. This is particularly true during a ritual or ceremony. I have seen rather insignificant rituals made impressive by solemn and earnest participation by both performer and observer, while on the contrary I have seen the effect of some of our most important rituals ruined by careless observance.[55]

For the church generally and the Independence congregations particularly, he strongly requested that his ideas of ritualistic austerity and dignity be adopted and practiced. One rite with which he was especially concerned was the Communion, Eucharist, or Lord's Supper, the "sign and seal" of the covenant made by Christians. The service was at once a token of remembrance of the Founder of Christianity, a renewal of the covenant made with him by the individual in the waters of baptism, a ceremonial meeting place for God and persons, a means to achieve the "greatest Christian desideratum—to have Christ's spirit to be with us,"—and a witness of fraternal concern and acceptance as people gathered at its common table.[56] It involved not only a vow of fealty and spiritual responsibility but also prepared the communicant for his own "Gethsemanes," whether they were large or small;[57] therefore he recommended that the service be anticipated seriously by members in good standing.[58]

Traditionally, the celebration of this rite was also attended by a period of spontaneous prayer and testimony following the serving of the emblems of remembrance—bread and unfermented wine—by selected priests who passed among the congregation. Since he thought that weekly public prayer-testimony services provided adequate opportunity for the self-expression of Saints thus inclined, and that its inclusion in the Communion disrupted the dignity of the service and detracted from the spiritually provocative nature of the ritual, he recommended its exclusion from the ceremony. To further concentrate on the life, death, and resurrection and message of Christ, to make the experience more beautiful, impressive, majestic and "soul-satisfying," and to insure continuity of "motive, theme and expression" and its observance, he added the austere music of meditation as the "handmaiden" of ceremony.[59] Some Saints who missed the midweek prayer services resented the loss of their Sunday mode of expression and criticized his reform as "high church" accommodation to the social and economic elite who usually supported him. Nonetheless he persevered, and his minor changes became the rule for the sacrament service of the Lord's Supper and the pattern for other ordinances of the church.

Much of his ritualistic proclivities derived from his Masonic connections with Orient Lodge and Ararat Shrine Temple of Kansas City from the late 1920s. By the time of his death in 1946 he had served as Illustrious High Potentate of the Ararat Shrine and as Grand Chaplain of the Grand Lodge of Missouri.[60] Fascinated by symbolism, he was particularly taken with the rites of the lodge and expended no small amount of energy researching their origins and nature and lecturing on their meaning.[61] From his Masonic and Biblical study, for example, he became intrigued with the idea of adding a ritual of "washing of the feet" as a preliminary to the Communion in the church. It was a ceremony of humility and brotherhood practiced by the Jews and reaffirmed by Jesus as he washed the feet of the disciples before the Last Supper. By this action Jesus "taught that no one is too highly placed to render fraternal service." Since Fred M. was not absolutely sure that this example of service in the Jewish custom was intended to become a "pattern" for all cultures and the seed for future ritual, he decided not to press for the idea.[62]

In the late 1920s he refined a "stewardship" ritual especially designed to solemnize the dedication of the Atherton/Holden stewards. The ritual followed a lengthy research of the candidate's compliance with the basic laws of the church to final certification as a steward, and it was intended to dramatize the significance of the steward's commitment to the social and economic ideals of the Saints. It contained a charge to the candidates, a covenant by which they "sealed" themselves to God and their task, and a "setting apart" by "laying on of hands" and prayer.[63] In addition to the advice of the members of the church hierarchy, Fred M. sought the counsel of attorney and Bishop R. T. Cooper regarding the construction of a specific stewardship covenant for the service.[64] The bishop listed and explored precedential covenants in the Bible and Doctrine and Covenants and concluded that the ancient use of these binding agreements between God and humans had been refurbished by new revelation to the Saints as "modern Israel." Under these circumstances, he concluded, a ritualized covenant for stewards was altogether appropriate.[65] Bishop Carmichael concurred that the covenant and "setting apart" were "the most solemn and sacred task that can be imposed on mankind and there should be proper . . . ceremonies to impress this fact on the minds of those who expect to take God as their partner."[66] President Smith then proceeded to draft a covenant document and institute its use as part of the stewardship ceremony of his institution.

This move toward formalism in religious services met his own basic preference and preferences of the elite who gave him their allegiance, but it provided those who already considered him "Papist" with another reason to complain further. For the latter, his changes were new examples of "despiritualizing" regimentation in the church. In all likelihood, formalization put into relief the social differences of his religious constituency and, rather than unify them, it had the opposite effect.

Closely related to his liturgical refinements in the church was a building program he calculated to beautify Independence and to enhance the quality of the worship of the Saints. His object was a "higher class of buildings" that were rich in the symbolism of the gospel and church history. He believed that the Greeks expressed their love for philosophy, reason, and beauty in the Partheon, and that the medieval cathedral represented the upward reach of that age of faith and belief to God.[67] Unique symbolism must also coalesce with utility, however, an even greater measure of progress:

> I have observed, in attempting to read history or to watch the factors by which people develop, that where spiritual group progress has been made it spells material progress as well. And public buildings and public lands are two of the chief factors which represent or spell group progress.[68]

His search for an architectural style led him to Europe and the Middle East in 1920-21 where he studied and photographed Gothic, Roman, Greek, and Byzantine structures.[69] After visiting the foundaries of Toorrerdam and listening to ninety-six carillons, he also expressed an interest in a two- to three-hundred-foot tower in Independence crowned with such bells.[70]

While the Utah Mormons had developed congeries of secret, esoteric temple rites they believed necessary to individual salvation or "exaltation,"[71] President Smith and the Reorganized church repudiated this part of Restoration tradition for the rituals of mainstream Protestantism. With the exception of baptism for the dead—a rite which was prescribed in the Doctrine and Covenants but which they did not practice[72]—they subscribed to no rituals that were so sacred that they required secrecy and a special edifice in which they were to be performed. For Fred M., a temple was a special church building wherein the ministry and the membership in good standing could meet for services and, because of their faith, consecration, and obedience, expect to be specially endowed by the Spirit of God for their unfinished kingdom-building tasks.[73] He anticipated that the church would erect a temple of this kind in Independence and surround it with a cluster of other buildings of distinctive architecture.[74] In 1926 he declared to the Conference that

> Still before us [is] the great task of building . . . the Temple to which we have all looked forward. I have not forgotten it. . . . For in my dreams of Zion it is always in a prominent place of perspective. I cannot look upon the buildings or upon the plan even of the buildings that shall be in this center place without seeing them clustered around that jewel of all our architectural achievements, the Temple.[75]

His yearning to the contrary, because of financial limitations and the pressing need for a more immediate, practical building, the closest he could come to achieving his wishes in the Center Place was the construction of the Auditorium for the housing of conferences and church offices. Even that was limited by the unavailability of funds and the church debt of the 1930s. What he originally had in mind was a building large enough to seat 10,000 with smaller models located throughout Independence, Kansas City, and Jackson County to meet local congregational needs and assist in "colonizing" these areas with nuclei of Saints. Temporarily, until his plan could be carried out, he advocated the construction of large, one-room, rectangular meetinghouses that could be readily converted into apartments, homes, or business properties when they were no longer needed.[76]

Ground was broken for the Auditorium in 1926, and the building was first used in its rudimentary stages of construction by the Conference of 1926. It was not nearly as large as Fred M. had hoped, and the ancillary buildings were never erected because of the financial contraction of the depression years. Located on part of the original Temple Lot purchased by Joseph Smith, Jr., in 1832, the Auditorium was built around an elliptical conference chamber 175 feet wide and 210 feet long and covered by a dome that rose above the floor 110 feet. The building could house approximately 7,000 people in its main chamber and accommodate another 1,700 in its basement. In September 1928 church officials moved into its enclosed spaces, and by April 6, 1930, the date of the Centennial Conference, 11,000 Latter Day Saints gathered there for the opening Communion service. By January, 1931, however, the work on the building virtually stopped because of a debt of $1,876,000, and construction was not resumed until the mid-1940s.[77]

Some of the Independence Saints made reference to the Auditorium as "Frederick's Folly," and his ubiquitous critic, T. W. Williams, parodied his efforts in a *Messenger* article entitled, "A Modern Great One Proposes His Pyramids."[78] He also assailed the President and Presiding Bishop for speculation in the future of the 228-acre Colorado White Marble Company near Aspen, Colorado, without consent of the Conference.[79] President Smith was interested in this company as a source of marble for the Auditorium and the future temple, and his "business sense" indicated it might be a profitable investment for the church at a time when other quarries in this area were thriving and their product was being used in large national monuments. Fred M. responded to the Williams charge with a brief history of the company, his interest in it, and its possible benefits to the church in a letter to the *Herald*. He explained to his readers that he first visited the tottering Colorado White Marble Company of White Horse Mountain in 1922 as a result of a long chain of events beginning in May, 1921. The Yule Marble Company had been reformed into the Colorado White Marble Company of Ohio, which sent a representative to visit Benjamin McGuire, James Keir, and Israel Smith of the Presiding Bishopric. He proposed that the church invest $15,000 in the company and receive in turn the marble needed for its proposed edifices at an "inside" price. The bishops presented the idea to President Smith, and with his concurrence, they made a tentative contract to that effect pending approval by the church. In October, however, an officer of the company visited Independence and divulged that the company was not using the money to develop the quarry as promised. After a year of litigation, the church gained title to the whole company, and the original $15,000 investment had now secured a $200,000 company and "good marble at a good price"[80]—if it could be efficiently and cheaply quarried. But the cost estimates for removing the marble were prohibitive, and virtually all mining companies ceased operating there during the 1930s. Thus, no marble for the "walls of Zion" was forthcoming. The church continued to hold this property as an important investment, anticipating profitable land development in the future.

Most of the church construction in his institution in Independence and the larger church was accomplished solely by local congregations before 1925. They built their own churches or purchased existing ones from other religious organizations, refurbished them according to their own tastes, and paid for them by their own resources or financial arrangements. In the years following, President Smith tried to inch the locals away from this practice and to centralize their planning and purchasing in the general authorities of the church. He and the Joint Council of 1930 urged the Conference of that year to adopt their resolution to the effect that the advice, consent, and a degree of financial aid by the General Church should be solicited and received before land was purchased or construction was begun on congregational levels.[81] The Conference complied, and General Church supervision and direction under the president became the rule for church construction during the remainder of his administration.

Financially, the enthusiasm of the president and the Bishopric for the gathering and the building of the Auditorium, together with the willingness of the conferences to vote appropriations that were in excess of what church receipts could fill, changed the moderate surfeit of 1926 into a debt of $1,876,000 by the beginning of the next decade. In part, the debt was the result of a new accounting policy that no longer listed local churches or congregational meeting halls as General Church assets, but the real problem centered in the dwindling receipts of the early thirties. Consequently, the institution was unable to service debts as scheduled or on demand.[82] To deal with the emergency, the president, Joint Council, and appropriations committee met in early 1931 to devise strategies and programs. In general, they agreed to a retrenchment policy to pare expenditures, limit building expansion, convert to cash all holdings that were not absolutely necessary to the operation of the church, and cut the missionary and administrative staffs while maximizing the efficiency of those who remained.[83] These moves preserved the church from the embarrassment of bankruptcy and saved both the confidence and the investment of those who held its bonds,[84] but they cut deeply into all of the developmental plans for the kingdom of God that Fred M. held dear: stewardship, missionary expansion, and construction. He lamented to the Joint Council, "Is this . . . one of the trials? I think so. We must be driven to the Red Sea before we can cross it. . . . We must move forward in *faith*."[85] In this case, it was the unexpected circumstances imposed by the depression that "temporarily" interrupted progress toward his goal and was the actual supreme, directionally controlling force of the church. Within ten years the austerity program of the institution had reduced its debt to $530,000, and Fred M. thoroughly expected to remove that remaining depressant by 1944[86] and, in the twilight of his life, resume the march to the kingdom.

With the exception of his formalization of church services and his centralization of church construction in the Presidency, little was new in his program through the mid-thirties. The continuity of dissent, departmentalization of the auxiliaries for youth, and the professionalization of the priesthood were older themes that he continued to emphasize until the latter part of that decade. From 1938 to 1946, however, he gave the ecclesiastical organization of the kingdom his final best effort. Efficiency was still possible.

Supreme Directional Control in Independence, Missouri, 1938 through 1946

In 1938, Elbert A. Smith was released as Fred M's counselor to assume the position as the Presiding Patriarch—or "spiritual father"—to the church, and

Floyd M. McDowell, the remaining counselor resigned to assume duties in the Department of Religious Education. Their vacant positions were filled by Fred M's brother, Israel, and L. F. P. Curry, a former Dallas businessman and Presiding Bishop of the church.[87] Of the two, Curry was the more assertive; while Israel provided legal advice and answered crank letters, he was reluctant to make decisions.[88] When Curry severed his business connections and moved to Independence he was in an ideal position to direct church operations in the Center Place because of Fred M's bouts with illness and the apparent unwillingness of Israel to exert the authority of the office. Fred M., however, preferred that Curry also be subordinate, and the two became so estranged by 1944 that he denied him any equality or responsibility except to "rubber stamp" his orders.[89]

Ultimately he found it difficult to share power with anyone or delegate responsibility except to those who were thoroughly subordinate, and he constantly lamented the absence of a loyal "young man to lean on" that had been his father's blessing in his declining years.[90] Of those in the Twelve, his favorite was John F. Garver, his traveling mirror-image and representative throughout the church.

On the other hand, he appreciated young, responsible, competent, efficient, and obsequious followers, and he encouraged them whenever possible. In Garland E. Tickemyer, the young appointee pastor of the Wichita, Kansas, branch of the church, he encountered such a person and made him his protégé. Garland had been leader of that congregation since he was twenty-one in 1934, and Fred M. was very impressed with the enthusiasm, efficiency, and the cooperative spirit he demonstrated in his assignment. Talented as well as dedicated, he was a lyric tenor and sang in the Wichita Civic Opera. Always open to opportunities to further the church work and increase its standing and prestige in the secular world, Fred M. instructed Garland to accept the roles:[91]

> We are very glad to have our men recognize their community responsibilities and make contribution such as this. It is good publicity and may bring you in contact with a number of people who may be able to reciprocate in such a way as to help build up the church work.[92]

In 1938 President Smith visited Wichita and spent a day with Garland Tickemyer, the effect of which was to transfer the latter to Independence as his special assistant. After the Conference of that year, when Arthur A. Oakman, the incumbent "Pastor in Zion" became a member of the Quorum of Twelve, Garland was called to the office of high priest and the vacant pastorship of the Stone Church, a job which carried with it the central control of the other congregations in the area. It was he who, in consultation with the other pastors and the president, nominated congregational officers, took the lead in choosing or silencing priesthood members, established systematic general educational programs for priesthood-regulated home visitation schedules, organized projects for youth, planned the content and structure of worship services, made preaching assignments, implemented missionary drives, and directed the radio broadcasts for the church from station KMBC. In effect, he controlled the Independence ecclesiastical organization as President Smith's right hand in all areas except those that directly involved financial matters. He proved to be the ideal administrator, keeping his chief informed through detailed weekly reports, advance calendars of activities, letters or conferences analyzing current personal or institutional problems.[93] He was unswerving in his loyalty and provided occasional ego-boosts, exemplified by his comments on President Smith's radio sermon on the sanctity of marriage in January 1939:

> I thought it was the best broadcast we have ever made. The authoritative way in which you spoke was indicative of . . . the deep personal convictions that you have on the subject. Satisfaction was written all over the faces of the two hundred or more people who were in the Stone Church to listen to the broadcast when you presented in a brief, forward and uncompromising manner the monogamous beliefs of the church.[94]

Fred M. gratefully responded, "I appreciate the hearty support you are giving me."[95]

In the Stone Church pastorate over which his influence was most direct, Garland was a meticulous administrator for his chief. He divided the membership of 2,750 into five subpastorates of 550, and each of these into four districts of approximately 150. Through carefully selected and nominated subpastors, their directional control was dispensed from the top of the congregation to its most basic unit and was carefully maintained and exercised whether the officer in consideration was pastor, solicitor, women's leader, music director, or scoutmaster.[96] In August 1938 they discussed the development of a young adult class to be organized under a competent superintendent; in six months the group was fully constituted and functioning in part as a recruiting center for the ordination of younger clerics.[97] The Independence Zion's League, under the Smith-Tickemyer leadership, assisted in reducing church debts by donating proceeds from its activities. One of these activities was the presentation of Israel Zangwill's play, *The Melting Pot*, to Independence residents. Both pastor and president agreed that the League should pay the church-sponsored White Masque Players at least five dollars for the use of their facilities and equipment, for "It does not develop the character of our young people to expect something for nothing."[98]

Fred M. was also satisfied with Garland's refinement of the services and rites conducted under his leadership. He appreciated his institution of printed bulletins, his insistence on decorum in all services, his use of responsive readings in worship, his selection of dignified men to occupy the pulpit in the Sunday preaching services, his separation of the Communion from the testimonial meetings, and his use of prominent businessmen of the church as welcoming committees before and after meetings.[99] For him, Pastor Tickemyer was typical of what he considered to be the good shepherd of his flock, and an elder "leading the services as the Spirit might indicate"—living evidence of the "divine authority of the priesthood" and in short, a good manager (the highest compliment the president could give anyone).[100]

Both men were limited by the debt reduction plan for the total institution, and no building program or improvements could be undertaken in the late 1930s. They encouraged youth groups to volunteer their time and energy to beautify the Stone Church and to make minor repairs. One project for which the pastor pleaded, however, was that of recording the voices and ideas of the "elder statesmen" of the church for the sake of history and to provide moral uplift for posterity. President Smith told his protégé that the project was indeed worthy, but no money was available to fund it. He was nonetheless sure that Garland would find a way to implement his idea. The usual method of supporting small but desirable propositions in this period of financial stringency was to find individuals or groups with the talent or the resources necessary and persuade them to donate either or both to the cause. Garland prevailed on F. G. Pitt and others to make their own recordings, pay for them, and then donate the final products to the church.[101]

Pastor Tickemyer was "known to stand in well with the Big Chief,"[102] and his organization of the Stone Church was more or less duplicated by the seven other congregations of the Independence Zion.[103] All of them reflected the president's basic governing philosophy of supreme directional control, but some members of the institutional hierarchy discerned a "revolt brewing." They observed what they thought to be "continued lack of administrative direction" in the city, finding L.F.P. Curry unable to give it his sustained attention, Israel Smith incapable of keeping up with necessary details, and Garland too much the alter-ego of Fred M. with "his eye on a place in the Twelve." Alienates from the crisis periods of the 1920s were still indefatigable in their critique of the Independence directional system. Best exemplified by B. L. McKim, these critics found the president's "Ensign of Peace" to be ludicrous. His "strongly centralized government" had brought the coveted kingdom of God no nearer to tangible reality, and his grandiose plans for the gathering, stewardships, and building expansion had all failed. The favor of God had vanished from the church, and in its place crept the errors of secularism and rule by edict. If God wanted the kingdom in this "dispensation," B. L. argued, then he must find a new leader. . . and possibly a different people.[104]

Fred M. ignored comments such as these and continued to believe that his direction was correct and that his methods were the most efficient means to the sacred ends he envisioned. Sincere expressions of support from his patrons cushioned the effect of his detractors and resuscitated the vapid state of his later presidency. One of his cousins who noted a "lack of punch" in his voice during a radio address in March, 1940, wrote that God was still with him in the work to which he had been called, in spite of the fact that he had been maligned by "wagging tongues."[105] His secretary forwarded a note to him and enclosed a poem by Grace Noll Crowell entitled, "Pain," the message of which was to praise his virtue of patience.[106] From a California admirer he received the message, "We have implicit confidence in you and faith in your leadership and are silently upholding you in our thoughts and prayers."[107] And from Willoughby, Ohio, came a written charge to stick with the ship until the very last.[108]

In the words of another, "I praise God. . . because he has prepared you and established you to defend his truth and lead his people."[109] *Herald* editor Leonard Lea anticipated that future histories would depict this leader as one of the most liberal and progressive produced by the church—one who recognized and stressed the importance of education, brought order, dignity, and peace to both the ranks and the hierarchy and moved his religious organization from an "atmosphere of medievalism" into the modern world.[110]

These encomiums were sincere but exaggerated demonstrations of friendship, faith, and affection, yet they were necessary ingredients for Fred M. to avoid depression and maintain his sense of direction. Sympathy, he realized, was more than a cognitive process, it was a "fellow feeling"[111] that could uplift the fallen, restore confidence, and provide a balm for damaged egos. Thus, with the help of his friends and supporters he was able to emulate the feat of one of his favorites, Gentlemen Jim Corbett, who could always rise from the canvas to "fight one more round."[112]

After Fred M. died of cardio-vascular disease on March 20, 1946, the organization of Independence as "Zion" under the Presidency returned to its original position as a stake with its own leadership in 1950. Supreme directional control continued to be the ideal, but it was not vigorously pursued by succeeding administrations there or elsewhere in the church. There was no real philosophical reconciliation effected in the church between the traditions of political democracy nurtured by the American experience and the authoritarian, theocratic principles of its Restoration heritage, and supreme directional control was as much a mesalliance in its application as it was in theory. It accentuated the differences between the social-economic elites and the "rank and file" of the institution, with the former usually supportive of President Smith and the latter in opposition. Respect and willing obedience could never be compelled from those who resented the exercise of power over them. Members of the congregations in the Independence area were never sure of the boundaries—if any—between their democratic rights and the overwhelming prerogatives of the Presidency, and many wondered if the church was following the theocratic pattern of its Utah counterpart in which democracy and dissent were taboo. Confronted with the Smith aristocratic bureaucracy in Independence, constituents on the congregational levels unconsciously followed the practice of early Spanish colonials who obeyed but did not carry out imperial regulations. The practice of theocratic democracy under supreme directional control did not facilitate progress; it perpetuated inertia.

Fred M's followers were basically "pietists" who emphasized personal faith, conversion, and feeling in their religious lives. They also worshiped emotionally and informally, and felt compelled to regenerate a sinful world through mission. Sure that their message of stewardship was socially relevant, they stressed correct moral behavior and tried to demonstrate that the sacred and the secular were intimately tied to each other. Their president shared some of these attitudes—notably the integration of the sacred and secular, the concept of mission, exemplary morality, and the social importance of stewardship—but he departed from the pietism of his church in that he was more intellectually committed to his faith, nonemotional, and preferred formal ritual to pentecostal services. These areas of departure between him and his religious constituency provided the latter with yet another reason to consider him an elitist and an autocrat who wanted to destroy the essential trappings of the faith. Fundamentally, leader and followers lived in different worlds.[113]

For these reasons, Fred M's efforts to apply his concepts of governance in the "best of times" of the twenties and the "worst of times" of the thirties met with little success in either decade, and his exemplary Zion of the forties was a form without substance.

NOTES

1. Independence *Examiner* (April 20, 1925), p. 1; Daniel Macgregor, "Supreme Directional Control in Operation," *Zion's Advocate* 2 (August 15, 1925): 2-5; ibid. (October 15, 1925): 8.
2. Independence *Examiner* (April 27, 1925).
3. T. W. Williams, "History of the Protest Movement in Independence," pp. 5-8; T. W. Williams, "A Declaration of Rights," *Messenger* 1 (November 1, 1925): 1.
4. R. J. Lambert, "Conference of Williams Followers," *SH* 73 (October 20, 1926): 997-1000.
5. T. W. Williams, E. D. Moore, and Vida E. Smith, "The Situation Clearly Stated," *Messenger* 2 (January 1, 1927): 59.
6. Williams, "A Declaration of Rights," 1, 7.
7. Long, p. 9.
8. T. W. Williams, E. D. Moore and Vida E. Smith, "No One Is Safe Under the New Regime," *Messenger* 1 (January 1, 1926): 1, 5; T. W. Williams, "Travesty of Supreme Directional Control," ibid. (December 1, 1926): 48; "Striking Men Down," ibid., 47.
9. T. W. Williams, "Group Organizes a Local Church," ibid., 1 (December 1, 1925): 10; T. W. Williams, "Independence Group Develops Social Spirit," ibid. (March 26, 1926): 76.
10. Thomas W. Williams, *The "New" Social Program of the Church* (Independence, Missouri: n.d.), pp. 1, 2, 12-13.
11. Long, pp. 14-16.
12. T. W. Williams, E. D. Moore and Vida E. Smith, "Story of the Conference of the Church of Jesus Christ," *Messenger* 1 (May 1, 1926): 93-94.
13. T. W. Williams, "No One Is Safe Under the New Regime," 5; T. W. Williams, "Warns America Against Autocracy," *Messenger* 1 (February 1, 1926): 45-46; T. W. Williams, "Under Supreme Directional Control," 83; T. W. Williams, "Pope and President Agree in Demand for Obedience,"

Messenger, 1 (June 1, 1926): 116; T. W. Williams, "Is the Church Democratic?" ibid. (July 26, 1926): 128.
14. T. W. Williams, "Coolidge Denounces Centralized Power," *Messenger*, 1 (July 26, 1926): 127.
15. FMS, "Address to the Conference," *GCM* (April 6, 1926), pp. 3907-09.
16. Ibid., p. 3909.
17. *GCM* (April 9, 1926), pp. 4063-64.
18. "Proposed Amendment," ibid. (April 10, 1926), pp. 4069-70.
19. The First Presidency, *An Open Letter to "Protesting Saints" and All Other Interested Persons* (Independence, Missouri: Reorganized Church of Jesus Christ of Latter Day Saints, May 18, 1926), pp. 1-14, passim.
20. The First Presidency, *An Open Letter to the Saints* (Independence, Missouri: Reorganized Church of Jesus Christ of Latter Day Saints, July 26, 1926), pp. 2-8.
21. The First Presidency, *Changes and Innovations: An Open Letter to the Reorganized Church of Jesus Christ of Latter Day Saints* (Independence, Missouri: Reorganized Church of Jesus Christ of Latter Day Saints, October 1, 1926), pp. 5-9, 13.
22. As cited in Paul M. Hanson, "Statement, Protest, and Notification," 45. See also T. W. Williams, E. D. Moore and Vida E. Smith, "The California Protestants Organize into Groups," *Messenger* 1 (March, 1926): 73-74; J. F. Garver to FMS, March 15, 1928 and FMS to Frank M. Weld, March 5, 1928, Rebecca Weld Noland Papers, Lamoni, Iowa; F. Henry Edwards to Alice M. Edwards, December 14, 1925, Edwards Collection.
23. E. J. Hayden, "The Situation at De Kalb, Illinois," *Messenger* 1 (July, 1926): 129.
24. Hayden, 129-30; E. E. Long, *The De Kalb Agreement* (n.p., n.d.), pp. 1-3.
25. Hayden, 130; Long, *The De Kalb Agreement*, p. 3; FMS to Frank M. Weld, March 5, 1928, Rebecca Weld Noland Papers; Tickemyer Interview.
26. Tickemyer Interview; FMS to Frank M. Weld, March 5, 1928, Rebecca Weld Noland Papers.
27. *History of the RLDS*, vol. 7, pp. 703-07.
28. FMS, Manuscript for an address to Conference, ca. 1940, FMS Papers; Tickemyer Interview.
29. FMS, Manuscript for Installation Address for Pastor Emery E.

Jennings at Walnut Park Church, Independence, Missouri, January 11, 1941, FMS Papers.

30. Richard Trowbridge, *Facts Which People Should Know and Earnestly Consider* (Independence, Missouri: n.p., 1927), p. 64.
31. Random jottings, August, 1943, FMS Papers.
32. F. Henry Edwards to Alice M. Edwards, February 13, 1939, Edwards Collection.
33. FMS, Manuscript for an address to Conference, ca. 1940, FMS Papers.
34. Ibid.
35. FMS, "7000 Hear President Smith Sunday," *SH* 83 (April 14, 1936): 97, 101.
36. F. Henry Edwards to Alice M. Edwards, February 8, 1932, December 12 and May 4, 1939, Edwards Collection.
37. *GCM* (April 6, 1927), pp. 4128-29; FMS, Notes on priesthood, ca. 1940, FMS Papers.
38. FMS, Notes for a 1932 Joint Council; "Suggestions for the Twelve," FMS Papers.
39. FMS, "Some Things Our Ministers Should Do," *SH* 75 (February 1, 1928): 113; FMS "Our Preaching Ministry," *Priesthood Journal*, vol. 2, (January, 1936), pp. 3-4.
40. Oral History Memoir of Daniel T. Williams, p. 69, RLDS Archives.
41. FMS, "Our Preaching Ministry," pp. 3-4; FMS, "Utilizing Quorum Organization for Education," *Priesthood Journal*, vol. 2 (July, 1936), pp. 27-29; FMS, "The Clinic," *SH* 88 (March 29, 1941): 387; FMS, "Official Report of the 'Clinic'," ibid. (August 2, 1941): 963.
42. FMS, "Some Things a Member of the Priesthood Should Know," *Priesthood Journal*, vol. 9 (July, 1943), pp. 3-8.
43. FMS, "Pastoral Ministry," ibid. 1 (October, 1934), pp. 7-8.
44. FMS to Garland E. Tickemyer, October 13, 1936, Garland E. Tickemyer Papers (hereafter cited as GET Papers), RLDS Archives; FMS, "Official," *Priesthood Journal*, vol. 4 (October, 1938), p. 5.
45. FMS, "Pastoral Ministry," 9-17.
46. *GCM* (April 6, 1926), p. 3914.
47. Ibid.; FMS, "A Call to Service," *SH* 77 (August 13, 1930): 898.
48. FMS to Mrs. B. M. Anderson, January 22, 1930, Edwards Collection; FMS, "Youth and the Tasks of Citizenship," *SH* 77

(September 3, 1930): 985; FMS, "A Seminar on Youth's Problems," *SH* 76 (March 27, 1929): 354.

49. "Young People's Discussions Started by President Smith," *SH: Conference Daily Edition* 83 (April 8, 1936): 58-59.
50. *History of the RLDS*, vol. 8, pp. 265-66; Oral History Memoir of Daniel T. Williams, pp. 5, 10; Daniel T. Williams, "Zion's Christian Legion," *SH* 82 (December 31, 1935): 1673; Daniel T. Williams, "Glad Tidings to the Legion," *SH* 84 (May 29, 1937): 678; FMS, "Exit Zion's Christian Legion," ibid. (December 4, 1937): 1450; FMS, Notes on Zion's Christian Legion and the Church, ca. 1937, FMS Papers.
51. F. M. McDowell, "Young People's Organization Suggested," *SH: Conference Daily Edition*, 83 (April 9, 1936): 65; *History of the RLDS*, vol. 8, pp. 265-67.
52. Elbert A. Smith, "Some Memories of President Frederick M. Smith," 442; Edward Larsen Interview; FMS, "Cathedrals or Auditoriums?" *SH* 75 (May 23, 1928): 610; He required the same dignity and decorum in secular activities while he was Illustrious High Potentate of the Ararat Shrine Temple of Kansas City in 1941. See FMS, "Potentate's Message: Decorum in the First Section," *Ararat Shrine News* 5 (May, 1941): 3.
53. The terms, "ritualist" and "pietist" as used here derive from Paul Kleppner, *The Cross of Culture: A Social Analysis of Midwestern Politics, 1859-1900* (New York: The Free Press, 1970), pp. 72-74.
54. FMS, "Church Decorum," *SH* 74 (March 16, 1927): 306.
55. FMS, "Church Decorum," 306; FMS, Random notes, n.d., FMS Papers; FMS, Lecture notes, 1930, FMS Papers, Masonic file. See also FMS, "Landmarks of Masonry," n.d., pp. 1-2; ibid.; FMS, "Across the Desk of the Editor in Chief," *SH* 86 (March 11, 1939): 293.
56. FMS, "Sacrament of the Lord's Supper," *SH* 60 (October 15, 1913): 1004; FMS, "Remarks of Frederick M. Smith Previous to Sacramental Service April 6, 1930," *SH: Conference Daily Edition* 77 (April 9, 1930): 35-36; "News of Church and Home," *SH* 77 (November 5, 1930): 1225; FMS, "Lord's Supper," 7-8, 10.
57. FMS, "The Covenant of the Lord's Supper," *SH* 78 (January 7, 1931): 1.
58. FMS, "Letter in Response to Query on Sacrament

Participation," *Zion's Ensign* 28 (April 19, 1917): 12; FMS, "The Lord's Supper on April 6," *SH* 77 (March 12, 1930): 298; FMS, "The Sacrament," *SH* 81 (March 13, 1934): 325.

59. FMS, "On the Communion Service," *One* 5 (June, 1919): 6-7; FMS, "The Lord's Supper," 10; FMS, Notes for a communion address, n.d., FMS Papers.
60. Millard D. Hamilton, Recorder of the Ararat Shrine to the writer, October 6, 1972; Recorder of Orient Lodge No. 546, A.F. & A.M. to the writer, January 12, 1976; Devere Love, Recorder of Mizra Temple, to the writer, November 1, 1972.
61. FMS, "What Is Masonry?" n.d., FMS Papers, Masonic file; FMS, "Landmarks of Masonry," n.d., ibid.; FMS, Notes on the ritual of the 31st Degree and the *Egyptian Book of the Dead*, Spring, 1929, ibid.; FMS, Address at Ft. Scott, Nebraska, November 18, 1930, ibid.
62. FMS, Notes on the 18th Degree, n.d., ibid.; FMS, Communion address, n.d., FMS Papers; FMS, "Across the Desk of the Editor in Chief," *SH* 87 (January 20, 1940). Among other ritual and ecclesiastical changes which he considered but did not push were the ordination of women and adding to the role of patriarchs that of father confessors for the church. (See interview with Garland E. Tickemyer, March 25, 1973.)
63. Albert Carmichael to FMS, July 18, 1928, FMS Papers; F. Henry Edwards to FMS, October 6, 1928, ibid.; J. A. Koehler to FMS, December 10, 1929, ibid.
64. FMS to R. T. Cooper, January 30, 1929, ibid.
65. R. T. Cooper to FMS, April 25, 1929, ibid. The modern revelation to which he referred was Doctrine and Covenants 81:4.
66. Albert Carmichael to FMS, May 25, 1929, ibid.
67. FMS, "Building Program of the Church," n.d., FMS Papers; FMS "The Importance of Local Church Buildings," *Priesthood Journal*, vol. 3 (April, 1937), p. 5.
68. FMS, *Address to the Seventy-First General Conference of the Reorganized Church of Jesus Christ of Latter Day Saints* (Independence, Missouri: Herald Publishing House), p. 11.
69. Richard P. Howard to the writer, March 15, 1973; T. W. Williams, E. D. Moore and Vida E. Smith, "What Has Become of the Auditorium?" *Messenger* 1 (January 1, 1926): 9.
70. T. W. Williams, E. D. Moore, and Vida E. Smith, "A Modern Great One Proposes His Pyramids," *Messenger* 1 (March, 1926): 73.

71. O'Dea, *The Mormons*, pp. 56-60.
72. Doctrine and Covenants 107:10-14. Baptism for the dead was relegated to history by the 1970 Conference of the church when it removed the document pertaining to it from the book of Doctrine and Covenants.
73. FMS, *Kirtland Centennial, March 27-29, 1936* (Independence, Missouri: n.p., January 1, 1936); FMS, Notes on the temple, n.d., FMS Papers; FMS, "Building Program of the Church," n.d., ibid.; Edward Larsen interview.
74. Smith, *Concerning the Prophet...*, p. 127; FMS, "The Auditorium Charted as a Landmark for Aviators," *SH* 75 (August 22, 1928): 978.
75. FMS, *Address to the Seventy-First General Conference...*, p. 11.
76. FMS to L. F. P. Curry, August 3, 1939, FMS Papers.
77. FMS, "Concerning the Auditorium," *SH* 73 (December 1, 1926): 1163; FMS, "President Smith Speaks of the Auditorium," *SH: Conference Daily Edition* 75 (October 3, 1928): 39; FMS, "The Auditorium," *SH* 78 (January 28, 1931): 73; FMS, "Cathedrals or Auditoriums?" 610; "The Shadow Passes from the Auditorium," *SH* 88 (January 11, 1941): 35; FMS, *Address to the Seventy-First General Conference...*, pp. 11-12; *GCM* (April 6, 1927), p. 4123; Roger Yarrington, *The Auditorium* (Independence, Missouri: Herald Publishing House, 1962), p. 82.
78. Edward Larsen Interview; Williams, Moore and Smith, "A Modern Great One Proposes His Pyramids," p. 73.
79. T. W. Williams, E. D. Moore, and Vida E. Smith, "General Church Officials Form Corporation," *Messenger* 1 (December 1, 1926): 2, 10.
80. FMS to the Church, March 8, 1926, as cited in FMS, "Little Journeys with the Editor in Chief," *SH* 73 (April 7, 1926): 318-23; "White Marble Company," *SH* 75 (July 18, 1928): 843; "Colorado White Marble Company," *SH* 75 (July 18, 1928): 843.
81. *History of the RLDS*, vol. 8, p. 163; General Conference Resolution 903, April 16, 1930, as cited in *Rules and Resolutions*, pp. 99-100.
82. *History of the RLDS*, vol. 7, pp. 154, 274, 278; FMS, "Fiscal Year Closes with a Substantial Surplus," *SH* 73 (July 21, 1926): 667-68; *GCM* (April 6, 1927), p. 4126; ibid. (April 14,

1927), p. 4273; Handwritten minutes of the January, 1931 Joint Council, FMS Papers.

83. Handwritten minutes of the January, 1931 Joint Council, FMS Papers; FMS, "Important Changes in the Financial Situation," 160-70; G. Leslie DeLapp, "Official: A Brief Summary of our Financial Policy," *SH* 78 (October 28, 1931): 1012; FMS, "The Way Out," *SH* 78 (March 4, 1931): 193.
84. FMS, "Church Bonds," *SH* 77 (May 21, 1930): 545; Albert Carmichael, "Church Bonds," ibid. (May 28, 1930): 584; L. F. P. Curry, "Official: Notice of Refunding of $25 and $50 General Church Bonds," ibid., 79 (May 25, 1932): 489.
85. Handwritten minutes of the January, 1931, Joint Council, FMS Papers.
86. *Kansas City Star* (January 6, 1941), clipping file, RLDS Archives. See also FMS, "The Financial Policy," *SH* 78 (October 28, 1931): 1011; L. F. P. Curry, "Five Year Plan of Debt Reduction," *SH: Conference Daily Edition* 83 (April 9, 1936): 65-69, 77; FMS, "Across the Desk of the Editor in Chief," *SH* 84 (January 16, 1937): 68; FMS, "The Report of the Bishopric," ibid. (February 13, 1937): 195; FMS, "A Report and Appeal," ibid. (May 29, 1937): 675; FMS, "The Incubus of Debt," *SH* 87 (August 3, 1940): 963; FMS, "The Progress in Debt Paying," ibid. (October 26, 1940): 1347.
87. Doctrine and Covenants 138; FMS, "Reorganization of the Presidency," *SH* 85 (November 5, 1938): 1141; Tickemyer Interview.
88. F. Henry Edwards to Alice M. Edwards, August 10 and 15, 1939, Edwards Collection; Tickemyer Interview. Except for a brief period in the mid-1920s wherein he opposed Smith in the SDC controversy, Israel A. Smith was usually in his brother's shadow, and often financially assisted by him. See Israel A. Smith to FMS, February 6, 1928, July 17, 1928, August 13, 1928, and August 18, 1928, FMS Papers.
89. Tickemyer Interview; FMS, "President L. F. P. Curry to Full Time Church Work Next Month," *SH* 87 (July 20, 1940): 900.
90. Ibid.; FMS, Notes for lecture on leadership, n.d., FMS Papers.
91. Garland E. Tickemyer (hereafter referred to as GET) to FMS, February 26, 1935, and January 22, 1936, GET Papers; F. Henry Edwards to Alice M. Edwards, August 15, 1939, Edwards Collection.
92. Telegram reply by FMS to Letter of GET to FMS, February 26, 1935, GET Papers.

93. GET to FMS, November 14, 1938, November 22, 1938, February 1, and March 1, 1939; FMS to GET, October 13, 1938; Overview of correspondence between GET and FMS, 1938-1946, GET Papers; FMS, "Across the Desk of the Editor in Chief," *SH* 86 (July 22, 1939): 900-01.
94. GET to FMS, February 1, 1939, ibid.
95. FMS to GET, February 27, 1938, ibid.
96. GET to the Presidency, July 11, 1946, ibid.
97. GET to FMS, August 18, 1938 and February 1, 1939, ibid.
98. GET to FMS, November 22, 1938, ibid.
99. Stone Church Bulletin (1943-1946); See also *Liberty Street Church Bulletin*, 1-4 (1943-1946); GET to FMS, September 21, 1938; FMS to GET, October 3, 1938, GET Papers.
100. FMS, "Across the Desk of the Editor in Chief," *SH* 86 (April 29, 1939): 517.
101. GET notes regarding a conference with FMS, November 22, 1938; GET to FMS, September 30, 1938, and October 12, 1938; FMS to GET, October 3, 1938, and November 16, 1938, GET Papers.
102. F. Henry Edwards to Alice M. Edwards, August 15, 1939, Edwards Collection.
103. These congregations were known as Second Church, Liberty Street Branch, Walnut Park Branch, Englewood Church, Enoch Hill Branch, East Independence Branch, Gudgell Park Branch, and Sugar Creek Branch. GET to FMS, October 7, 1938, GET Papers; FMS, "Across the Desk of the Editor in Chief," *SH* 86 (January 21, 1939): 70.
104. B. L. McKim, *An Appeal* (Independence, Missouri, n.d., 1940), pp. 7, 24-25; B. L. McKim, *Explanation and Statement* (Independence, Missouri, n.p. 1943); B. L. McKim, *Succession of Ministerial Authority: Where to Be Found?* (Independence, Missouri: n.d.) p. 3.
105. Letter of a cousin "Emma [last name illegible]" to FMS, March 28, 1940, FMS Papers. See also W. S. Hettrick, Charge to FMS at the Kirtland Centennial, March 28, 1936, ibid.
106. Grace L. Krahl to FMS, December 6, 1942, ibid.
107. Dora Pankey Glines to FMS, April 1, 1934, ibid.
108. James E. Bishop to FMS, August 18, 1943, ibid.
109. FMS, "Across the Desk of the Editor in Chief," *SH* 86 (April 9, 1939): p. 420; FMS, "Across the Desk of the Editor in Chief," ibid. (April 1, 1939): 388-89.
110. Leonard Lea, "President Smith Celebrates a Birthday," *SH* 88

(January 18, 1941): 67-68; Lea, "Our President's Contribution," *SH* 87 (April 20, 1940): 484.

111. FMS, Random jottings, n.d., FMS Papers.
112. "Fight One More Round," typewritten story of Gentleman Jim Corbett, FMS Papers.
113. Kleppner, pp. 72-74.

Chapter VII

THE CONTINUITY OF MUGWUMPERY

Beyond the religious questions he considered so seriously, Fred M. also commented on other leading issues of his day and was moderately active in attempting to redress the evils he observed surrounding him, his church, and modern American society. With the exception of instances in which his sectarian proclivities subsumed all else, his response to contemporary social and political questions was almost identical to that ascribed to mugwumpery by historians. These elite reformers were confronted with massive urban-industrial problems they could neither understand nor accept, and they responded to them with a series of reforms that were calculated to salvage what they considered to be the older, more legitimate, moralistic base of America.

Mugwumpery was part of the more conservative, traditional side of that larger, many-faceted movement known as progressivism, the ethos of which saturated Smith's formative years. Except in rare cases, mugwumps rejected the power of the state as a force for reform and proposed that character was more important to social change than environmental variables. Character could be developed only by direct appeals to the individual through the moral suasion of education, the pen, or elocution. These reformers were concerned about efficiency, order, honesty, professionalism, and expertise in government and society, and social harmony and Victorian morality were their goals. Content with imprecision and innuendo, they felt that mugwump reform was to be accomplished by public men above party—men they considered a talented, educated elite who possessed vision and authority—and aristocracy who despised the corrupted rich as well as the democratic masses, and who had caught the vision of their stewardship of social regeneration.[1]

While mugwumpery was a fragment of the larger progressive movement, it differed from the latter in several significant aspects. Mugwumps relied on their own elites to guard public morality and virtue. They stressed ethical codes, avoided partisan activities, and expended their energies in denouncing recreant individuals. Progressives looked to government regulation and to legislation to promote social and economic justice, and they often resorted to mass, collective action from producer and/or consumer bases. Although the two movements met in the settlement houses of the late nineteenth century, they differed in temperament, methodology, and goals. Progressives labored in the present and looked to the future while mugwumps looked backward to the past. Mugwumps were content to march in place while the twentieth century rushed past them. They worked in good government clubs, city reform leagues, the National Municipal League, and tenement reform groups, antivice campaigns, and purity crusades to fight evils on their own terms.[2]

More often, mugwumps were content to engage in fights for clean government against "bossism"—"getting the rascals out" and replacing them with "good men" who would then cleanse the system—rather than attempting to discipline and control the corporate interests that backed these miscreants. Occasionally mugwumps such as President Smith could applaud a legislative enactment that enforced morality. In the case of prohibition, the morality of dry, middle class, Protestant Americans coalesced with his Restoration concept of the inviolability of law and its own proscriptions against alcohol and overcame his distaste for change by legislation or amendment.

To him, stewardship and mugwumpery were the most compatible of reform components. They were both based in voluntarism and stressed the power of example, character, and moral suasion over legislative programs or political commitments to improve the social order. Furthermore, both movements were economically orthodox in that they accepted the free enterprise system and laissez faire. They also accepted honesty as the most valuable trait of character required for social service, and the efficiency ideal was repugnant to neither movement. Finally, both reflected the antebellum America from which their basic approaches to legitimacy, order, and change were derived. The only significant difference between them was the antidemocratic character of mugwumpery that found no place in stewardship. In Fred M., however, even stewardship accommodated the elitist qualities of mugwumpery.

In his campaigns for education and character development, social convention, Victorian morality, and reform through benevolent, elite administrators, his religion and his mugwumpery each supported the other and produced a meliorist.

Education and Character Development

His earlier career had already deeply underscored his abiding interest in education, its benefits for the Saints and the world at large, and its necessity for personal development. He delivered a series of lectures at the Stone Church in Independence that were calculated to uplift the members and stimulate the priesthood members of the institution to develop their talents and upgrade their ministry.

Underlying all of these efforts was his controlling assumption that individual character and innate ability far outweighed environmental factors in determining the course of life and society, and only when individuals had caught the vision of their potential could their creative forces be released under intelligent control.[3] Character—or "spirituality"—was a combination of susceptibility to the will of God, breadth of mind, depth of personality, sound morality, and superb discipline that put the individual into "accord" with the all-permeating reason of the universe.[4] Physical or psychic environments could only fortify or retard these inherent qualities:

> I have almost been more inclined to attach less significance to the environmental factor than I have to heritage alone. . . [but] sooner or later this child, governed by its instincts, is beginning to look out beyond itself and think about the things with which it comes into contact.[5]

Ultimately, then,

> character and environment are interactionary. A more highly developed character looks for and creates a better environment, and

the better environment in turn makes possible a better character. So we go on to perfection.[6]

Superior character development began with the nurture of a good home and a Christian atmosphere early in life and was perpetuated by educational processes in formal schooling or self-discipline.[7] "To develop spirituality means to develop character," he told the Saints, but that was not a goal in its own right; rather, it was a means of establishing the kingdom of God.[8] He was convinced that education "in its broadest sense is essential to spirituality," and

as I understand it, is more than the amassing of knowledge. It is more than the reading of books. It is more than the mastery of books. It has to do with the application of the knowledge. . . . It is an inseparable part of our life.[9]

The goal of education was to develop the total person spiritually, physically, mentally, and vocationally, and fit him or her into the social unit according to divine intention.[10] The resultant "spiritual culture" could bring the kingdom a step nearer.[11] In this broad sense, education could implant within individuals a poignant awareness of their own potential as well as their limitations, inculcate the basic principles of "right living" and the ideal of what "ought to be," and clarify the moral requisites of a truly Christian society.[12] Considering modern educational systems he declared:

Education must have an uplifting effect upon the moral forces of the community, and it is to be regretted . . . that in the educational process of to-day the factor of morality has a smaller coefficient than formerly. I mean this, that we are neglecting to teach morals in our schools, and we are allowing those who do not stand for the morals, such as the churches have always stood for, to have too large a say in our educational processes, thus lessening the moral content of our social fabric to-day.[13]

As leader of his church, President Smith hoped that every Saint would receive forms of secondary and higher education, but he asked that the programs followed by each individual be selected "technically and methodically." There were too many "misfits" in social, economic, and academic life because the choice of vocation had been left up to individual caprice rather than reliance on a scientific and socially purposive method. In lieu of laissez faire in education, qualified church leaders should counsel members in choosing a vocation or a career that would fit their own abilities and maximize their contribution to the kingdom.[14] He concurred with Professor Hall that an academic education was not needed, required, or desirable for every person; education must be adapted to the "needs and natural endowment. . . of each individual," whether that aptitude was for "tilling the soil" or for practicing medicine. Beyond that point the energy and effort expended were wasted; it was "like stuffing food down a capon after he has reached the maximum of his weight."[15]

Fred M. encouraged prospective students to avail themselves of the opportunities for them at Graceland College and pioneered the organization of the Graceland Extension Institute in Independence and its successor, the Independence Institute of the Arts and Sciences, in which he served as a lecturer. He was also elected president of the Kansas City School of Social Service in July 1916 by representatives of the Associated Charities, the City Board of Public Welfare, and the educational institutions of the city. Among those institutions were the Universities of Missouri and Kansas, Park, William Jewell, and Washburn Colleges, and

Kansas City Baptist Theological Seminary. The school was instituted in September 1913 to help supply the city's need to educate at least two hundred new welfare workers, and offered courses in sociology, economics, psychology, hygiene, industrial problems, aesthetics, political science, moral reform, eugenics, immigration, criminology, and municipal government in three-month terms at Central High School, the Public Library, and the Waterworks. Among the duties levied on President Smith was the presentation of lectures in general psychology and ethics to classes held at the school during that year. He applauded these efforts of the city to professionalize its social workers through formal, academic training. He felt this educational opportunity would not only upgrade the quality of their service to the city, but would assist them to develop more efficient means to stimulate character growth in their "clients." By late fall, 1916, he expressed the hope that the new institution would eventually become a formal college to increase the efficiency of contemporary and future social workers.[16]

His basic goal for Graceland was that of helping to promote a "broader mental culture" among the membership generally and the ministry particularly.[17] In his message to the Conference of 1919 he categorically stated:

> It is time we forever drove from our midst the idea that God's glory lies not in intelligence, or that God cannot use an educated man. We should stand for mental, physical, and spiritual culture. Our salvation lies not in the cultivation of our emotional sides alone, but in the well-balanced culture of mind, body, and spirit. We should stand firmly for higher standards of education as a prerequisite for the work of the ministry.[18]

He agreed with J. A. Gunsolley that the mission of the college was not to manufacture "trained preachers";[19] rather, the institution should help to generate an awareness of social problems and stimulate the thought and the enthusiasm required for their solution. While the church worked for Zion, it was also a part of the world and was responsible for the improvement of its social and economic conditions.

As the center for the "theological evolution"[20] of the church, the Religious Education Department of the college was the place for the "consecrated young men and women" who planned to prepare for future service and to begin their career. Too often, he maintained, the institution had unfairly sent clerics into various fields of ecclesiastical labor with no training at all,[21] and some of these were of little benefit to the church or the community. To fill this need among those especially designated for clerical or missionary work he recommended a strict regimen of course work at Graceland that included heavy doses of sociology and psychology.[22] More important than any of this, however, was his assessment that young people of all nations who attended Graceland left it with a sensitivity to ineluctable ideals and an unremitting drive to realize them both within the church and in the world external to it. As an instrument for character development and enrichment, the college was as indispensable to the church as its doctrine;[23] therein secular learning was made holy, tools were perfected, and lives were consecrated to the meliorization of the social order:

> Let me repeat, It should be the ideal of Graceland to teach that all life, body, muscle, wealth, land, pen, or tools must be made to

> glorify God, to bring his kingdom by being devoted to the service of man with no other thought of reward than the consciousness of having lived good by thus serving man. This task as the solution of our educational problem can only be approached through a unified, consecrated corps of workers together with God, and that Graceland is developing this corps is my firm belief and great joy.[24]

It was therefore with no little enthusiasm that he exhorted Latter Day Saint youths to attend their church college and boycott those that had "thrown religion out the window."[25]

From another perspective, President Smith's sanguinity regarding Graceland's value was not universally shared by all members of his faith. Richard Trowbridge, the estranged church auditor of the early 1920s, typified the basic revulsion of some of the more fundamental Saints against their leader, his educational emphasis, and the centrality of Graceland in his plans for the future of the total institution. For Trowbridge, Fred M. wanted the whole church to "bow down to his idol [secular education]" and sacrifice "primitive Latter Day Saintism with its faith in the simple fundamental truths as taught and exemplified by Jesus Christ" to abstruse educational programs outlined by "this *Doctor* or that *Professor*" who insouciantly scoffed at basic divine laws.[26]

President Smith considered the emotional outbursts of such critics as classic illustrations of the validity of his arguments in support of Graceland, and their persistence merely galvanized his sense of urgency to proliferate the educational opportunities readily available to thc Saints of Independence and its immediate surrounding areas. By April 1914 Graceland was already offering extension courses there for those who wished to enhance their abilities to serve humanity and the church. In 1916 he appointed an education commission consisting of him and his wife, Bishops Ellis Short and Mark H. Siegfried, Eunice W. Smith of the Sunday school, Eva B. Short of the Women's Auxiliary, and Alonzo Parsons of the Religio to survey and report the educational needs of the Center Place. The commission met through the summer and fall of that year and agreed that there was abundant demand for classes, and qualified people who could teach them were willing to donate their talents.[27] He looked upon the proposed college as a "supplement" to Graceland which could provide college and high school options for those of the age of fourteen and beyond and, with the exception of requirements for "good moral character," willingness to work, and adequate prerequisites, not even church membership was a necessity for attendance.[28]

By its second year of operation, it was given the title, "Independence Institute of the Arts and Sciences." By September 1921 it had a total enrollment of 142 in classes in kindergarten, home economics, religious education, sociology, and psychology meeting in small rooms and corners of the Stone Church.[29] The Institute charged no tuition and the faculty of twenty-seven donated their services and expertise to what they thought was a good cause. President Smith gave the new venture his unequivocal support; in a sermon at the Stone Church in October 1921 he explained the nature of the Institute and asked:

> Are you enrolled? I do not care how old you are, are you enrolled? I would advise you to enroll for this season. Every man and woman of

the church ought to be studying something. A man cannot develop his brain without applying himself to brain exercise.[30]

In 1922-1923 course offerings increased in quantity and quality. Most of the faculty members possessed at least a bachelor's degree and several had graduate degrees. President Smith and Floyd M. McDowell had earned doctorates, and J. A. Etzenhouser and Mabel K. Smith had each obtained master's credentials.[31] Among the selection of courses for 1923 were art, music, biology, bacteriology, physiology, mechanical and architectural drawing, physics, practical engineering, English composition, literature, speech, history, political science, sociology, social service, economics, algebra, trigonometry, geometry, calculus, surveying methods, mothercraft (home economics), psychology, mental hygiene, pedagogy, philosophy of education, school curriculum, school administration, moral education, church history, doctrine, institutions, and literature.[32] By fall 1927 the school had expanded to a faculty of fifty-three and a student body of 376, and President Smith, elated with its progress, publicly expressed his hopes for its future:

It is. . . essential that we who are looking forward to Zion and its improved social organization shall have our educational institutions in which are dominant our spiritual ideals and cultural standards. I am happy, therefore, to see evidences of the steady progress of the Institute towards the university I hope ultimately to see emerge from it.[33]

One of his more specific hopes centered in the possible coalescence of the Institute with the Independence Sanitarium, its School of Nursing, and a future medical school.[34]

A physical location for the Institute was established in

the spring of 1923 when a twenty-acre plot of land on South Pleasant Street was purchased from Mrs. Margaret Swope. The property included a large, neo-Gothic mansion that contained sixteen large rooms and an auditorium that could seat approximately two hundred people. The Swope family sold the acreage and home to the Institute for $50,000, two-thirds of which was donated by Bishop John Zimmermann of Philadelphia, and the remainder—including $5,000 for repairs—was pledged by the city of Independence. Designated as "the Campus," the property served not only the needs of the Institute but also as a public park, a recreational center for the church and city, and a location for outdoor preaching services.[35]

When the Institute moved its headquarters to the Campus, it was also duly incorporated according to Missouri law as an organization of "academical and collegiate" nature to instruct in the "Arts, Sciences and Letters," to build Christian character, and to be governed by seven trustees selected by the church in Conference. Fred M. was president of the board of trustees which included Elbert A. Smith, the Presiding Bishopric, and George N. Briggs, president of Graceland College.[36] By 1928 many of its students qualified for junior college credit through Graceland, and research facilities were increased by the availability of the church library of 15,000 volumes, the Lambda Delta Sigma Society Library at the Institute and the Ruth Lyman Smith Memorial Collection established by President Smith and his daughters in 1927.[37]

The years following the stock market crash of 1929 brought the rapid demise of the Institute as a college and as a moral-intellectual influence in the church and community. In the context of depression its annual operating budget of $5,000 was difficult for the church to bear. Instructors needing money found their time more difficult to allocate freely, and the same was true for potential students who paid minor tuition costs. Most of all, the campus was a competing academic institution with Graceland at a time when the college desperately needed student tuition to continue its own existence. With the church operating budget cut from $716,462 to $393,430 in 1930, there was little room for support for Graceland or any other academic organization.[38] The fledgling Institute was therefore dropped in 1931, and those it served were encouraged to take the parallel courses offered at Graceland. President Smith, however, never abandoned the idea of a college in Independence, and as late as 1942 he remained an advocate of Graceland expansion into the Center Place. To him education was still the handmaiden of the Lord to perfect the tools of the Saints for social regeneration and moral reform.[39] He believed that people who *knew* what was right would *do* what was right. The tasks of education, therefore, were to inform them regarding the ultimate verities and provide them with the means to express their convictions. For him, education was another means of bridging the gap between the sacred and the secular.

The Morality of Reform

Throughout his public career Fred M. Smith consistently reacted against what he considered to be emerging social disorganization and disrespect for authority caused by individual greed, selfishness, and ruthless ambition. In the tradition of his father and grandfather, he sustained the legitimacy of American constitutional law and held that governments had been instituted by divine power for the benefit of men and societies.[40] Law represented the power of community over the excesses of individualism,[41] and even Christ rendered unto Caesar that which belonged to him as the sovereign of the state.[42] Furthermore, from the scriptural canons of the church, President Smith emphasized the commandment:

> Let no man break the laws of the land, for he that keepeth the laws of God hath no need to break the laws of the land; wherefore be subject to the powers that be, until He reigns whose right it is to reign, and subdues all enemies under his feet.[43]

Nevertheless, he observed in his own country and in others that governments were in turmoil, and the insidious forces of social and moral disintegration were at work.[44] Revolutionaries and "short-sighted reformers" put their "marring hands" against every institution with little regard for the consequences of their actions. Presumably, these "short-sighted" individuals were any reformers beyond the purview of mugwumpery. He also accused "civil libertarians" of using "liberty of speech" to justify license under the guise of freedom, and the baneful result of that practice, he feared, would be anarchy.[45] In concurrence with Ellwood, former Attorney General John G. Sargent and Solicitor General James M. Beck, he explained to the Conference of 1930:

> In America the outstanding factor promoting disturbed outlook is the wave of rebellion which has saturated our social order, and

which finds expression in lawlessness and revolt against constituted authority, and which in trying to find justification seeks shelter under the cloak of personal liberty.

But unrestricted personal liberty can not be had in any social order, however primitive may be the form or simple the group objective. With growing complexity of organization and breadth of scope of endeavor, the restrictions upon personal liberty grow larger, and there is to be found in its place the great significant truth that safely lies in obedience to law and in respect for properly constituted authority. This revolt exists in other countries, but at present it finds its most violent outcrop in America if we exclude unfortunate Russia.[46]

Throughout these remarks his primary concern was that of social "safety"—the prevention of disobedience of law, social disharmony, and revolution—rather than social justice, the overriding concern of progressive reformers. The Conference forwarded these remarks to President Herbert Hoover along with its pledges of support of him in his "onerous duty" of law enforcement,[47] feeling that Hoover would appreciate these sentiments.

What Fred M. downgraded in this palladium of statutory inviolability was the equally important processes of creating good laws, repealing bad ones, and protecting the rights of the dissenting minorities or oppressed majorities such as consumers within the existing legal structure. Dissenters and reformers of all types other than fellow mugwumps were irreverent, selfish iconoclasts who, because they could not—or would not—fulfill the law, sought to destroy it. He was so concerned with obedience to absolute law that he was blinded to the positive effects that new statutes could have in the crusade against poverty and injustice.

He deplored the rising incidence of crime in the

twenties and often spoke of it as an "index of social righteousness" and stability in America. He noted that in crimes wherein federal courts alone had jurisdiction that cases had increased from 9,503 in 1912 to at least 80,000 in 1923, and that homicides were so frequent in large cities that newspapers reported only those that were the most sensational or scandalous.[48] On the microcosmic level, he asked his Masonic brothers as well as his fellow Saints how often they had "ignored or broken the laws requiring jury duty, violated prohibition laws or 'dodged' taxes" they owed to the local, state, and federal government.[49] He also excoriated the powerfully rich whose arrant greed impelled them to step beyond the bounds of the law, dishonor the courts, and derisively mock government.[50] He was convinced that the public safety and liberty of the United States rested in obedience to law and that it was one of the prime duties of a minister to promote respect for duly constituted authority. Even though obedience to law implied restriction of personal liberty, it was the only ultimate source of what he valued as public security.[51] Therefore, he hoped that the Saints would find themselves

> standing four square for law enforcement and helping our magistrates so inclined to carry through to a successful administration of the law and the punishment of all violators thereof. Our ideals of the past demand it. To reach our goals will demand that we demonstrate our love for law and order and our respect for properly constituted authority and the conventions and safeguards of society. . . . Every man a worker and every man a law-abiding and useful citizen.[52]

As he formulated his own view of the secular world in his confrontation with the acids of modernity, he turned a jaundiced eye toward American urban government. At a meeting of the Independence, Missouri, Men's League in 1910 he lamented that American municipalities were among the worst governed in the world because of a dearth of expertise and little cooperation between the moral or religious elements within those communities. Consequently, "politicians and citizens of low moral standards" reaped the spoils because they had earlier learned to cooperate to control civic affairs to benefit themselves.[53] He encouraged altruistic cooperation under Christian auspices within cities in order to "speedily decapitate the hydra-headed monster, civic graft, that greatest curse in American government today."[54] Forms of local government, whether they were of the new commission-manager type or the older ward system, mattered little. What did matter was that city government base itself in the "higher" cooperation of its religious/moral elements in order to purge the system of its evil. He urged his fellow citizens to

> hail with delight the present day movements looking towards . . . civic reform and community cleanliness. . . . Let the men of the churches forget their sectarian quarrels and as religious men and Christian citizens work for purer, cleaner civic and social conditions; let them actively and intelligently cooperate against the forces of graft and community vice and it will not be long until America's cities would be the best governed in the world, not the worst.[55]

Typical of most mugwumps, President Smith was personally above politics, but he encouraged the membership and the priesthood of the church to work in local politics to preserve the sanctity of areas not "already besmirched" and to "undertake the herculean task of cleaning up politics where they have already become rotten."[56] He urged them to use the pulpit to promote economic and political progress, harmonizing the demands of "good morals and deeper spirituality."[57] It was the duty of the Saints to participate in all elections and caucuses to help insure that the best persons possible were chosen to represent or govern the people; from the mugwump perspective, good civil servants were absolutely essential to good government.[58] Furthermore, they must denounce sordidness in any form. In reaction to a judge in Kansas City who advised ministers to "stay out of public affairs, especially politics," he asked:

> Shall ministers close their eyes to corruption in high places, and say nothing when men on the bench, in the city halls, in the nation's legislature go wrong? Shall we see rotten politics corrupting ward and city, state and nation, and remain silent because some would say that politics are taboo for advocates of the gospel? . . . And shall the men of the cloth remain silent and say all such matters are extraneous to the gospel? No! There is crying need for the voice of the pulpit to be raised in a loud, clear, insistent, irresistible plea for cleanliness, for morality. Any minister who, seeing evil, fails to denounce it, is derelict in duty; he is weak in purpose if seeing a wolf steal in among the sheep he makes no effort to destroy it; he is small in character if, sensing immorality and wrong, he fears because of position to cry out against it.[59]

With respect to his own geopolitical environment of Independence and Kansas City, Missouri, he requested all good citizens to restore "integrity and probity" to their government: "We must clean up this place politically . . . and I tell you that is some job but it can be done."[60]

He was fully cognizant of the totalitarian dangers that could spring from the abuse of power by those who used political position as an instrument of personal aggrandizement,[61] but he tenaciously advocated that the more immediate danger was flagrant violation of the law by those who would be a "law unto themselves" and disrupt or destroy social harmony. He was wary of "machine-made political tricksters" and "grafters" such as those produced by the Pendergasts of Kansas City who "winked" at the spoils system. He had friends among those who had worked with Pendergast—the most notable was Judge Harry S. Truman with whom he served on a county beautification committee—and he generally respected his use of power, but he could not accept the social, moral, and economic costs of the machine as a legitimate demonstration of the best potential of the American political system. He put his confidence more in the virtues of "good men" who could administer public laws with equity and justice with no "interest" other than that of the public at heart. In agreement with William Penn and mugwumps of the late nineteenth century, he claimed that the presence of good men in political offices helped to guarantee that the government would not be malevolent in character or delinquent in its application of moral principles.[62]

Distrustful of reformers, fearful of the "pitfalls of radicalism," and aware that no governing body would "legislate the people good,"[63] he was sure that the Christians—and especially Latter Day Saints—had a pivotal role in assuring the moral progress of his country.[64] From that perspective he all but endorsed Herbert Hoover as the candidate for the Saints over Alfred E. Smith in the presidential election of 1928. Basically a political independent, he was impressed by

Hoover because he was a Christian gentleman of impeccable character and a trained engineer of broad experience who took a scholarly, "scientific," and altruistic approach to problems, working from a solid base in general principles toward their detailed implementation. He was therefore a statesman of Woodrow Wilson's stature and not a provincial, machine politician like Al Smith. The latter chose politics as a career and fought fierce political battles east of the Hudson River, but he had few of the requisites for disinterested statesmanship (i.e., he did not stand above selfish political, economic, or provincial interests). Moreover, Hoover stood firmly on his party's platform to enforce the "great moral experiment" of prohibition, whereas Smith repudiated the Democratic platform, took a "wet" stand, and called for modification of existing law. Because the Saints were prohibitionists by religious tradition and concerned with social meliorization, their president presumed that they would cast their votes for Hoover in this "battle royal between a politician and an engineer."[65] Prohibition was one of those few instances in which this mugwump applauded the coercive powers of the state. He was elated with Hoover's victory and his subsequent attempts to enforce the law.

President Smith and the church hierarchy made efforts to work cooperatively with other denominations wherever they had a significant number of members congregated in an urban setting. Depending on the context, some communities permitted the church to participate in ministerial alliances, but others—protesting that the "Mormons" were not Christian in their orientation or their soteriology and that they had expanded their canon of scripture beyond the Bible—refused any form of cooperation with them. Even the Federal Council of Churches in 1908 and the International Council of Religious Education in 1948 refused the Saints membership for these same reasons.[66] For their part, most of the Saints were not particularly anxious to participate in the ecumenical movement; if decadent public morality and social problems could be alleviated only by cooperation with other movements at the expense of their doctrines, then they too were as exclusive as the ecumenicists proved to be. President Smith did send delegates to the Iowa Interchurch World Movement at Des Moines in 1919, but they were not impressed by its decisions to evangelize the world and "stop stealing each other's sheep."[67] He and Garland Tickemyer were active in the Independence Religious Council for Community which included Jews, Protestants, Christian Scientists, and their own church, and the latter was invited to join the local Ministerial Alliance during the 1940s.[68] But the "Christian cooperation" he praised in the abstract was never realized due to mutual exclusiveness on the part of the denominations and the Saints.

Reformers had long supported the movement toward prohibition not only because they believed that removal of the "liquor evil" would relieve the poverty of the working classes, uplift them morally, preserve the sanctity and integrity of the family, and eradicate the causes of vice, but because it would also curb the power of plutocracy by destroying the liquor "interest" and remove the causes of political corruption and graft by an attack against the bastion of the political boss: the saloon.[69] The Saints wholly concurred with this sentiment. As support for local, state, and national prohibition intensified in the early twentieth century, they were the largest and most active cadre for the dry forces in the city of Independence. In the first and fourth wards in which they were the majority, they held prayer services for "dry" power and assisted in patrolling the streets to prevent election fraud in the July 21, 1914, vote on the local prohibition question.[70] President Smith insisted that only unfermented wine or water be used in the sacramental ordinances,[71] and before the election he encouraged the Saints and citizens of Independence to vote dry. He believed that the use of alcohol and saloon patronage were followed by poverty, crime, and "racial" degeneracy; therefore he considered it the duty of the Saints to vote against the liquor industry at all times.[72]

> There is no argument to be offered for the existence of the saloon, and if I have any influence on you I want every Latter Day Saint to go to the polls and vote for a dry town in the most emphatic manner. We should be lined up constantly against the saloon. . . . For every dollar we get from the saloon we pay from two to four dollars to care for the consequences.[73]

He further cautioned that the "wets" may try to "steal the vote of the fourth ward if they cannot get it any other way, and it is for us to see that they can't."[74] The drys won the election by a narrow margin, and he credited the Saints with the victory.[75]

When prohibition was enacted nationally with the ratification of the Eighteenth Amendment, he favored vigorous enforcement of the law if it was to successfully demonstrate its value for the American populace.[76] The law and its execution was more than simple enforcement of a constitutional and statutory mandate; it was "a recall of the people as a mass to a sense of moral and spiritual values in religion, in politics [and] in our social life,"[77] and represented a legitimate operational expression of the church in its mission of character development and social regeneration. He agreed with President Hoover that prohibition was a piece of legislation that foreshadowed moral and economic progress, therefore "it is our duty to commend right and denounce wrong"[78] in support of it. When he overheard a businessman comment at a luncheon that no statute could regulate what he chose to imbibe, he angrily interjected:

> Brother, you have no right to put in your mouth that which will lessen your moral resisting power. You have no right to be unclean as long as your uncleanness has a deleterious effect on someone else.[79]

He thoroughly detested the insidious "interests" and lobby groups that exerted their influence to repeal or revise the law, and for those such as "Governor 'Al' and his allies" who openly opposed it he had nothing but unremitting scorn.[80] In the midtwenties he estimated that the annual profit from bootleg violation of the law was at least $500,000 annually and growing.[81] For him, the church was the chief influence in the communities where it was predominant to educate the public to accept enforcement:

> The battle against the liquor traffic goes on. It may have to be largely one of education, but it is on. And Latter Day Saints because of their traditions as well as teachings are or should be in the ranks fighting for clean communities and clean living.[82]

A *Literary Digest* poll of Independence in 1932 indicated that the city was still "in the ranks fighting" when its citizens voted 426 to 358 to continue prohibition.[83] At the 1919 church Conference B. H. Macbeth, a representative of the Iowa Anti-Saloon League, was invited to speak; he elaborated on the measures currently being undertaken (such as the drive for 3 percent beer in Michigan) by opponents of the new amendment and expressed his appreciation for the cooperation of the Saints.[84] Eight years later the Conference stated that prohibition was an example of constitutional law designed and drafted by God for the "safety and freedom" of humankind; therefore it should be rigidly enforced.[85] President Smith was pleased with this concluding statement of the resolution:

> The responsibility of each Latter Day Saint is to exert his mind and strength to the end that good and wise men be selected for office in local, state, and national capacities. Each must therefore seek to exercise the franchise extended to him. . . . He should also make insistent demand upon officers selected that they exert themselves to enforce the dry laws. We pledge ourselves to support men who make strong and consistent records for upholding and enforcing the prohibition laws, and to exert ourselves for the removal of any officer who is tardy or weak in these matters.[86]

When prohibition was repealed by the Twenty-first Amendment in 1933, he was grievously disappointed and anticipated that the darkness of night was about to descend on America.[87] In response to inquiries from the Saints relating to what their role—if any—should be in the "liquor traffic," he replied that the traditions, scriptures, and moral responsibilities of the church emphatically demanded that the Saints (especially if they were in the priesthood) not engage in any form of manufacture, sale, or use of intoxicants. As special exemplars of propriety in the institution, clerics were responsible to call the membership to the highest planes of conduct. "Moral suasion is and has been with us the great force in raising moral standards," and in the face of its liquor proscriptions the church could not demand less than the highest standards for its own people if it expected to "appeal to reform conduct" in its external environment.[88] He never relaxed his stand on the liquor issue and for the rest of his life it remained for him and his church a fundamental point of departure for ensuent social reform. In this case, his sectarian, prohibitionist background prevailed over his mugwump aversion to strong government.

From Charles Ellwood and others who influenced him through their courses and writings while he was a student at the Universities of Missouri and Kansas, Fred M. developed an enduring interest in penal reform. In *Sociology and Modern Social Problems* (1910 and 1924) Ellwood proposed that every state reorganize its prison system to include reform schools for children under the age of sixteen; "industrial reformatories" for first-offending adults between sixteen and thirty; "special reformatories" for vagrants, inebriates, and prostitutes; hospital institutions for the criminally insane; and maximum security enclosures for "incorrigibles." Additionally, he anticipated a "reformatory without walls" to be used in cooperation with an enlightened parole system.[89] With ideas such as these in the background of his mind, on August 15, 1910, he and his family visited the federal prison at Leavenworth, Kansas. There he was favorably impressed with the cleanliness, order, and provisions available to the 1,400 inmates, one-third of whom were black, and he praised Warden R. W. McClaughry for his excellent work.[90] His inspection tour extended to the prisons at Jefferson City, Missouri, and Ft. Madison, Iowa. (He gained entrance to the latter by giving a Masonic signal to its officials.)[91] The former institution he described as backward due to its failure to modify its procedures in harmony with the new reform impulse. Most salient of all the defects he noted was the failure of Missouri officials to provide a reformatory or "half-way home" for juvenile offenders. Those beyond the age limit for the children's homes at Boonville and Chillicothe were sent directly to the penitentiary at Jefferson City—the least progressive of Missouri's penal institutions. Of particular repugnance to him was the lack of prisoner differentiation and placing young first offenders in the same cells with inveterate criminals—a practice which he felt made the prison at Jefferson City the "crime university" of the state. He also found sanitary conditions so neglected that long-term inmates, even when discharged, were usually tubercular. While he wrote to reform these abuses, at the same time he categorically denounced "grandstanding politicians" who, with no real knowledge of needed penal reform, put the "poor prisoner" in the condition of martyrdom. He felt that more systematic research into prison conditions was needed by concerned citizens if significant change was to be engendered; politicians were content to ride the crest of sentiment to be elected, but their adamant convictions dissipated quickly after victory.[92]

He selected as a model for a penal reformer Warden Thomas Mott Osborne of Sing Sing who introduced a form of self-government among the inmates of his prison in December 1915. Prisoners could help in assigning punishments for infractions of rules, take classes in telegraphy, industrial drawing, and languages, and avail themselves of temporary freedom to attend family funerals. In addition, sanitation patrols were formed and prison uniforms abolished. As a result, covert use of alcohol and drugs diminished, the incidence of insanity decreased, discipline problems were reduced, industrial output increased, and attempted escapes dwindled.[93] He always cautioned, however, that the ultimate reform was the prevention of crime itself; but that goal evolved slowly through educational process and moral uplift.[94]

The Social Service Bureau of the church was its instrument for providing direct aid or assistance to the indigent, the poor, the ill, the unemployed, deserted children or spouses, and the mentally disturbed. Established under the leadership of M. A. Etzenhouser in 1922 with offices in the Battery Block of Independence, it included a commodity shop, an employment agency, and a day care center for children, with voluntary services from physicians, dieticians, school specialists, and attorneys. According to a report to the 1925 Conference it had 190 cases, 141 of which were related to health problems, thirty which centered in "unfavorable home conditions," and, in all, only eighty-one which were concerned with financial difficulties. President Smith was pleased to hear that cases in Independence had declined almost half compared with the previous year; this was attributed to the "higher plane" of social conditions in the city because of the moral influence of the church, the effectiveness of the Bureau in meeting outstanding needs before they reached problem proportions, improved general employment conditions, and 354 Bureau-sponsored lectures in the field of "education and prevention."[95] With the vast influx of Saints into the Independence area in the early 1930s, however, unemployment cases were "all too numerous" because of lack of skills and the aggravation of an already depleted job market by the ill-advised migration of "gatherers."[96] Through the medical assistance provided by local physicians the Bureau continued to meet some of the needs of the physically or mentally ill, but its financial resources were strained beyond their limits and its functions were returned to the office of the Bishopric.

President Smith considered reform to be a divine obligation in the world of which he and the church were a part. As an enlightened citizen, he believed that he was required to enunciate the ideal for others to follow. The voluntary, melioristic reform he postulated was a combination of the sectarian and mugwump traditions he embodied and represented in his church and community. He upheld law and order as inviolable, requiring absolute obedience, and those who sought to change its structure were "short-sighted" civil libertarians seeking their own self-interest. He gave no thought to the processes whereby good laws were passed and those of negative effect were repealed. Nor did his interpretation of law provide an avenue for the aggrieved—dissenting minorities, consumer majorities, or collectivist groups—to influence how they were governed or the formation of laws which affected them directly or indirectly. "Social safety" was much more significant to him than social justice. Those who openly campaigned or worked on the state or local level for fair tax laws, more direct political democracy, regulation of corporations that corrupted government, or public ownership of utilities were simply applying their "marring hands" to institutions that should be left to enlightened administrators. The culprit was not the political-economic system but the men who had taken charge of it. True to his mugwump leanings, he declared that the only significant reform, the only permanent change, would be derived from principled men who were elected to public office. The enlightened individual was his answer to mass, collective problems, and Herbert Hoover was the prime example of all that he admired and respected: he was Christian, educated, principled, concerned with efficiency, and skilled in administration. However, when his mugwump proscriptions against coercion by government conflicted with his sectarian stand on prohibition, President Smith relented and accepted the great "moral experiment" as a positive use of law for moral purposes. In this instance the Saint overshadowed the mugwump.

Victorianism and Social Convention

Another phase of the president's melioristic approach to reform was his abiding faith in morality and the social conventions of Victorian America that he carried with him from the nineteenth into the twentieth century. Throughout his life he condemned the use of tobacco and intoxicants (with the limited exception of peyote among American Indians), saloons, sexual license, prostitution, pornography, social dancing, and lewd plays or entertainment. He was also concerned about the rising incidence of infidelity within marriage, increasing divorce, illegitimacy, and a declining birth rate, all of which he thought were the concomitants of the decay of home and family value structures and the rise of the "new" woman.[97] All of these evils he attributed to

> growing disregard for authority and disobedience to law with a . . . break in morals and revolt against religion . . . for people will be inclined to follow their own desires and exercise "personal liberty" irrespective of any socially bad effects.[98]

If society was to survive, he maintained, then it must give attention to the "social conventionalities" which "have their roots in that which has been set up to defend and protect society against disintegration . . . even if times have changed. . . ."[99] For the truly converted Christian whose altruism was directed not only for present society but to needs of future generations, "taboos" had immense value for the benefit of the "race," and he hoped to place his own church in the forefront of all institutions that resisted the forces of evil and stood for social cohesion, fraternity and "clean living."[100]

In the twenties he warned the youth of the church to avoid such modern dances as the Fox Trot and the Charleston and to boycott the entire "jazz" culture—otherwise they would be led into environments where Saintly lives might be compromised.[101] He found both modern dance and its accompanying music barbaric, and "We must frankly admit that attendance at modern dances is activated by lusts of the flesh."[102] The church issued no absolute formal mandates against dancing, but he specifically requested that priesthood members constantly warn the young people of the covert dangers therein that threatened their propriety and their souls.[103] Yet, he realized that a mere "negative attitude" toward this "commercialized recreation" would not suffice to protect them, and he beseeched the conferences and departments of the church to develop creative and attractive recreational alternatives to the ones he considered destructive.[104]

Another entertainment that he found distasteful and morally degrading not only in the twenties but throughout his life was the motion picture and the life-style it portrayed. The Conferences of the church in 1916 and 1918 had already discussed motions to the effect that this mode of entertainment had a "tendency to lead people away from Christ"[105] and was "detrimental to spiritual development."[106] In the late thirties, after Hollywood had already cut sex and violence in its products through self-censorship, he expanded those arguments. Even though he did not attend movies and never specified which ones were particularly offensive, his basic complaint about them was that they presented "scandalous and salacious" portraits of American home life and created a factitious normality to the public which was degrading as well as demoralizing to the family.[107] The Hollywood home was decorated with

> glamorous stage beauties and amorous men lounging around in luxurious surroundings, constantly using cigarettes and tobacco, bibbing wine and drinking liquors, seeking and finding, as surcease from the *ennui*, thrills from illicit and home destroying social concourse through broken vows and faithlessness.[108]

To him, one of the socially redemptive missions of the church was to use its pulpit to "thunder against the vile presentations" of the movies and demand cleaner and more wholesome representations in visual art for the American consumer.[109] He would have helped his followers more if he had been specific about his criteria for "wholesome representations."

Dress fashions of the day also evoked his critical reactions. He expressed shock that the Saints were becoming slaves to the fashion designers of New York and Paris—people "who had forgotten God" in their search for sartorial splendor.[110] He had little admiration for the seductive, male-inspired attire of the free-living "flapper," but his judgment was not restricted to that sex, for he observed that "men are as much slaves to fashion as are women; witness the balloon trousers, not to say anything about the starched collars."[111] "Need and just want," not wealth, status, or the desire to imitate, should determine the degree of "personal adornment" of those who would build the kingdom.[112]

His denunciation went beyond attire, personal immorality, and the "musical crime of jazz"[113] to include the literary art of the age of prosperity and depression:

> The principles of our classic music have been violated. . . . The old rhythm of poetry has been distorted, and today the greatest license is taken in free verse. Literature, which it was the universal determination to keep clean and pure, has grown in indecency and license until even history and biography have been entered by writers of the muck-raking variety, and the most scurrilous things pass off under the head of biography and history. Everywhere the revolt against authority is apparent.[114]

Although he never specifically mentioned titles which were scurrilous or rife with license, he would probably have included the works of T. S. Eliot, Ernest Hemingway, and H. L. Mencken in these categories. In January 1923 he pleaded with the Kansas City Fine Arts Institute for purification of art and literature and called for a return to the dedication and perfection that he believed was Michelangelo's. Literature particularly suffered from a "paucity of ideas" hidden "beneath the modernity of style."[115] Contemporary writers pandered to publishers who were "greedy to supply the people's maw with loads of trashy literature"[116] for commercial gain. The short story, the novel, and even the cartoon had all succumbed to the commercial blight. Writers no longer applied their talents under the creative urge but pushed their pens only for gain. Before the end of that same year he advised the Kansas City Quill Club of an exodus needed from the "literary fleshpots of Egypt" into the promised land long since vacated by Michelangelo. He implored the club to maintain the high standards of those who knew the ideals of "true art" and detested the inroads of greed. Members should "stand ready to nourish genius and denounce the prostitution of a holy calling . . . [and] encourage artistic story building and the divine sport of versification for the pure love of it."[117] While not as Victorian as Smith, and much more concerned about the dearth of democratic themes, Bernard DeVoto agreed that the literature of the twenties was bankrupt and trivial.[118]

Ever the dilettante who once told his cousin, "I have more poetry in my sole than in my soul,"[119] Fred M. composed the words for two hymns to be used for worship by the Saints[120] and scratched two pages of plot for a western novel, short story, or biography he contemplated writing sometime in the future. The plot included the character of Frank Dickens, a Colt revolver and a "Mr. Dinkel" who originally owned the gun and had "done much 'to make me [Dickens] so I could live among civilized people.'"[121] This inauspicious beginning was similar to one of Mark Twain's short stories with a dash of Owen Wister added, but Fred M. aptly demonstrated his own "pure love" of literature by trying his hand at criticism in a 1933 radio lecture on Edgar Allen Poe's *The Raven*. According to his judgment, this poem was one of the author's best literary productions. Its structure and style clearly illustrated to him "mechanical and literary perfection," but its enduring value was the "sense of having stood in holy places"[122] that it imparted to the reader. The poem revealed, he believed, a deep remorse that accompanied infidelity to higher ideals—a more profound remorse than that produced by lack of faith to friendship, vows, or morals. The maiden in the poem symbolized those lofty, higher ideals, and the raven was infidelity to them and awareness of their irretrievable loss. "Nevermore" would the raven of infidelity leave the presence of the fallen narrator.[123]

Conditioned to thinking in terms of moral absolutes, he encapsulated the poem as one that elucidated the despair of those who failed to transcend omnipresent evils and prostituted their highest aspirations. To him, great literature always held such lessons of moral excellence and provided a "glimpse of what is not often revealed to man." Poe had laid bare his great genius, but critics had only partially grasped the significance of the poet and the meaning of his masterpiece. Through education the world might come to appreciate such deeper meaning in the arts.[124] Not particularly original in its scope, this exposition was drawn in part from a lecture on the same topic at Lincoln-Jefferson University in Chicago by Professor Hubert M. Skinner.[125]

In his fulminations against illicit sex, marital infidelity, "trashy" literature, and art of questionable value, President Smith resembled one of the more outstanding vice crusaders of Victorian America. Anthony Comstock spent his entire life eliminating pornography, prostitution, and nudity from the cities of America; he was a paragon of virtue during a time when bare table legs were considered to be of possible prurient interest.[126] Anthony was already an anachronism in the first two decades of the twentieth century, an age that historian Henry F. May has described as the "end of American innocence,"[127] and Fred M.—no less Victorian—continued his crusade from the pulpit and the lectern.

Most of his condescending statements and activities in regard to women and their status were confined to his dissertation and were somewhat tempered in his earlier years. He was pleased, however, when the women of the church organized new departments of self-improvement, home and child welfare, literary and educational development, eugenics, and domestic science within the Women's Auxiliary for Social Science. This auxiliary had succeeded in creating sixty-nine local and twenty-two district organizations by 1913, and two of its subsidiaries—the Ladies' Aid Society and the Laurel Club of Independence—had earned $1,111.09 for the benefit of the needy within the church.[128] Herein women were attending to their "proper" responsibilities in establishing Christian nurture in the environments of their homes and in supporting the charitable efforts of the institution of which they were members.

During the Conference of 1915 an address written by Mrs. Smith on "The Woman Movement" was read before the body. She acknowledged that education had changed the lot for women, and for that reason "our women as individuals should give a little more serious study to the real problems which confront us, as women."[129] If they desired to mingle the good of the old with the good of the new and "make paradise of the present," then they must transcend their inertia and respond with "externally feminine nature to a changed environment."[130] Not only traditional domestic duties but professions and careers were available to women of all classes, particularly in such progressive states as Wisconsin. She urged her sisters not to forsake their social service efforts but to relate to newer activities and organizations such as the National Conference of Mothers, the Parent Teachers Association, and the Consumers League to help define their identities and present roles.[131] Fred M., in temporary ill health and consumed by his studies, responded with silence. There was little place in his Victorian frame of reference for women outside the home.

He halfheartedly supported women's crusades for the right to vote until the Nineteenth Amendment became a part of the Constitution in 1920, but he had scant sympathy for any movements that tended to loosen the ties of women to marriage, home, and family. As fearful as Ellwood that emancipation of the moral guardians of the race would cause social chaos and convert the home into a dormitory, he counseled the Saints to stay in the forefront of the feminist movement and direct it into "safe channels."[132]

One of the social dangers he attributed in part to feminism was the "wave of infidelity" and divorce that he thought to be sweeping the United States in the twentieth century.[133] For him marriage was not "a capricious mating for fugacious pleasure but the formation of a companionship to outlast storm and discouragement,"[134] and it was made for life:

> When the Almighty created the Garden of Eden . . . he placed therein *one* man and *one* woman, and assigned them to the task of multiplying and replenishing of the earth, and there was no indication that it was in any way a companionship of convenience. Adam and Eve were mated for life.[135]

Burgeoning divorce connoted a lack of respect on the part of the public for the sanctity of marriage as a divine covenant and was another example of the "general decay of morals . . . and the breakdown of rectitude,"[136] yet he was determined to save as much "human wreckage" as possible. The church permitted divorce and remarriage of the "innocent" only when the "offending party" was an inveterate, unrepentant adulterer beyond redemption. His solution was not confined to more legislation or to more intensified judicial severity but included "marriage education" for young people before they consummated "improper unions" made in haste and without wisdom.[137] Since marriage was the "core of social responsibility," no amount of time or resources spent in the spiritual, physical, and economic preparation for it or in the establishment of criteria for the selection of a compatible mate was wasted.[138]

Another related "national menace" he noted was a decline in the American birthrate in the thirties. He credited this to the "insidious work of the Neo Malthusians" and birth control pioneers such as Margaret Sanger who myopically undercut future generations. With the average size of families decreasing from five in the early part of the century to three and one half by the thirties, he foresaw his church losing its "natural" increase.[139] He therefore asked the Saints for "larger and better" families, and to assure their children of "good birth" and nurture. In the *Bulletin* of the National Republican Club, March, 1940, he bracketed and underlined the statement of a nineteen-year-old "Future Wife of America" who wanted nine children, all boys, and who lamented that she hadn't begun her mothering career two years earlier.[140] Such stalwarts were following the divine command to "multiply and replenish the earth."[141]

Basically, his ideal for women was enshrined in "cult of true womanhood" of the Victorian America in which he was born and nurtured to adulthood. From this perspective the "true woman" was a pious devotee of her religion, pure in her moral conduct, submissive to authority generally and to that of her husband specifically, and meticulously domestic. Outside of the home, her only acceptable work was in the fields of religion and charity. Within the home she was considered the giver of life. Composed of essentially "finer clay," she was morally superior to man—hence the creator of future "good men"—and the guardian of the family.[142] In his grandmother, Emma Hale Smith, he found the epitome of the true woman. She had the courage to marry the "fanatic" Joseph and stay by him through all his trials. Avoiding trouble because she was not "inordinately ambitious," she was completely devoted to her home and family and taught her children the principles of the faith. Furthermore, she was gracious, hospitable, responsible to her community, and accomplished her church work with minimal ostentation. She was the woman who represented all the qualities he felt should be part of a Latter Day Saint home, and her model was a "*must* for Zion."[143]

Although he considered the man as the provider and regulator of the family as a social unit,[144] it was the woman who, because of her "natural endowments and biological status," was its backbone. Children became largely what they were taught in their formative years, and it was in the home that they were provided their most significant learning context and imparted respect for significant conventions as well as the moral fiber necessary to maintain them. The chief ingredient of that salubrious environment was the woman; he quoted the Chinese proverb, "A hundred men may make an encampment, but only a woman can make a home," and the chief task of that homebuilder was to bring her children to God and the church.[145] He could not have been less than pleased when he heard Dora P. Glines, a personal friend and head of the Department of Women, report to the Conference of 1923:

> The Christian home is really the greatest success that Christian teaching has yet produced.
>
> Women have in their hands the children of the world. The infancy of humanity is yours to train. Humanity itself is in your hands.[146]

But he was also forced by circumstances to concede that on rare occasions the fair sex could be achievers external to home. When Agnes Macphail, a member of the church from Canada, became the first woman member of that country's parliament, he forwarded his congratulations and wished her success in her "work for better home conditions."[147] He also gave his accolades to Jessie Ward, city clerk of Centralia, Washington, for her role in helping to procure a hydroelectric generating plant to provide cheap power for her community.[148] Most of his paeans were reserved, however, for the domestic achievements and quiet contributions of his ideal woman.

Within the structure of the church, the preeminent themes of homebuilder, begetter, and teacher of the young permeated women's activities and goals in its Department of Women, Women's Council, and Social Purity Board. The latter was created at the Conference in 1912 to supplement the work of the Religio and the Sunday school in health and "effective moral prophylaxis" and to crusade for a social life that was "pure, true and undefiled."[149] In 1917 a member of the Women's Auxiliary was selected to serve on the board to assist in selecting books and pamphlets for young readers, developing "clean life clubs" and promoting sex education through lecture-discussion sessions with young females. One male and one female lecturer were chosen for each district or stake to guide young people in "the vital matters of sex and personal purity"; herein women had the opportunity to fulfill one of their nurturant roles.[150]

President Smith believed that the church should give its primary attention to its own people first, and its women were the logical candidates for the responsibilities entailed in keeping the "physical temples" of God's people holy through self-denial and discipline.[151] He was also pleased with their personal efforts in Independence in 1933 that resulted in a $6,000 contribution toward the church debt.[152] Although their basic duties in the institution were to

> sit in preaching services, sing in the choir, pray, sing, and testify in the prayer services; teach in the Sunday school; play with the youth; live with their children; cook in the kitchen (home and church), and even see that their husbands' attire is not awry as they go to their quorum meetings or into the pulpit,[153]

he realized that they needed opportunities for their own—special group expression and activities to vent their splenetic frustrations or "feminine mind." For this reason he advocated the formation of a Women's Council in 1934 to create opportunities to that end, to coordinate subsequent meetings or seminars, and to consolidate their energies.[154] The council planned its own meetings for the Conference of 1936 and dedicated itself to his goals of unreserved support of the general church program, of "Zionic" homes, and of teaching loyalty to the next generation,[155] but it implemented few—if any—of its original therapeutic purposes. These select ladies gave President Smith that which they thought he really wanted to hear from them, and he, in response to their "cooperative" spirit mused the idea of a special priesthood of deaconesses—the order of "Dorcus"—to minister to the physically and spiritually ailing. While he recapitulated that idea often for the next ten years, once making reference to it as a change that would require formal revelation, he was unwilling to stimulate more controversy at conferences, hence he made no overt move to institutionize this new rank of clerics.[156]

In the main he enjoined his followers to be chaste, frugal, and honest; to refrain from the use of intoxicants and tobacco; to avoid dancing and attending the theatre; to dress with taste and austerity; and to conduct their social and private lives with decorum. He spoke out against the dissolution of marriage, the corrupt nature of modern society, and the pusillanimity of Christian ministers when they failed to condemn it resoundingly. Fred M. believed that God wanted the Saints to be a happy people but not given to levity: "To properly draw the line between happy exuberance and levity becomes one of our spiritual duties."[157] Sobriety was particularly incumbent on priesthood members. Physically and spiritually clean men were necessary if a soiled world was to be whitened. Using indiscreet language and telling stories of "doubtful propriety" within which obscenity was "thinly veiled" were prohibited to men of that station: "Let your humor bubble up spontaneously when proper, but avoid humor which is strained."[158] He threatened to enforce clerical conformity to these standards by suspending the ministerial licenses of offenders. Always concerned about "public image," he threatened this censure of "ministerial silence" to any man who thought "more of his chew of tobacco" than his privilege to minister; to those who had "unsavory reputations" in their neighborhoods, "even if we cannot prove anything" against them; to those who dishonored the church in order to "go out and ride hobbies"; and to those who indulged in inconstructive criticism or in attacks on other members or leaders of the faith. "Some men," he postulated, "distort liberty of speech into license of speech."[159] In more muted tones he noted the "spirit of democracy . . . abroad in the land," but urged that the exercise of free speech entailed in that political philosophy be contained by proper discipline: "Let us remember that we are brethren and should be working together with God. Let brotherly love abound."[160]

His probity ascended to its greatest heights, however, when he entreated member and priesthood member alike to resist temptation and remain chaste. The truly regenerate Saint could control his inordinate desires and gain strength for future tests by overcoming his weaknesses:

> There comes [from] that sublimation through self-denial . . . greater intellectual and spiritual, as well as physical power. . . . We cannot help a bird alighting in our hair; we can prevent the building of nest. We cannot prevent an occasional thought; we can prevent its retention.[161]

Those who were "first offense" adulterers by confession or by the judgment of the High Council were forgiven and retained their membership by church tradition, scriptural injunction, and Conference resolution; but any who committed a "second offense" were to be summarily excommunicated by the same authority. President Smith recoiled from this strictly Draconian interpretation of church law, however, because he recognized that such weaknesses were part of the essential quality of being human. From his own view the person who was "excommunicado" was not forever barred from membership but could eventually be reinstated with a proper demonstration of repentance and restitution.[162]

A widower at the age of fifty-two, Fred M. was extremely circumspect and exemplary in his relationship with women. Although he had several female friends with whom he corresponded and who helped to meet part of his own ego needs,[163] the relationships were basically one-sided. He accepted their pledges of affection and support, but he always reciprocated in the same manner that he would write a colleague in the church hierarchy or a business associate. In the case of Mae Yoder, a woman with whom he cosponsored the Harmony Chapter of the Order of the Eastern Star in Kansas City and from whom he received a series of letters throughout the 1930s, his token of esteem was an autographed picture of himself bedecked in a "goatee" beard, mustache, and his Shriner's Fez.[164] Such conduct made him almost invulnerable to public criticism, and his family, friends, and followers were all sure he would not "fall from grace."

Regardless of his external circumstances or surroundings he was a man of personal and moral integrity, but even he needed release from the strain of his demanding life. In the late 1920s[165] he joined the Masonic Lodge and the Ararat Shrine of Kansas City as a respite from the "thankless . . . demands" of his church work;[166] he maintained his membership in good standing until his death.[167] When he was elected and installed as Illustrious High Potentate of the Ararat Shrine in 1941, he assured his Noble brethren that

> he stood for certain ideals but he preferred that they forget that he was a preacher and think only that he was their Potentate. He stated that he would be preaching to them all through the year anyway.[168]

In the confines of the Lodge he did not miss the "knocks, disappointments, criticism and worse" that were so often part and parcel of his church experience. Masonry was his retreat from the "storms and stresses of life's battles," and it was in that fraternity that he was extended the appreciation he failed to receive from his own people.[169]

His desire for ritual found sufficient satisfaction in the esoteric practices and ceremonies that were the marrow of the institution. The symbology of the tokens, signs, ornaments, and ceremonies of initiation and elevation were part of the "operative art" that made it unique and attractive to him.[170] The themes he constantly reiterated as an officer in these fraternal organizations, however, were essentially the same ones he presented to his church and community; and, in his order of importance, he relegated both the ritual and the conviviality of the Lodge to secondary status. It became simply another front for his moralistic reform motifs.

Always the ally of order and decorum, he insisted on the enforcement of rules forbidding levity, smoking, and raucous behavior during rituals. While the Shrine was "the playground of Masonry," the behavioral principles of the order were "Pleasure without intemperance, hospitality without rudeness, jollity without coarseness," and the Fez was to be worn to no place where the member could not be accompanied by his family.[171] As long as Shriners could laugh, he told them, they could overcome any of their troubles, but when their behavior at card parties, dances, dinners, and conventions was negatively exacerbated by overuse of alcohol the situation quickly ceased to be humorous.[172] His own deportment at Shrine dances or card games was, in his daughter's words, that of a "wallflower"[173] who considered his brothers a "fine bunch of fellows" but did not participate with them in some of their more "degrading" habits.[174]

More important to him than mere decorum, however, was the moral obligation of all Masons to be good citizens and to fight injustice. He admitted that in all probability they would not be asked as the ancient Knights Templar to take up the shield and the sword, but "armed with the shield of devotion, the sword of righteousness, and the buckler of truth, we must stand against the injustice of man to man."[175] Particularly, he saw that "injustice" stemming from

> a danger which springs from the onward sweep and prosperity and industrial organization based on the appeal to self aggrandizement, and . . . individualism, if carried to the extreme will sweep aside the landmarks of social progress.[176]

The interjection of selfish business interests into politics had caused a "decay of political righteousness," and innocent citizens were those who suffered. They were not only exploited in political realms but also manipulated by businesses that put quantity before quality, production before craftsmanship, and profit before service.[177] Basically, he reacted to the competitive values of capitalism and called his brothers to a "group consciousness" to stand against these "unsocial forces."[178] Presumably by "group consciousness" he implied the mutual protection and assistance that Masons had long afforded each other and the same fraternal awareness that allegedly characterized the stewardship of the Saints. Yet, in the broader sense,

> To discover that man is our brother and his need is our opportunity is to see the Son of Man in the leper.

To share with the needy our crust is to learn that none is so poor but that he can contribute to the relief of man and thus share the richest blessing of God.[179]

He felt that the surest sign of social decay was the selfishness of individuals who acquiesced in their sordid appetites and forgot the glaring needs of their brother man.[180]

"Higher obligations" called Masons to "join hands" and contend against "wrong, ignorance and evil, and for the dominance of righteousness and light."[181] Fred M. directed them to look into the mirror, note the "grained spots" of their own lawlessness and shame and resolve not to "keep within the law alone, but to rise above it."[182] He complained in the Shrine's monthly periodical about the disruption, disunity, disintegration, and moral decay that characterized world conditions; then he called his readers to national loyalty, domestic fidelity, and renewed zeal for religion—the ultimate sources of power for order, fraternity, and constitutional government.[183] It was obvious to him that the United States must be governed by law or by force; the alternatives were clear. The former was based in liberty and the latter in tyranny and, since the challenges of the age were theirs to meet, he appealed to the members of the Lodge to actively seek the spiritual vigor that could assist them to make the right choice: "Masons, to your knees in petitions for divine strength; and arise and to your tasks."[184]

Innocuous as it was, Smith knew that his Masonic connection increased his vulnerability to criticism from members and fellow clerics in his church. Although acquainted with the Lodge much earlier, he had—for this reason—delayed his affiliation with it until 1927.[185] He was aware that the temple rites of the Utah Mormon church were possible derivatives of the intimate association of his grandfather and the leading members of the church quorums with the Masonic Lodges of Nauvoo, Illinois, and Montrose, Iowa, and of their beliefs that the practices were "corruptions" of ancient Hebrew temple rites that needed purification. Some Saints believed that this flirtation with Masonry had deprived the church of the full attention and energies of its leaders at a crucial period in its history, perhaps hastening the destruction of the community.[186] Furthermore, Fred M. had given due attention to writings in the Book of Mormon that made reference to "secret societies" as covert institutions that subverted religious and national governing structures for their own selfish gain, and the titillation that came from possession of political and economic power.[187] The "Gadianton Robbers" was one such secret organization that created havoc in ancient American societies and reflected the anti-Masonry Jacksonian America's state of New York, site of the Restoration's birth.[188]

In 1906 the Reorganized church experienced a wave of revulsion against the Masonic order when Leon A. Gould, assistant editor of the *Herald* alleged that U.S. Senators who were members of the Lodge were biased in favor of Senator Reed Smoot because of his ritualistic Mormon background.[189] This and subsequent articles on the same topic were printed in the *Herald* while Joseph Smith III was traveling in the East. When he returned he advised the church that Masonry was a matter of "this world" and that their religion was concerned with time and eternity as well; therefore fraternities such as that of the Masons were of little ultimate consequence. Saints could give equal attention to both.[190] His counsel notwithstanding, the General Conference of 1907 resolved that "we discourage . . . membership in any society or order which requires the taking of oaths or entering into a covenant or obligation to guard the secrets . . . of its organization."[191]

After Fred M. had been a member of the Masonic order for three years his sister wrote that she was impressed with his ability to achieve recognition in his Lodge work, and that she was proud of his accomplishments. She warned him, however, that it was extremely difficult to serve two masters and, now that he had the confidence in himself for success in the external world, he should "let well enough alone" and give his undivided attention to the progress of the church.[192] Others were not so diplomatic in the temper of their advice. One postulated that the president had absented himself from church leadership when he "went through the chains of the Masonic Lodge,"[193] and another wondered how he could justify the time he gave to "Mammon" when the local, unpaid ministry worked to support their families and gave their remaining free hours to the work of the church and its mission.[194] His response to these inquiries and didactic assertions from the Saints was always the same; Masonry was simply another front for the crusade against wrong: "We must fight on to victory,—or defeat. I'm still battling. Trying to get a reserve of strength for another 'charge' on the ramparts of wrong."[195]

In his respect for the social conventions of the late

nineteenth century, he was as much a Victorian gentleman as his father. His comments on sexual morality, popular culture, and the role of women in the home and society placed him squarely in the moralistic tradition of Victorian America and made him an anachronism in the twentieth century. This posture, cojoined with his abiding concern for government through law and his penchant for order and social control, further attested to the continuity of mugwumpery in his reform message.

Race Relations

The church during Fred M.'s thirty-one years of leadership shared the basic racist heritage of the America that spawned it. The theory that Blacks were the descendants of the sons of Cain and Ham in the Bible, thus inheriting their "curse" of darkness and proscribing lineal rights to priesthood participation was apparently taught by some during the period of the leadership of Joseph Smith, Jr.[196] His son, Joseph III, modified that stance in the early Reorganized church at the end of the Civil War:

> Be not hasty in ordaining men of the Negro race to offices in my church, for verily I say unto you,
>
> All are not acceptable unto me as servants, nevertheless I will that all may be saved, but every man in his own order, and there are some who are chosen instruments to be ministers to their own race.[197]

When Blacks did become ordained ministers in the church, they were sent to areas where they could work among their own people to establish congregations of Saints.[198]

By the time Fred M. became president, segregation had become well-cemented into its tradition. As late as 1944 his former counselor and then Presiding Patriarch maintained that segregation was the best policy for the well-being of both races, and any immediate change from that practice was most unlikely:

> Thoughtful Negroes are not so much concerned about social equality or entrance into white homes and churches, as they are about equality of opportunity for service and development. Before they reach equality of opportunity in politics, education, and industry there is a long and difficult process of interracial adjustment to be made. If it is made peaceably, sanely, justly, well and good for our country—if not, the blood of dark and white people will be mixed in the dust of more than one street.[199]

Fred M. made few comments on that general policy toward Blacks, but he did fear the future racial violence it portended. In 1944 he collected and read several articles on race riots[200] and expressed his concerns to members of his family regarding that ultimate result of discriminatory practices.[201] He publicly condemned the lawlessness of lynch mobs[202] and noted that the exclusion of Blacks and other minorities from clubs, associations, and prominent positions in government was inconsistent with the ideals upon which his country was founded, epitomizing the very evil against which it was currently crusading in Europe.[203] When Edmund Wong, a Hawaiian youth who attended Graceland College was mistakenly harrassed in 1942 by law enforcement officers in Umatilla County, Oregon, President Smith suggested to *Herald* readers that prejudice was an ugly side of American society and all should "endeavor to control . . . propensities to hate our enemies and learn to hate evil without hating individuals."[204]

With respect to race, he was a "midroad" mugwump compared to Thomas Wentworth Higginson and Charles W. Eliot who were more openly racist and segregationist, and to Moorefield Storey and Felix Adler, who were more liberal in their attitudes toward race and served in the founding of the National Association for the Advancement of Colored People.[205] On the one hand, he did not question segregation because of his primary concern for "social safety." On the other, he disliked discrimination and violence based on racial prejudice.

War and Peace

When the first guns of World War I were fired, the Saints followed the admonition of President Woodrow Wilson to remain neutral and impartial.[206] Restoration scriptures enjoined them not to be hasty in making war and to be long-suffering in the cause of peace and universal good will. According to one source they were to "renounce war and proclaim peace" for the benefit of future generations.[207] When Wilson presented his war resolution to Congress on April 6, 1917, President Smith supportively addressed the church then assembled in Conference. Like most mugwumps[208] he ascertained in Wilson's speech a "statesmanship" and "deep pathos" unequalled in American state papers since Lincoln:[209]

> We deplore war; but if this country must enter the conflict as now appears inevitable, may we thank God that we do so under the leadership of one with a clear envisagement of the great principles at issue, and who will wage war not against a people, but against corrupt government and in the interests of democratic freedom.[210]

His disdain for democracy in the church and his desire to avoid its dangers to the domestic welfare of his country made his use of the concept as a justification for war seem inconsistent. Nevertheless, he went on to reassert the church belief that the United States had been created by divine power and that its destiny was still guided by the "omnipotent hand" as the "champion of liberty" and the guardian of the "principle of freedom." While it was founded for the purposes of peace, the country was "sanctified" and preserved by the sacrifices of external and fratricidal wars, and once again its people were "compelled to wage sanguinary battle" against corruption and for the right.[211] The Conference voted to endorse President Smith's comments and forward them to President Wilson, who responded with a note of appreciation.[212]

When he was asked about enlistment and exemptions, Fred M. replied that nations, not individuals, were ultimately accountable for war and its bloody results, but that the individual must obey the laws of the land and register for the draft. Enlistment was entirely an individual matter, however, and the conscience, or "the guiding overruling power of the Deity" was the companion of the devoted Saint to help in decisions of that import. Technically, he and the church respected the right of members to give or withhold their allegiance to the war on the basis of individual conscience, but they could not expect automatic exemptions from military service. Exemption did not inhere simply in membership or priesthood status in the church; it included only those who were full time General Church officers or local ministers who were absolutely necessary to the spiritual needs of their communities.[213]

At the end of one year of war the Conference of 1918

convened to hear their leader explain to them and the president of the United States—

In no church should greater loyalty to the United States be found than among the . . . Latter Day Saints . . . with few exceptions our people are doing their full individual duty towards the Government . . . We therefore stand for loyalty to our Government, and for its fullest expression I plead.[214]

He believed the more appropriate result of freedom of conscience was loyalty, not dissent. On April 12 F. M. Sheehy and R. C. Russell demonstrated their "fullest expression" by sponsoring a resolution in which the term "recreant" was applied to any church members who looked with favor on Marxian Socialism, the Industrial Workers of the World, or anarchist organizations—all of which they thought to be inimical to the interest of the United States government.[215] A substitute to the motion was offered the following day that deleted specific names of groups dissenting from American policy but specifically committed the American citizens of the church to give undivided loyalty to their country's war aims against the "Teutonic allies."[216] When the substitute passed without debate and became part of the public record of the church, President Smith was very pleased indeed.

Encouraged by this action he addressed the Conference again during the following evening in yet more ebullient tones. The United States had gone to war in times past for reasons that were both selfish or altruistic, but "never before have we gone to war for so high an ideal as is that which is directing and guiding our statesmen today."[217] Unstinting in his support for Wilson he declared that "no man in the wide world has a clearer vision of the ideals for which this country stands than the magnificent man who is in the chair as our chief executive."[218] For him, President Wilson was the greatest statesman the world had yet produced—one who envisioned the principles of international liberty and cooperation in government, law, and economy in lieu of competition, who was the stern foe of military autocracy, and who presided over the nation that was freer than any other from the stain of selfishness.[219] Because of the high standard of liberty, President Wilson comprehended as the American goal in war, Fred M. predicted that one day even the Germans would "salute our flag in all earnestness . . . and with reverence."[220] Therefore, he concluded,

> We must not be found short even one per cent in our sympathy with the allied governments as they are organized to-day, but with the principles for which they are fighting we must be one hundred per cent pure for liberty and the ideal which has been erected by this Nation.[221]

He was aware that his patriotic stance was not uncritically accepted by all of the faithful, many of whom could not conscientiously support a war they considered immoral from every perspective. For him, these myopic Saints had not peered far enough into the future to see that the war would eliminate the military masters of corrupted political structures and replace them with the machinery for enduring peace and liberty. He complained that such critics had intimidated him sufficiently enough to temper his plans to ask the army for a "Latter Day Saint Battalion" in which the dedicated Saints could exemplify their conviction and mettle before the world.[222] To those who carried their protest to seditious limits, he served notice that the Federal government was observing the Saints to assess their attitude toward the prosecution of the war. His position toward government investigation of the church was one of unqualified support":[223]

> I have sent word to the Secret Service in Kansas City that if any of our people, according to their observation, are expressing sentiments that approximate sedition, I shall be found, as an officer in this church, assisting the secret service department to apprehend them.[224]

Legitimate governments demanded loyalty and had the right to take extraordinary measures to defend themselves in times of emergency, he declared, and reading Doctrine and Covenants 112 bolstered his opinion.[225] With considerable aplomb he warned,

> We are neither slackers nor cowards. In the past some of our men who, as elders in the church, have attempted to speak for this church, and from the mouths of slackers and cowardly pacifists have gone out expressions in regard to the attitude of the church which do violence to our real position. I give warning now, as your leader, I will not stand for it.[226]

The new world order that he anticipated with an Allied victory and a "just and lasting peace" never materialized, and even while the Treaty of Versailles was in the process of negotiation he observed the "chaos of reconstruction at home and the terror of Bolshevism abroad. The doctrine of discontent is being systematically and energetically propagated, and from its dangers neither the nation nor the church is free."[227] When he visited Germany in the winter of 1920 he observed malnutrition, sickness, and extreme bitterness against France, all of which boded ill for the future.[228] The finished treaty and the League of Nations had not been ratified by his own country; the French army was still on German soil; the Balkan situation was still "uncomposed"; and unsatisfied minorities kept the "European kettle still boiling. . . . The world is war-weary, and yet it cannot rest."[229] Why was this? President Smith found his answer in the psychological roots of national and international insecurity:

> The world . . . is struggling to find the foundations of peace, but the seekers find themselves thwarted by psychological factors. . . . Peace conferences fail because assurances of political security run counter to the goals and objectives held in view by those who envisage national functions through goggles colored by selfishness.[230]

Absent was the fraternal acceptance, the sense of community, necessary for real international understanding and for that deficiency he faulted a languid, self-eviscerated Christianity that had not taken its mission seriously enough.[231]

In the thirties the world again careened toward war. Cautiously wary of another abortive crusade, he voted with the Conference in 1934 to condemn war as an instrument of policy.[232] Arbitration—not war—he found, was the least costly means of settling international differences.[233] He was also influenced in this direction by "The Arms Inquiry" of Senator Gerald P. Nye reprinted in the *Christian Century* in 1935. Long distrustful of "selfish" industrialists and "profit hungry" capitalists who cared nothing about public interest, Nye wrote with a poignant ring of truth. Among that which Fred M. considered to be "startling revelations" in Nye's document he included in his own *Herald* abstract of the article. Munitions manufacturers sold secret patents to enemy nations, frustrated peace negotiations, started wars in Latin America, bribed public officials, and sowed hate, distrust, and suspicion—all to promote their profits. He concluded his synopsis with the observation that "The arms manufacturers are our real international villains and traitors."[234]

Collaborating with those profit-motivated miscreants, superpatriots and "flaming orators" such as Adolf Hitler was subverting nationalism and statesmanship into a forum for aggressive emotionalism and paranoid hysteria that was bringing civilization to the edge of the volcano of war. Only patriotism tempered by the "benign influence" of the love of God was productive of international cooperation and peace; its godless expression merely created or prolonged wars and strife.[235] Against the context of blatant aggression and expanding wars of the latter part of the decade, he reevaluated his concept of loyalty: "loyalty to a nation is demanded of its citizens. . . and may at times blind us to national errors or misguided statesmanship."[236] Egregious examples of man's inhumanity to man had been perpetrated under the guise of such extreme loyalty, and Hitler's persecution of Jews in Germany was the most recent instance of such barbarity.[237]

In these years immediately preceding World War II, President Smith observed that the nations had drunk too deeply from this flask of godless nationalism, and he feared that the narrow interests inspired by such nationalism would expand local conflicts into a general war.[238] National traits were, after all, merely individual ones "written large," and the selfishness that manifested itself in individual and industrial relationships was also an inherent part of international diplomacy. Eventually such selfishness brought war:

> It has been stated by some economists that besides freedom of the seas, the right of international barter and trade, etc., there are about a score and a half elements of substances which are of prime essentiality to independence. . . . Of these no nation can produce all or find all within its boundaries. Only a few have a large majority of them, while many have less than half, and quite a number of even the major powers have only a few. Those which have not, must in some way secure what they lacked. . . . When conditions become so disturbed that trade courses are broken or disrupted, or when tariff barriers become impractical hurdles, then national solidarity and security become threatened, and nations so threatened are tempted to resort to drastic measures sometimes not even short of war. War is thus resorted to in order to *take* what it could not otherwise secure.[239]

Woodrow Wilson, the "liberal international capitalist" who deplored tariffs and international competition, could not have stated the ultimate causes of war more succinctly or clearly.[240]

During the first year of the war President Smith expressed sympathy for the oppressed peoples and defenseless citizens who were bitten by the iron teeth of the dogs of war. He was horrified that the nations of the twentieth century could be as brutal as those of the Dark Ages, and with more complete disclosure of the persecution of Jews in Germany he admitted that Americans "might for the time being at least, submerge our feelings of good will toward the Germans."[241] He advised the Saints that war's confusion and ruthless devastation had been presaged in prophetic writings and that it was their particular responsibility to work for world peace by removing the causes of war and illustrating in concrete form the social application of Christianity in Zion, the kingdom of God.[242] With respect to their antiwar resolution of 1934 he said:

It [is] useless for us to adopt resolutions concerning peace when we [have] failed to take the great step toward peace by establishing Zion, which would hold up the ensign of peace to the whole world and be a living testimony that the church as an interpretation of the Christian message would, through the promulgation of fraternity in industrial relations as well as civic affairs, promote the condition of society from which war will be forever excluded.[243]

When the United States entered the war with the Japanese attack on Pearl Harbor, his faith in the mission of the church and his country never wavered: "It is no time for us to lose faith in the goals of the church, for the purposes of the Almighty will not be frustrated, and our divinely imposed tasks still weigh upon us as responsibilities which must be discharged."[244] Since the church traditions favored constitutional, democratic, and republican forms of government, and especially that of the United States, he directed the Saints to support their country in its attempt to universalize those principles through a just war.[245] To be successful in war, the country needed the loyal, willing help of all its citizens, and he asked the Saints to be good Americans, buy war bonds, and join the armed services.[246]

Because war was ultimately attributable to the failure of Christianity to regenerate the social order locally and generally, he believed that the time had come for an "all out" mobilization of religion for the purpose of engendering a nonvindictive and lasting peace. Ignoring the Soviet Union because of his distaste for its form of communism, he directed this challenge to "America and Great Britain" and "other English speaking peoples" who were going to determine the nature of the settlement[247] The divisive forces apparent before December 7, 1941, he cautioned were not yet vanquished and would reappear during the postwar years if the stipulations of the peace were founded in hatred and revenge for Nazi brigandage.[248]

> We must exert all necessary efforts to avoid the mistakes of the peace treaty following the last great war . . . the peace treaty must not contain the seeds of another war. . . . Surely it must be held that the spirit of the peace treaty must be that of fraternal intercourse. Anger and hate cannot be the basis for such fraternity, however prominent they may be in winning the war.[249]

From his vantage point, the peace plans that were first articulated by Woodrow Wilson and resurrected in the Atlantic Charter and the Allied conferences at Quebec and Teheran were tainted by the mistrust and national self-interest he saw emerging at Dumbarton Oaks, Yalta, and Chapultapec.[250]

It was his conviction that the true elements of Christian peace were not materially different from those of the individual as he functioned in the "social fabric of which he is a thread."[251] As the individual surrendered rights detrimental to the group, so must nations surrender rights and prerogatives dear to them if the friction and heat that generated conflict were to be avoided.

Under the guidance of the benevolent, brotherly principles of the gospel of Christ, nations as well as individuals could allay "racial and national hatreds and prejudices" and avoid the dangers of power politics.[252] President Smith counseled the church that it should ceaselessly endeavor to work and pray for these factors to be present at the peace table, "for a godless treaty, one devoid of the principles of brotherliness, will be but a pause before more war. We are our brother's keeper, for of one blood hath God made the nations of the world."[253]

We would not live long enough to be disappointed again.

NOTES

1. John G. Sproat, *The Best Men: Liberal Reformers in the Gilded Age* (New York: Oxford University Press, 1968), pp. 5-8, 278-79; Gerald W. McFarland, *Mugwumps, Morals and Politics*, 1884-1920 (Amherst, Massachusetts: University of Massachusetts Press, 1975), pp. 7, 36-38, 48, 50-51, 120, 174; David P. Thelen, *The New Citizenship: Origins of Progressivism in Wisconsin, 1885-1900* (Columbia, Missouri: University of Missouri Press, 1972), pp. 11, 13-16, 18-21; David P. Thelen, "Rutherford B. Hayes and the American Reform Tradition in the Gilded Age," *American Quarterly* 22 (Summer, 1970): 151, 155, 157; Geoffrey Bodgett, *The Gentle Reformers: Massachusetts Democrats in the Cleveland Era* (Cambridge, Massachusetts: Harvard University Press, 1966), pp. 35-38. For a concise profile of mugwump reformers see Richard Hofstadter, *The Age of Reform: From Bryan to FDR* (New York: Random House, 1955), chapter 4, and George E. Mowry, *The Era of Theodore Roosevelt and the Birth of Modern America, 1900-1912* (New York: Harper and Row, 1962), chapter 5.
2. Gerald W. McFarland, *Mugwumps, Morals and Politics, 1884-1920* (Amherst: University of Massachusetts Press, 1975, pp. 86-100, 105, 147; David P. Thelan, *The New Citizenship: Origins of Progressivism in Wisconsin, 1885-1900* (Columbia, Missouri: University of Missouri Press, 1972), pp. 13-16, 18-21.
3. FMS, *The Higher Powers of Man*, pp. 213, 229-30.
4. FMS, "The Educational Problem of the Church," *SH* 70 (July 11, 1923): 653-56, passim.
5. FMS, Interpretation of "Panathenaicus," by Isocrates, FMS Papers.
6. FMS, "Notes for an address to the women's meeting of the 1940 General Conference," ibid. Smith's opinion also reflected

that of his University of Missouri mentor, Charles Ellwood. See Charles A. Ellwood, *The Social Problem: A Reconstructive Analysis* (New York: The Macmillan Company, 1922), pp. 263-65.

7. FMS, Notes for a speech to the "Women's Department," n.d., FMS Papers; FMS, "Education—'With the Goal of the Church Always in View,'" *SH* 68 (December 6, 1921): 1153.
8. FMS, "The Educational Problem of the Church," 653-65.
9. FMS, "Obedience to Law," 532-33.
10. FMS, "Education—'With the Goal of the Church Always in View,'" 1153.
11. Ibid., FMS, "The Church, the Youth, and the Religion," *SH* 66 (February 5, 1919): 121.
12. FMS, "Obedience to Law," 354-55; FMS, *Marriage and the Church* (Independence, Missouri: n.p., 1929), p. 8; FMS, Annotations by Smith on Letter of E. J. Gleazer, Jr. to FMS, December 3, 1945, FMS Papers. See also Charles A. Ellwood, *Christianity and Social Science: A Challenge to the Church* (New York: The Macmillan Company, 1923), pp. 147-51, 167.
13. FMS, "Obedience to Law," 355.
14. FMS, "The Educational Problem of the Church," 654. (See also Smith's underlinings in a clipping from the *New York Times Magazine* [January 3, 1937], treating the elitist educational philosophy of Nicholas Murray Butler of Columbia University, and the typescript of an editorial in the *London Spectator* [July 23, 1943], FMS Papers.)
15. Ibid.; FMS, "Education—'With the Goal of the Church Always in View,'" 1153; Ross, pp. 311-12, 318.
16. G. Stanley Hall to FMS, July 25, 1916; FMS to G. Stanley Hall, July 12, 1916, August 8, 1916 and October 4, 1916, CULP, FMS Student file; *Kansas City Star* (September 25, 1914); *Kansas City Times* (September 28, 1915); *Kansas City Journal* (September 14, 1913); Kansas City Board of Public Welfare, *Annual Report of the Board of Public Welfare of Kansas City, Mo., April 21, 1913-April 20, 1914* (n.p., n.d.), pp. 10-15.
17. FMS, *The President's Message to Conference, 1919, Lamoni, Iowa*, p. 8.
18. Ibid.
19. *GCM* (April, 1919), pp. 2908-09.
20. FMS, Notes for an address at a Graceland College Homecoming, n.d., FMS Papers.

21. *GCM* (April 6, 1927), p. 4131.
22. FMS, "Suggested Program for Training in Applied Religion," n.d., FMS Papers.
23. FMS to Mrs. Francis Davis, April 4, 1932, Marietta Walker Papers, RLDS Archives; FMS to Mrs. B. M. Anderson, March 22, 1921, Edwards Collection; FMS, "A Greater Internationalism," *SH* 72 (October 7, 1925): 1061-63.
24. FMS, "The Educational Problem of the Church," 654.
25 Ibid., 653-54; FMS, "Attend a Church College," *SH* 84 (August 28, 1937): 1091.
26. Trowbridge, pp. 28, 35.
27. Salisbury, 396-97; Independence Institute of the Arts and Sciences, "The Campus," unpublished loose-leaf binder, 1927-1928, RLDS Archives.
28. *Independence Institute of the Arts and Sciences: Seasons of 1917-1918* (n.p., n.n.), RLDS Archives; FMS, "Education—'With the Goal of the Church Always in View,'" 1155.
29. Independence *Examiner* (September 24, 1921), 1.
30. FMS, "Education—'With the Goal of the Church Always in View,'" 1155. See also Independence *Examiner* (May 30, 1923), 1.
31. Independence Institute of the Arts and Sciences, "The Campus," unnumbered; "The Independence Institute," *SH* 74 (September 28, 1927): 1147-48.
32. *Bulletin of the Independence Institute of the Arts and Sciences: Announcements of Courses for 1922-1923* (n.p.), p. 5, 7-19, RLDS Archives; "Fourteen Special Courses Are Offered at the Institute," *SH* 74 (May 25, 1927): 596, 622.
33. FMS, "The Independence Institute of the Arts and Sciences," *SH* 74 (October 12, 1927): 1186. See also *GCM* (April 6, 1927), p. 4131.
34. *GCM* (April 6, 1927), p. 4131.
35. Pearl Wilcox, "Independence Retrospect," Part 9, *SH* 106 (November 2, 1959): 1048; Independence Institute of the Arts and Sciences, "Tentative Working Program," unpublished typescript, RLDS Archives; Independence Institute of the Arts and Sciences, "The Campus," unnumbered; Letter of Institute Workers in Support of the Campus, March 28, 1924, as cited in ibid.
36. Independence Institute of the Arts and Sciences, *Articles of Incorporation* (Independence, Missouri, n.p., 1923), pp. 1-6;

FMS, "The Independence Institute of the Arts and Sciences," 1186.

37. FMS, "The Campus," unnumbered; "Ruth Lyman Smith Memorial Library," *SH* 75 (June 27, 1928): 755.
38. Paul M. Edwards, *The Hilltop Where. . . : An Informal History of Graceland College* (Lamoni, Iowa: The Venture Foundation, 1972), p. 88.
39. FMS, "Conference Address Looks to the Future," *SH: Conference Daily Edition* 71 (April 9, 1924), 94.
40. FMS, "Conference Address Looks to the Future," *SH* 89 (April 18, 1942): 487; FMS, "Loyalty in Time of War," *SH* 88 (December 20, 1941): 1603; FMS, "Sanctity of the Law," 1224; Doctrine and Covenants 95:2; 98:11h; 112; FMS, "Obedience to Law," 533-36, passim.
41. FMS, *The Higher Powers of Man*, pp. 223, 225-26; FMS, Notes for a Masonic Lecture, 1930, p. 7, FMS Papers; FMS, The Value of Statutory Precepts," 113.
42. FMS, "Allegiance to the Laws of the Land," n.d., FMS Papers.
43. Ibid.; Doctrine and Covenants 58:5.
44. FMS, "Looking to the Redemption of Zion," 527.
45. FMS, "Christianizing Society," *SH* 71 (February 14, 1924): 124; FMS, "Looking to the Redemption of Zion," 527; FMS, "Safety in Law and Liberty in Respect," 1305; FMS, Notes for Masonic Lecture, 1930, pp. 1-6, FMS Papers.
46. FMS, "The President's Address," *SH: Conference Daily Edition*, 77 (April 8, 1930): 17. See also FMS, "Questions and Answers," *SH* 79 (May 11, 1932): 449; FMS, *The Sublimation of Labor*, p. 3; FMS, "Respect for the Law," pp. 737-38; Ellwood, *The Social Problem*, pp. 2, 45.
47. "Letter to Herbert Hoover," *SH* 77 (April 10, 1930): 49-50.
48. FMS, "Forces For and Against Crime," *SH* 76 (November 6, 1929): 1344-45; FMS, Notes of Speech to Masonic Lodge on Dues, n.d., FMS Papers, Masonic file; C. L. Olson to FMS, September 19, 1930, FMS Papers.
49. FMS, Notes for a Masonic Lecture, 1930, p. 10, FMS Papers, Masonic file; FMS, Notes for Masonic Lecture, n.d., ibid.
50. FMS, "A Danger Before Us," *SH* 75 (April 25, 1928): 489.
51. FMS, "Respect for the Law," 737-38; FMS, Notes for a Masonic Lecture, 1930, pp. 27-28, FMS Papers, Masonic file.
52. FMS, "Sanctity of the Law," 1227. See also FMS, "The President's Address [April 8, 1930]," 17.

53. FMS, "The Value of Cooperation," *SH* 57 (December 21, 1910): 1248.
54. Ibid., 1249.
55. Ibid.
56. FMS, "Forces For and Against Crime," 1345-46.
57. FMS, "Moral Economic Progress," *SH* 75 (August 29, 1928): 1002-03.
58. FMS, "Our Duty as Citizens," *SH* 69 (July 12, 1922): 639-40.
59. FMS, "Cleanliness in Individual and Social Life," *SH* 71 (May 28, 1924): 508.
60. FMS, Notes for Address to Bishops of Holden Stake, May 12, 1940, FMS Papers; T. W. Williams, Vida E. Smith, and E. D. Moore, "Should the Church Go into Politics?" *Messenger* 1 (January 1, 1926): 5.
61. FMS, "Respect for the Law," 737-38.
62. FMS, Notes for an address on government, n.d., FMS Papers; FMS, Notes for a lecture on the Pendergast Machine, n.d., ibid.; FMS, Notes for an address to the Lincoln Club of Jamesport, Maine, November 3, 1939, ibid.; FMS, Notes for a Masonic lecture, 1930, pp. 1-4, ibid., Masonic file; Tickemyer Interview; Alice M. Edwards Questionnaire, 1972; William Penn, "Frame of Government for Pennsylvania," as cited in Daniel J. Boorstin, *The Americans: The Colonial Experience* (New York: Vintage Books, 1958), pp. 42-43.
63. FMS, "Christianizing Society," 527; FMS, "The Value of Statutory Precepts," 113; FMS, "The President's Address," *SH: Conference Daily Edition* 81 (April 7, 1934): 40.
64. FMS, "Moral Economic Progress," pp. 1002-03.
65. FMS, "Across the Desk of the Editor in Chief," *SH* 80 (May 30, 1933): 676; FMS, "Hoover or Smith," *SH* 75 (August 29, 1928): 1001; FMS, "An American Election," ibid. (November 7, 1928): 1266; FMS, "The Approach in Thinking," ibid. (July 18, 1928): 841; FMS, "Cleanliness in Individual and Social Life," 507-08; FMS, "Sanctity of the Law," 1225-26.
66. Leland A. Negaard, "Our Relationship to the Ecumenical Movement," *SH* 109 (August 1, 1962): 17, 34; Leland A. Negaard to the Writer, March 26, 1974; Tickemyer Interview.
67. T. W. Williams, "Forward Movement Among the Churches," *SH* 66 (December 31, 1919): 1263-64; Editorial, "Quotations from the Iowa Interchurch World Conference," ibid., 1266, 1271; C. E. Wright, "The Interchurch World Movement," *SH*

67 (March 17, 1920): 246; R. J. Lambert, "The Eternal Question, Christian Unity," *SH* 73 (June 23, 1926): 565-66; Samuel A. Burgess, "Church Union," *SH* 67 (January 14, 1920): 26; Samuel A. Burgess, "On What Basis Shall the Churches Unite?" *SH* 68 (June 7, 1921): 531; Samuel A. Burgess, "The Probable Future of Church Union," ibid. (August 30, 1921): 818; FMS, "Is Church Unity Probable?" *SH* 74 (May 11, 1927): 530; *History of the RLDS*, vol. 7, p. 43.

68. Tickemyer Interview; GET to FMS, October 1, 1938, GET Papers.
69. James H. Timberlake, *Prohibition and the Progressive Movement, 1900-1920* (Cambridge, Massachusetts: Harvard University Press, 1963), pp. 100-24.
70. *History of the RLDS*, vol. 6, p. 552. Few numbers of the *Saints' Herald* or *Zion's Ensign*, 1900-1920 were set to print without treating the subjects of prohibition or temperance originally or by reprint. For examples see Walter W. Smith, "Probibition by Law," *Zion's Ensign* 27 (November 2, 1916): 1; "What Prohibition Has Done for Two Camps," ibid. 28 (November 15, 1917): 15; William Jennings Bryan, "Why Wait," ibid., 29 (February 21, 1918): 15; "National Prohibition Nearing," ibid. 30 (January 16, 1919): 1; "Why I Am an Abstainer," *SH* 55 (May 13, 1908): 468-70; "Governor Hanley on the Liquor Traffic," ibid. (May 6, 1908): 448; "Brewers Attacking the Drink Peril," ibid. (July 1, 1980); "Ready for the Fray," Independence *Examiner* (July 20, 1914), p. 1; "Mammoth 'Dry' Petition," ibid. (July 18, 1914).
71. FMS and F. A. Smith, "Use of Wine in the Sacrament," *GCM* (April 8, 1913), p. 1701.
72. FMS, "Preparation," *SH* 61 (August 19, 1914): 785; See also FMS, *The Higher Powers of Man*, pp. 48, 52; and Charles A. Ellwood, *Sociology and Modern Social Problems*, (New York: The American Book Company, 1924), pp. 330, 337-40.
73. Ibid.
74. Ibid.
75. Editorial, "Saloons Close in Zion," *SH* 62 (December 22, 1915); 1228; *History of the RLDS*, vol. 6, p. 552; "Give Women the Credit," Independence *Examiner* (July 22, 1914).
76. FMS, "Wet or Dry? Dry!" *SH* 74 (February 23, 1927): 1.
77. FMS, "The Sanctity of the Law," 1226.
78. FMS, "Moral Economic Progress," 1002-03.

79. FMS, "The Direction of Our Resolution," *SH* 75 (May 16, 1928): 591.
80. FMS, "Wet or Dry? Dry!" 1.
81. FMS, "Forces For and Against Crime," 1343.
82. FMS, "Across the Desk of the Editor in Chief," *SH* 80 (May 30, 1933): 675; FMS, "Holding to Our Standards," *SH* 79 (December 14, 1932): 1286.
83. Leonard J. Lea, "Independence Votes 'Dry' in the 'Literary Digest' Poll," *SH* 79 (April 27, 1932): 394-95.
84. GCM (April 5, 1919), p. 2765.
85. Ibid., (April 11, 1927), p. 4248; ibid. (April 18, 1927), pp. 4286-87.
86. *GCM* (April 18, 1927), pp. 4286-87. For other statements from church literature in support of prohibition see: Editorial, "Law Enforcement," *SH* 71 (June 4, 1924): 529; Editorial, "National Prohibition," *SH* 66 (February 12, 1919): 148; Cyril E. Wright, "Educate for Battle," *SH* 79 (October 19, 1932): 1037.
87. FMS, "Across the Desk of the Editor in Chief," *SH* 81 (February 20, 1934): 228.
88. FMS, "Latter Day Saints and Liquor," *SH* 82 (February 5, 1935): 163.
89. Edward Larsen Interview; Ellwood, *Sociology and Modern Social Problems*, pp. 349-51; FMS, "Missouri's Need for a Reformatory," *SH* 73 (October 20, 1926): 996; Editorial, "Prevention of Crime," *SH* 70 (August 15, 1923): 770; FMS, "Prison Reform," ibid. (September 5, 1923): 842.
90. Editorial, "A Visit to the Federal Prison at Leavenworth," *SH* 57 (August 31, 1910): 845, 848.
91. Edward Larsen Interview; FMS, "Missouri's Need for a Reformatory," p. 996. Smith cited his earlier visits to this institution in this short article.
92. FMS, "Missouri's Need for a Reformatory," 996.
93. Smith reprinted two articles in support of Warden Osborne, "Progress at Sing-Sing," *Outlook* (May 12, 1915), and "After Warden's Scalp," *Des Moines Register* (August 11, 1915) in *SH* 62 (June 16, 1915): 585-86 and ibid. (October 13, 1915): 989.
94. FMS, "Missouri's Need for a Reformatory," 996.
95. M. A. Etzenhouser, "Social Services Bureau, Report," *GCM* (April, 1925), p. 3989; *History of the RLDS*, vol. 7, p. 527.
96. M. A. Etzenhouser, "Report of the Social Service Bureau," *SH:*

Conference Daily Edition 77 (April 9, 1930): 43.

97. FMS, "Christianizing Society," 124; FMS, Notes for a sermonette, ca. May, 1933, FMS Papers; David J. Pivar, *Purity Crusade: Sexual Morality and Social Control, 1868-1900* (Westport, Connecticut: Greenwood Press, 1973), pp. 3-12.
98. "Questions and Answers," *SH* 79 (May 11, 1932): 449; FMS, "Forces For and Against Crime," 1346.
99. FMS, "The Redemption of Zion," *Zion's Ensign* 34 (August 10, 1922): 501.
100. FMS, Notes for a sermonette, ca. May, 1933, FMS Papers.
101. FMS, *A Message to the Young People of the Church* (Independence, Missouri: Herald Publishing House, 1922), p. 4; FMS, *Address to the Seventy-First General Conference*. . ., p. 12.
102. FMS, "The Redemption of Zion Explained," n.d., Reprint from *Ogden Standard Examiner* (January, 1923), RLDS Archives.
103. FMS, "Shall Our Young People Dance?" *Priesthood Journal* vol. 8 (April, 1922), pp. 49-50; FMS to Mrs. B. M. Anderson, April 28, 1932, FMS Papers.
104. FMS, *Address to the Seventy-First General Conference*. . ., p. 12.
105. *GCM* (April 12, 1916), p. 2220.
106. Ibid. (April 13, 1918), p. 2637.
107. FMS, *Marriage and the Church*, p. 7.
108. Ibid.
109. Ibid., p. 8.
110. Ibid., pp. 13, 15-16; FMS "Dress Styles?" *SH* 74 (March 2, 1927): 243; FMS, "Stewardship and Dress," ibid. (July 13, 1927): 793-94.
111. FMS, "Stewardship and Dress," 793-94; FMS, *Address to the Seventy-First General Conference*. . ., pp. 15-16.
112. Ibid.
113. FMS, "Forces For and Against Crime," 1345.
114. Ibid.
115. FMS, "Michelangelo," *SH* 70 (November 14, 1923): 1080.
116. FMS, "Vocation Versus Avocation," ibid. (September 5, 1923): 846.
117. Ibid.
118. Bernard DeVoto, *The Literary Fallacy* (Boston: Little, Brown, and Co., 1944), pp. 99-105.
119. Smith, "Some Memories of President Frederick M. Smith," 440.

120. FMS, Manuscript for "Onward to Zion," and "Come, Oh Come Sweet Comforter," n.d., FMS Papers. See also *The Hymnal*, pp. 452-53.
121. FMS, Handwritten manuscript on "Frank Dickens," n.d., ibid.
122. FMS, "The Raven: A Spiritual Interpretation," *SH* 80 (October 31, 1933): 1387.
123. Ibid., 1388.
124. Ibid.
125. Hubert M. Skinner, *An Old Poem Re-Studied* (Lincoln-Jefferson University: Chicago, Illinois, June 10, 1909), pp. 1-23, passim, copy in FMS Papers. For his other comments on literary figures see FMS, "Retreat," *SH* 76 (January 30, 1929): 114.
126. Ralph K. Andrist, "Paladin of Purity," *American Heritage*, 24 (October, 1973): 4-7; Heywood Broun and Margaret Leech, *Anthony Comstock: Roundsman of the Lord* (New York: Literary Guild of America, 1927), pp. 55-58, 75-84.
127. Henry F. May, *The End of American Innocence: A Study of the First Years of Our Own Time, 1912-1917* (Chicago: Quadrangle Books, 1959).
128. D. J. Krahl, "Report of the Women's Auxiliary for Social Science," *GCM* (April 15, 1913), 1737-38.
129. Ruth Lyman Smith, "The Woman Movement," *Autumn Leaves* 33 (August, 1915): 369, 373.
130. Ibid., 373.
131. Ibid., 370-71.
132. FMS, *A Message to the Young People*. . ., p. 6; Smith, *Concerning the Prophet*. . ., pp. 207-08; Ellwood, *Sociology and Modern Social Problems*, pp. 158-59.
133. FMS, "President Smith Addresses Women," *SH: Conference Daily Edition* 83 (April 7, 1936): 54; *GCM* (April 6, 1926), p. 3914.
134. FMS, Notes for a Father's Day Sermon, n.d., FMS Papers.
135. FMS, *Marriage and the Church*, pp. 4-5.
136. Ibid.
137. FMS, "President Smith Discusses Marriage Problems—Problems of Divorce Settled By Education, Not By Legislation," *SH: Conference Daily Edition* 83 (April 8, 1936): 57, 62; *GCM* (April 6, 1926), pp. 3914-3915.
138. FMS, Notes for sermon on marriage, n.d., FMS Papers.
139. FMS, "Birth Control and Families," *SH* 74 (March 2, 1927):

224; FMS, Notes regarding family sizes, July 28, 1934, FMS Papers.

140. FMS, Underlinings in clipping from *Reader's Digest*, "Is Birth Control a National Menace?" n.d., FMS Papers.

141. FMS, "Birth Control and Families," 224.

142. Barbara Welter, "The Cult of True Womanhood," *American Quarterly*, 18 (Summer, 1966): 151, 152-74, passim.

143. FMS, "The Contribution of Emma Hale Smith," *SH* 91 (August 12, 1944): 1029-32. He also found some of these same qualities in the character of Martha of Bethany, the sister of Mary and Lazarus of Biblical lore. See FMS, Notes on Martha of Bethany, FMS Papers.

144. FMS, Notes for a Father's Day Sermon, n.d., FMS Papers.

145. FMS, "The Family Circle," *SH* 77 (July 9, 1930): 77; FMS, "Home Builders," *SH* 85 (August 13, 1938): 85; FMS, Typewritten Pastoral Address, n.d., p. 1, FMS Papers; FMS, Notes for Address to the Women of the 1940 Conference, April, 1940, ibid.

146. Dora Pankey Glines, "Report of the Department of Women," *GCM* (September 14, 1923), pp. 3365-66.

147. FMS, "The First Woman Member of the Canadian Parliament," *SH* 76 (March 20, 1929): 323.

148. FMS, "Centralia and Its New Hydro-Electric Plant," *SH* 77 (November 12, 1930): 1234.

149. *GCM* (1912), pp. 1588-91; "Report of the Social Purity Board," ibid. (July 22, 1914), p. 1849; Charles Woodstock, "Report of the Social Purity Board," ibid. (July 28, 1915), pp. 2011-12; Pivar, pp. 10-12.

150. Ruth Lyman Smith, "Report of the Women's Auxiliary," *GCM* (1917), p. 2327; Charles B. Woodstock, "Report of the Social Purity Board," ibid. (March 1, 1918), pp. 2575-77; "Social Purity," ibid. (October, 1922), pp. 3147-48; Ralph W. Farrell, "Social Purity Board," ibid. (February 26, 1918), pp. 2753-64.

151. S. A. Burgess "The Duty of the Church Toward the Morals of Today," *SH* 69 (March 15, 1922): 249-50.

152. FMS, "Independence Women Reach a Goal," *SH* 80 (June 13, 1933): 739.

153. FMS, "A Program for the Women's Work," *SH* 82 (November 12, 1935): 1447.

154. Ibid.

155. P. J. Arnson and M. S. Hoecker, "The Women's Council," *SH*:

Conference Daily Edition, 83 (April 6, 1936): 19. The members of the Council were Blanche Mesley, Emma McConley, Mildred Grabske, Dora Glines, Audentia Anderson, Ruth Clegg, Alice Edwards, Margaret Hoecker, Lulu Carmichael, Agnes Fisher, Charlotte Koehler, Mable Carlile, Inez Smith Davis, Vera Thompson, A. Faye McLean, and Pauline Arnson.

156. FMS, "President Smith Addresses Women," 54; Tickemyer Interview.
157. FMS, "What Exercises May Be Held in Our Churches," *SH* 60 (December 17, 1913): 1217.
158. FMS, to the Presidents of the Quorums, August 21, 1913, RLDS Archives, letter file; FMS, "Charge to the General Conference Appointees," *SH* 89 (May 2, 1942): 548.
159. FMS, *An Address to the Priesthood*, pp. 11-12; FMS to the Quorums, May 29, 1918, RLDS Archives; FMS, "Use of Tobacco and Liquor," *SH* 81 (March 13, 1934): 325; FMS to District and Branch Pastors, n.d., FMS Papers.
160. FMS, "Statement for the First Presidency," *GCM* (April 7, 1909), p. 1179.
161. FMS, "The Duty of the Church Towards the Morals of Today," 249-50.
162. Standing High Council, "Adultery," *GCM* (April 12, 1926), pp. 4076-77.
163. For the most outstanding examples, see the sixteen pieces of correspondence from Dora Pankey Glives of Orange, California, April, 1929 through May, 1936, and another twelve from Mae Yoder of Kansas City, Missouri, from July, 1931 to October, 1936. FMS Papers.
164. FMS to May [*sic*] Yoder, May 14, 1945, FMS Papers.
165. DeVere Love, Recorder of Mizra Temple to the writer, November 1, 1972; Millard D. Hamilton, Recorder of Ararat Temple to the writer, October 6, 1972.
166. FMS to Mrs. B. M. Anderson, July 30, 1930, Edwards Collection; FMS, "Potentate's Message: Our Entertainments," *Ararat Shrine News* 5 (March, 1941): 3.
167. Recorder of Orient Lodge to the writer, January 8, 1976; *Kansas City Star* (June 7, 1931), and the Independence *Examiner* (February 28, 1941), RLDS Archives, clipping file; Edward H. Hashinger to FMS, December 10, 1934, Alfred Ludlow to FMS, December 13, 1934, and Darious Brown to FMS, February 19, 1935, FMS Papers.

168. "Minutes for the Years 1941-1942," January 8, 1941, Ararat Shrine Temple, Kansas City, Missouri, unnumbered.
169. Mrs. B. M. Anderson to FMS, March 7, 1930, Edwards Collection; FMS, Random notes on Herbert Hoover, 1929, p. 1, FMS Papers; Tickemyer Interview.
170. Charles S. Lobinger to FMS, March 4, 1928, FMS Papers, Masonic file; FMS, "What Is Masonry?" 1929, ibid.; FMS, "Ritual of Initiation," 1929, ibid.; FMS, Notes on "Ahiman Rezon," n.d., p. 27, ibid.; FMS, "Landmarks of Masonry," n.d., pp. 1-12, ibid.
171. FMS, Notes and quotations on the nature of Masonry, n.d., FMS Papers, Masonic file; FMS, Notes on the responsibility of Masonry to self and society, n.d., ibid.; FMS, "Potentate's Message: Decorum in the First Section," *Ararat Shrine News* 5 (May, 1941): 3; FMS, "Potentate's Message: The Shrine and Masonry," ibid., (February, 1941): 3.
172. FMS, "Potentate's Message: Our Entertainments," 3; FMS, "Potentate's Message: Shrine Rehabilitation," *Ararat Shrine News* 5 (June, 1941): 3; "Minutes for the Years 1941-1942," October 1, 1941, Ararat Shrine Temple, Kansas City, Missouri, unnumbered.
173. Lois Larsen to Alice M. Edwards, March 13, 1930, Edwards Collection.
174. "Minutes for the Years 1941-1942," December 3, 1941, Ararat Shrine Temple, Kansas City, Missouri, unnumbered.
175. FMS, "Suggestions for a K [Knights]. T [Templar]. Talk," n.d., FMS Papers, Masonic file.
176. FMS, Notes on "storms and stresses," ca. 1929, ibid.
177. FMS, Notes for a Masonic Lecture, 1930, pp. 18-19.
178. Ibid., p. 13.
179. FMS, "What Is Masonry?" 1929, FMS Papers, Masonic file.
180. FMS, Notes on the responsibility of Masonry to self and society, n.d., ibid.
181. FMS, Notes for a Masonic address at Fort Scott, Kansas, November 18, 1930, ibid.
182. FMS, Notes on the Masonic Ritual of the Thirty-First Degree, Spring, 1929, ibid.
183. FMS, "Dr. Fred Smith on Radio Coast to Coast," *Ararat Shrine News* 5 (May, 1941): 3; FMS, "Shriners Must Be Loyal Citizens," ibid. (May, 1941): 3.
184. FMS, Notes for a Masonic Lecture, 1930, p. 32, FMS Papers, Masonic file.

185. Joseph E. Morcombe, "Religious Tests in Masonic Lodges: Is Utah Justified in Challenging Craft Standing of Brothers on Account of Their Church Affiliations?" *The Masonic World*, 18 (October, 1936): 7-10; O'Dea, *The Mormons*, p. 57.
186. Mrs. B. M. Anderson to FMS, March 7, 1930, Edwards Collection; FMS, annotations "Masonry" and "Utah Temple Work" in his Book of Mormon, p. 564; Joseph E. Morcombe, *Masonry and Mormonism* (n.p., Grand Lodge of Iowa, n.d.), pp. 448-452; *History of the RLDS*, Vol. 6, p. 236; FMS, Notes on the Question of the Church and Masonry, n.d., FMS Papers, Masonic file.
187. Book of Mormon, Helaman 2:142-155; *Journal of History*, 1 (July, 1908): 287-88.
188. Cross, pp. 76, 114-20; O'Dea, *The Mormons*, pp. 23, 35.
189. *History of the RLDS*, vol. 6, p. 166.
190. Joseph Smith III, "In Question—Secret Societies," *SH* 53 (March 7, 1906): 220.
191. General Conference Resolution 593, April 6, 1907, as cited in *General Conference Resolutions, 1852-1915* (Lamoni, Iowa: Herald Publishing House, n.d.), unnumbered.
192. Mrs. B. M. Anderson to FMS, March 7, 1930, Edwards Collection.
193. W. D. Gillen to FMS, January 13, 1946, FMS Papers.
194. N. V. Anderson to FMS, November 17, 1941, ibid.
195. FMS to Mrs. B. M. Anderson, July 10, 1932, Edwards Collection.
196. Church of Jesus Christ of Latter Day Saints, *The Book of Abraham* (Salt Lake City: Deseret Publishing Company, 1962), chap. 1, vss. 21-27.
197. Doctrine and Covenants 116:4.
198. *History of the RLDS*, vol. 6, pp. 77, 187, 268.
199. Elbert A. Smith, "More About Racial Minority Problems," *SH* 91 (March 4, 1944): 278; See also Leonard Lea, "The Racial Problem," ibid. (October 28, 1944): 1267, 1275.
200. See Earl Brown, *Why Race Riots?* (New York: Public Affairs Committee, 1944), Albert Deutsch, "The Negro's Fight in the North: A Tale of Four Cities," n.p., Basil Mathews, "America's Negroes," *The Spectator* (August 28, 1942), unnumbered, FMS Papers.
201. Edward Larsen interview.
202. Editorial, "Mob Law," *SH* 70 (July 18, 1923): 685.

203. FMS, Random jottings, 1944, FMS Papers; FMS, "The Stirrings of Patriotism," *SH* 79 (August 24, 1932): 801.
204. FMS, "Control Racial Prejudices," *SH* 89 (September 5, 1942): 1124.
205. McFarland, pp. 139-41.
206. Joseph Smith, "Neutrality Enjoined," *SH* 61 (September 16, 1914): 873.
207. Doctrine and Covenants 95:3-6. See also James E. Yates, "Abhorrence of War," *SH* 61 (November 25, 1914): 1117-18; *History of the RLDS*, vol. 6, p. 625.
208. McFarland, p. 168.
209. FMS, "Report of the First Presidency [April 6, 1917]," 2288.
210. Ibid., 2289.
211. Ibid., 2288.
212. Ibid., 2302, 2419.
213. FMS, "The War: Who Should Enlist? Who Is Exempt?" *Zion's Ensign* 28 (July 19, 1917): 1-2.
214. FMS, "President's Report," *GCM* (April 6, 1918), pp. 2491-92.
215. Ibid. (April 12, 1918), p. 2639.
216. Ibid. (April 13, 1918), p. 2642.
217. FMS, "Address—F. M. Smith," ibid. (April 14, 1918), p. 2651.
218. Ibid.
219. Ibid., pp. 2651, 2653.
220. Ibid., p. 2655.
221. Ibid., pp. 2655-56.
222. FMS, "Loyalty," *SH* 74 (March 16, 1927): 305-306.
223. FMS, "Necessity for an Ideal," ibid. (May 2, 1918), 5.
224. Ibid.
225. Ibid.; Doctrine and Covenants 112. President Smith summarized this section as follows:

> . . . governments were instituted of God for man's benefit and that he holds men accountable for their acts in relation thereto; that governments are to protect by law the free exercise of conscience, the right to control and own property, and protect life; that civil officers must be upheld by the people, and good men sought for such offices, that religion is instituted by Deity, and that neither man nor law can be permitted to infringe upon the right to worship according to conscience; that all men are bound to sustain and uphold the respective governments in which they reside; that sedition and rebellion are unbecoming and punishable; that rules and magistrates should be honored in their stations as protectors of the innocent and punishers of the guilty, that all men owe respect and deference to the laws, that rulers, states and governments can and should enact laws for the protection of citizens in the right to their religious beliefs, that crime should be punished by adequate penalty, that men should use their abilities in bringing offenders to punishment; that religious influence should not mingle

with civil government; that religious societies have a right to deal with delinquent members, providing such dealing be for good standing and fellowship, and not for right of property or life, that men should appeal to civil law for redress of wrongs and grievances; that all men may rightfully defend themselves, friends, and government from unlawful attacks and encroachments, where immediate appeal cannot be made to the laws, and relief afforded.

FMS, "Our Attitude in War," *SH* 86 (November 18, 1939): 1443.

226. Ibid.
227. FMS, "Message to the President," *GCM* (April 6, 1919), p. 2691.
228. FMS, to Mrs. B. M. Anderson, December 30, 1920, Edwards Collection.
229. FMS, "Address to the Conference," *GCM* (April 6, 1920), p. 2860.
230. Ibid.
231. Ibid.
232. "Conference Unanimously Declares Against War," *SH Conference Daily Edition* 81 (April 14, 1934): 105-06.
233. FMS, "Questions and Answers," *SH* 79 (May 11, 1932): 449.
234. FMS, "The Munitions Business," *SH* 82 (June 11, 1935): 741.
235. FMS, "Nationalism and War," *SH* 84 (November 27, 1937): 1507; FMS, "President Frederick M. Smith Addresses Conference [April 7, 1936]," 53-54.
236. FMS, "Across the Desk of the Editor in Chief," *SH* 86 (November 25, 1939): 1477.
237. FMS, "Peace on Earth," ibid. (January 14, 1939): 38.
238. FMS, "Nationalism and War," 1507.
239. FMS, "The Church and Peace," *SH* 89 (March 21, 1942): 359-60.
240. For an elaboration of Wilson's views on the causes of war, see N. Gordon Levin, Jr., *Woodrow Wilson and World Politics: America's Response to War and Revolution* (New York: Oxford University Press, 1968), pp. 1-10, or Sidney Bell, *Righteous Conquest: Woodrow Wilson and the Evolution of the New Diplomacy* (Port Washington, New York: Kennikat Press, 1972, chaps. 1, 5-10, passim.
241. FMS, "Peace on Earth," 38.
242. FMS, "The Confusion of Conflict," *SH* 87 (July 13, 1940): 867; FMS, "The President's Address," ibid. (April 20, 1940): 487.

243. FMS, "Across the Desk of the Editor in Chief," *SH* 86 (October 7, 1939): 1252.
244. FMS, "Loyalty in Time of War," 1603.
245. Ibid.; FMS, "Conference Address Looks to the Future," *SH* 89 (April 18, 1942): 487; FMS, "Peace and War," *SH* 91 (March 25, 1944): 372; FMS, "Some Thoughts on Peace and War," ibid. (June 10, 1944): 741-42; FMS, "Our Attitude in War," 1443-44.
246. FMS, "The Torch of Loyalty," ibid. (July 11, 1942), 867.
247. FMS, "The Church and Peace," 360-61.
248. FMS, "The World After War," *SH* 89 (August 15, 1942): 1031; FMS, Notes on "German Brutality," spring, 1945, FMS Papers.
249. FMS, *The Church and Change*, p. 6.
250. Ibid., pp. 7-8; FMS, Notes for a speech on the postwar world, 1945, FMS Papers.
251. FMS, *The Elements of Christian Peace* (Independence, Missouri: Herald Publishing House, 1945), pp. 5-9.
252. Ibid.
253. FMS, "The Church and Peace," 361; FMS, "The Confusion of Conflict," 807.

CONCLUSION

In its larger perspective, this dissertation contains not only a portrayal of the life of a sectary as mugwump but also a support of Gerald W. McFarland's thesis that mugwumpery continued well into the twentieth century. Although Frederick M. Smith was a religious—rather than political—figure, he blended McFarland's two poles for twentieth century mugwumpery: the "orthodox" (those who were extremely independent of politics, advocates of laissez faire, and Victorian in morals) and the "innovative" (those who stressed newer areas of efficiency, professionalization and, on occasion, centralization of power and authority as a means to those ends). His innovative mugwumps represented the conservative side of progressivism or the liberal side of mugwumpery, while the more orthodox version of the genre represented the continuity of Victorian moralism, individualism, and the economic conservatism of the Grover Cleveland era.[1]

Specifically, the preceding chapters have shown that a person of Restoration extraction could be a willing participant in the reform ethos common to his own time. He appropriated the reform themes of efficiency, centralization, and professionalization, and added them to the conservative and melioristic frame of reference that was already part of his sectarian heritage. In the theocratic, centralized side of theocratic democracy and in stewardship, the voluntary act of truly converted Saints, President Smith tied mugwumpery and his sect together. He merged them in his own reform ideology, combining social meliorism in the broader community with exemplary stewardship in his church, and he hoped that on these two fronts he and his religion could move from their insularity and make a mark in the world.

One of the problems for that fusion was his departure from the basic pietism of his sect. Through his educational experience he combined intellect with faith and moved toward ritualism in a church that demanded more emotional commitment, and because of that he was neither understood nor appreciated by many of his followers. Conjunctive with this, he drew upon the older Restoration tradition of centralized, authoritarian leadership to enhance the efficiency of his religious organization in what he believed to be its call to uplift the secular world. That authoritarian emphasis was repugnant to the Saints of the Reorganization who had built the institution and accustomed themselves to democracy and autonomy. To his followers, his ritualism and authoritarianism made him an "intellectual" and an autocrat, a betrayer of the spirit of the faith. Paradoxically, the majority of the members of the church continued to support him in spite of what may have been their distaste for his personality or his methods. They believed, after all, that God had chosen him specifically to be their leader, and while he was imperfect and made mistakes his repudiation was not warranted nor acceptable to them. Coupled with the external forces of economic depression, internal dissent, and the fact that centralization in itself did not guarantee efficiency, his reform plans for the church were perpetually frustrated.

The foregoing chapters have demonstrated some of the problems that were part of his life and career. In his early years he accepted the parameters of his branch of the Restoration as well as his own lineal responsibility to lead it. He also assumed its premise that free enterprise in the hands of voluntary stewards was the mortar for building the exemplary kingdom of God. His early life was also characterized by an interest in the practical application of science and technology, an interest which he expanded into a study of social science and psychology for his master's and Ph.D. degrees. Through his studies he wanted to reconcile faith with intellect—something which the Saints did not value as pietists—and correlate knowledge with service, something which was admired.

His academic and intellectual development moved him toward ritualism and attitudes central to mugwumpery, confirmed his interest in efficiency and scientific management, and buttressed his confidence in the regenerated individual as the key to progress and change. His dissertation with G. Stanley Hall was firmly based on the premise that higher ideals, particularly those of a religious nature, could generate the enthusiasm, the drive, and the effort necessary to overcome normally overwhelming environmental barriers. Individual character was the key to spiritual, intellectual, and activist strength. Through the idealistically-motivated individual, scientific management, and economic orthodoxy, he believed more could be done to remedy the ills of society than special legislation or regulation through governing agencies. Change was the responsibility of disinterested idealists and good managers in the church and in the world external to it.

In his reform analysis, President Smith was totally a mugwump and a sectary, not a fellow traveler with social gospelers. He was close to the latter only in his assumption that the ultimate basis for a legitimate social order could be found in the Christian religion alone. Social gospelers relied on more than the regenerated individual as the catalytic agent to purge society of such injustices as poverty. They advocated collective action and/or resort to the legislative or coercive powers of the state, and considered urban-industrial environments as the fundamental problem with which they had to cope. He disavowed almost all concrete programs for reform that involved government except for prohibition—a proposition he supported for religious reasons—and centered his hope for future change in the sublime efforts of the regenerated individual. When confronted with any concrete legislative or administrative programs, he disparaged them as unnecessary expenditures of public money and erosive to personal character. In his concern for "social safety" and obedience to existing law over social justice, he overlooked the suffering of those who could be helped by legislation, collective bargaining, strikes, or consumer crusades. He was also against most variants of socialism because he saw them as threats to private property and individual initiative. To him real reformers were those who advocated law and order to protect the righteous, who enunciated purer ideals because they were elite and above party or interest; these should be elected to office and trusted to administer as good Christians. There was no room in his reform analysis for dissenting minorities, oppressed majorities of consumers, citizens, or taxpayers, or collective groups to develop countervailing power. Moreover, social conventions and proprieties in sexual conduct, marriage, and the purely nurturant role of women were verities that had to be recognized if social harmony—a concomitant of order and social safety—was to prevail.

Ultimately, he posited the stewardship of his sect as the answer to the specific problems of excess competition, poverty, and industrial injustice, and for the most part it fit into the configurations of mugwumpery. He sincerely believed that individuals who had caught the vision of the future kingdom of God would voluntarily "consecrate" their surplus resources to the church and assume the managerial positions over their property for God and the institution. Their "socialized surpluses" would be used for the benefit of those who did not have the talents or ability to produce their own. They, too, would have an inheritance in Zion because of the conscience and cooperation of the more productive individuals. Throughout all, the initiative of free enterprise would be preserved while the stewards used its benefits to promote equality and justice for the group as an example of what God had intended for the broader world. This was Fred M.'s answer to the excesses of the competitive, industrial world, and it was not incompatible with mugwumpery. Both stressed voluntarism, free enterprise, reform without the use of legislation, and the meliorative role of the individual. Stewardship was his institutional answer to world problems—an exemplary, voluntary process that all could see, emulate, and, after a contagion of example, help to precipitate the kingdom of God on earth.

As one of the primary goals of his administration, he wanted to develop concrete examples of stewardship in Independence, Missouri, the traditional gathering place of the Saints. In the initial Restoration communitarian experiments free enterprise had been stressed as an alternative to the "all things common" principle that characterized the early nineteenth century communitarian experiments. The Reorganized church drew on the same tradition to establish the "Order of Enoch" as a means of providing cheap land for the Saints, a community locus for church headquarters, and a demonstration of free enterprise as a positive, valuable, and godly system. Fred M. was never content with that interpretation of stewardship, although he applauded its temporal gains for the church. What he wanted was to blend the social idealism of the faith with managerial stewardships in an orderly, rational, process and to demonstrate the practical economic goals of the institution. He believed that the free enterprise system in stewardship could demonstrate to the world how God intended that stystem to function and would obivate the need for charity. While he contemplated convoking commissions of experts to survey the needs and resources of the area to implement such a project, the initial experiments at Holden and Atheron, Missouri, failed in the late twenties and early thirties because of financial retrenchment due to the depression, and because he was too tied to the existing capitalistic order and his own interpretation of how stewardships would operate. He would allow no deviation or cooperative experimentation outside the auspices of the church or sanctioned procedure.

The first ten years of his administration, however, were consumed by attempts to centralize and rationalize the governing structures of the church, and here he employed what McFarland called "innovative" mugwumpery to that task. Within the church from 1915 to 1925, the president embarked on his own crusade to make his institution fit for the dual task of building Zion within the church in stewardships and channeling its remaining energy toward making an impact in the broader world. To accomplish that, he initiated "reform" moves that focused on two themes, one inherent in Restorationism, the other in the reform ferment of his own time. From his religious traditions, he emphasized the centralizing, authoritarian premises of theocracy and reversed the generally cautious, democratic approach of his father's leadership.

From a more secular perspective, Fred M. was motivated by the popular efficiency motif of the late nineteenth and early twentieth centuries and its connected themes of centralization, professionalization, and order. As a good manager he could not tolerate the seeming inefficiency of democratic and—as he saw it—obstructionist traditions in the quorums when he considered the socially regenerative mission he thought belonged to the church. The glue that bound the movements together was his own authoritarian personality. Essentially, he wanted to make the church the "cutting edge" of social change and, similar to other authoritarian leaders, he centered that effort in his own messianism and his belief that the people of the church had a plebescitarian function only. For him democracy diffused power and wasted resources, while autocratization consolidated power and used all resources efficiently and with purpose. Even though mainstream mugwumps deplored the use of coercion, he combined their innovative side with his authoritarian traditions and personality, labeled it "supreme directional control," explained it as efficiency, and called it reform. In the name of centralization he subordinated the Quorum of Twelve, organized a coordinating committee to rationalize the church auxiliaries under his general management, and attempted to center the nominating power for church offices in himself and other administrators rather than in their constituencies. At the General Conference of 1925 he put his prestige on the line before his retinue with his "Document of Church Government," and that body, faced with supporting their prophet president or rejecting his supreme directional control, voted to support him.

He emerged from that Conference with total administrative control of the institution, including its personnel, bureaucracies, publications, councils, and finances. That control, however, gave him very little in practice. Opposition to "autocracy" continued; his directives were effectively ignored by many bureaucrats, and theocratic democracy functioned very much as it had in the past outside of the Independence area. It was at this point that he turned his attention to organized stewardships, professionalizing the ministry, and formalizing church ritual. The latter activity was motivated by his own ritualistic deviation from the pietism of his faith and exacerbated the differences between him and the larger group of his followers in Independence. It gave them another reason to oppose him as an elitist who wanted to "despiritualize" the church along with establishing an autocracy. It also accentuated the differences between the social and economic elites in Independence who supported him and the majority who questioned his wisdom. In one last attempt to provide for a smoothly operating, efficient government under his control in Independence he abolished the stake organization and governed it directly through select subordinates who followed his basic dictates. Through it all, efficiency still eluded him and the kingdom was no nearer in 1946 than it was in 1915.

Though Frederick M. Smith's life and career illustrated the continuity of mugwumpery into the twentieth century, was it really significant? Granted, this authoritarian personality combined his mugwump and sectarian heritage into a reform ideology and transformed Restoration authoritarianism into centralized efficiency, thereby providing it with a modicum of respectability. Beyond the boundaries of his religious institution he achieved little, and the "reforms" within that institution were of questionable value. The problem of centralization versus autonomy is still a part of the RLDS church, surfacing from time to time with varying degrees of intensity. Actually, Fred M. demonstrated more paradoxes than achievements. As a mugwump he deplored the use of power by government, yet as a sectary he used all the power he could muster within his institution to fight democracy, and decentralization and to support the prohibition movement in Independence. Moreover, he illustrated the difficulties that a religious leader of ritualistic leanings experienced in presiding over a pietistic faith, especially one that was tied to the philosophical contradiction of theocratic democracy—an almost impossible task. He also illuminated a conflict inherent in the Reorganized church throughout his administrative career. His followers criticized, maligned, and vehemently opposed him as an autocrat, but at the same time they could not—and would not—reject the person that they believed was a divinely appointed leader. The prophetic voice was too revered to repudiate.

More than this, he demonstrated that much in the American reform tradition is really conservatism, and that Hofstadter and McFarland, at least in some respects, were right. He tied the church to mugwumpery and provided for it a degree of middle class respectability, but that achievement did not represent reform or the responsibility of a Christian religious organization to the needs of thousands of Americans who suffered from poverty or injustice. While he was centralizing his institution, fighting his battles with the bureaucracies, or attempting to establish organized stewardships, the liberal religious world external to his organization expended its energies differently. Churchmen, denominational conferences and presses, and ecumenical associations kept the Christian social conscience from being consumed by the "lesser causes" of the fundamentalist-modernist controversy, prohibition, and resurgent Victorian prudery, and subsumed by an undisciplined capitalist civilization that sought to strangle all critics. The Federal Council of Churches, for instance, fulminated against capitalist excesses, denounced poverty and materialism, opposed the Ku Klux Klan, and spoke out in such *causes celebre* as the Sacco-Vanzetti case. More importantly, the council fought for the recognition of the legitimate demands of the repressed labor movement—the twelve-hour day, child labor laws, and the closed shop—and even helped to fund some strikes.[2]

Reinhold Niebuhr, a Smith contemporary, shared his belief that individuals could be reached by moral suasion, but he went on to declare that rarely had nations, groups, races, or power blocks voluntarily relinquished a favored position for other individuals. Power, coercion, and political commitments were necessary concomitants of reform in a conflict community. All that could be realistically expected of reform was a Madisonian pluralism within which power was evenly distributed, modifying the domination of any single group and maintaining a tenuous balance of interests. In the moral relativities of the "real" world, to Niebuhr the best that could be expected of any crusade was a relativistically better situation. Reformers must strive for the least evil among relative evils, fully aware of the good in every evil and the evil in every good. The church was the collective community of believers who stood over and above immoral society and was in constant tension with it, calling all institutions into judgment.[3]

Typical of a sectary and a mugwump, Fred M. looked to distant utopias of righteousness, rather than accepting the existing world and striving to eliminate gross injustices through means which were immediate and available.

As a reformer, he was always a Saint.

NOTES

1. McFarland, pp. 1-10, 173-77.
2. Robert Moats Miller, *American Protestantism and Social Issues, 1919-1939* (Chapel Hill: University of North Carolina Press, 1958), pp. 18-28, 31, 34-35, 39, 169-73, 221-22, 270-73, 346; Paul A. Carter, *The Decline and Revival of the Social Gospel, 1920-1940* (Ithaca: Cornell University Press, 1956), pp. 34-44.
3. Ibid., pp. 106-09; Carter, pp. 151-58; Reinhold Niebuhr, *Moral Man and Immoral Society* (New York: Charles Scribner's Sons, 1960), pp. xi-xii, 27, 36, 40-42, 47, 83-85, 117, 141, 226-27, 272.

SELECTED BIBLIOGRAPHY

Books

Abell, Aaron I. *The Urban Impact on American Protestantism.* Cambridge, Massachusetts: Harvard University Press, 1943.

Ahlstrom, Sidney E. *A Religious History of the American People.* New Haven: Yale University Press, 1972.

Anderson, Mary Audentia Smith and Hulmes, Bertha Audentia Anderson, eds. *Joseph Smith III and the Restoration.* Independence, Missouri: Herald Publishing House, 1952.

Anthony, Joseph P. *Lamoni's Passing Parade.* Lamoni, Iowa: Blair Printing Co., 1948.

Baldwin, D. R. *The Angel's Message and Socialism.* Robert, Montana: n.p., ca. 1918.

Bell, Sidney. *Righteous Conquest: Woodrow Wilson and the Evolution of the New Diplomacy.* Port Washington, New York: Kennikat Press, 1972.

Bergh, Albert E., ed. *The Writings of Thomas Jefferson.* 20 vols. Definitive ed. Washington, D.C.: Thomas Jefferson Memorial Assn., 1907.

Bernstein, Barton J., ed. *Towards a New Past: Dissenting Essays in American History.* New York: Random House, 1969.

Biographical and Historical Record of Ringgold and Decatur Counties, Iowa. Chicago, Illinois: The Lewis Publishing Co., 1887.

Blodgett, Geoffrey. *The Gentle Reformers: Massachusetts Democrats in the Cleveland Era.* Cambridge, Massachusetts: Harvard University Press, 1966.

Boorstin, Daniel J. *The Americans: The Colonial Experience.* New York: Vintage Books, 1958.

Brodie, Fawn M. *No Man Knows My History: The Life of Joseph Smith.* New York: Alfred A. Knoph, 1963.

Broun, Heywood, and Leech, Margaret. *Anthony Comstock: Roundsman of the Lord.* New York: Literary Guild of America, 1927.

Carter, Paul A. *The Decline and Revival of the Social Gospel, 1920-1940*. Ithaca: Cornell University Press, 1956.
Cheville, Roy A. *They Made a Difference*. Independence, Missouri: Herald Publishing House, 1970.
__________. *Through the West Door*. Independence, Missouri: Herald Publishing House, 1946.
Church of Jesus Christ of Latter-day Saints. *The Book of Abraham*. Salt Lake City: Deseret Publishing Co., 1962.
Clark, Elmer T. *The Small Sects in America*. Nashville, Tennessee: Cokesbury Press, 1937.
Conkin, Paul K. *The New Deal*. New York: Thomas Y. Crowell Co., 1969.
Cotton, Edward H., ed. *Has Science Discovered God?* New York: Thomas Crowell, Co., 1931.
Croly, Herbert. *The Promise of American Life*. New York: E. P. Dutton and Company, Inc., 1963.
Cross, Whitney R. *The Burned-Over District: The Social and Intellectual History of Enthusiastic Religion in Western New York, 1800-1850*. New York: Harper and Row, 1950.
Davis, David Brion, ed. *Ante Bellum Reform*. New York: Harper and Row, 1967.
Deuffer, Carlyle F., ed. *Stories of Our Hymns: Latter Day Saint Hymns and Their Composers*. Independence, Missouri: Herald Publishing House, 1938.
DeVoto, Bernard. *The Literary Fallacy*. Boston: Little, Brown and Co., 1944.
Edwards, Paul M. *The Hilltop Where . . . : An Informal History of Graceland College*. Lamoni, Iowa: The Venture Foundation, 1972.
Ellwood, Charles A. *Christianity and Social Science: A Challenge to the Church*. New York: The Macmillan Co., 1923.
__________. *The Reconstruction of Religion: A Sociological View*. New York: The Macmillan Co., 1922.
__________. *The Social Problem: A Reconstructive Analysis*. New York: The Macmillan Co., 1922.
__________. *Sociology and Modern Social Problems*. New York: The American Book Co., 1924.
Flanders, Robert B. *Nauvoo: Kingdom on the Mississippi*. Urbana: University of Illinois Press, 1965.
Geddes, Joseph A. *The United Order Among the Mormons: An*

Unfinished Experiment in Economic Organization. Salt Lake City: Deseret News Press, 1924.

Gladden, Washington. *Applied Christianity: Moral Aspects of Social Questions*. Boston, Massachusetts: Houghton-Mifflin and Co., 1899.

Goldman, Eric F. *Rendezvous with Destiny: A History of Modern American Reform*. New York: Vintage Books, 1956.

Gould, Lewis L., ed. *The Progressive Era*. New York: Syracuse University Press, 1974.

Haber, Samuel. *Efficiency and Uplift: Scientific Management in the Progressive Era, 1890-1920*. Chicago: University of Chicago Press, 1964.

Hall, G. Stanley. *Adolescence: Its Psychology and Its Relations to Physiology, Anthropology, Sociology, Sex, Crime, Religion and Education*. 2 vols. New York: D. Appleton and Co., 1904.

__________. *Jesus the Christ in the Light of Psychology*. 2 vols. New York: Doubleday, 1917.

__________. *Recreations of a Psychologist*. New York: D. Appleton and Co., 1920.

Havell, J. M. and Smith, Heman C., eds. *History of Decatur County, Iowa and Its People*. Chicago: The S. J. Clarke Publishing Co., 1915.

Hofstadter, Richard. *The Age of Reform: From Bryan to FDR*. New York: Random House, 1955.

Hook, Sidney, *The Hero in History: A Study in Limitation and Possibility*. Boston: Beacon Press, 1955.

Hoover, Kathleen and Cage, John. *Virgil Thompson: His Life and Music*. New York: Thomas Yoseloff, 1959.

Hopkins, C. Howard. *The Rise of the Social Gospel in American Protestantism, 1865-1915*. New Haven: Yale University Press, 1967.

Hurst, James Willard. *Law and the Conditions of Freedom in the Nineteenth-Century United States*. Madison: University of Wisconsin Press, 1967.

Kelley, E. L., and Hilliard, George. *The Law of Christ and Its Fulfillment*. Independence, Missouri: Herald Publishing House, 1911.

Kleppner, Paul. *The Cross of Culture: A Social Analysis of Midwestern Politics, 1859-1900*. New York: The Free Press, 1970.

Koehler, J. August. *Problems of Industrial Zion*. Independence, Missouri: Herald Publishing House, 1927.

Levin, N. Gordon Jr. *Woodrow Wilson and World Politics: Ameri-*

ca's Response to War and Revolution. New York: Oxford University Press, 1968.
May, Henry F. *Protestant Churches and Industrial America.* New York: Harper and Row, 1949.
__________. *The End of American Innocence: A Study of the First Years of Our Time, 1912-1917.* Chicago: Quadrangle Books, 1959.
McCloskey, Robert G. *American Conservatism in the Age of Enterprise, 1865-1910: A Study of William Graham Sumner, Stephen J. Field, and Andrew Carnegie.* New York: Harper and Row, 1951.
McFarland, Gerald W. *Mugwumps, Morals and Politics, 1884-1920.* Amherst: University of Massachusetts Press, 1975.
McKiernan, F. Mark; Blair, Alma R.; and Edwards, Paul M., eds. *The Restoration Movement: Essays in Mormon History.* Lawrence, Kansas: Coronado Press, 1973.
McLoughlin, William G., ed. *The American Evangelicals, 1800-1900.* New York: Harper and Row, 1968.
Meyer, Donald B. *The Protestant Search for Political Realism, 1919-1941.* Berkeley: University of California Press, 1960.
Miller, Robert Moats. *American Protestantism and Social Issues, 1919-1939.* Chapel Hill: University of North Carolina Press, 1958.
Morcombe, Joseph E. *Masonry and Mormonism.* n.p.: Grand Lodge of Iowa, n.d.
Mowry, George E. *The Era of Theodore Roosevelt and the Birth of Modern America, 1900-1912.* New York: Harper and Row, 1962.
Niebuhr, Reinhold. *Moral Man in Immoral Society.* New York: Charles Scribner's Sons, 1960.
Niebuhr, H. Richard. *The Social Sources of Denominationalism.* New York: Henry Holt and Co., 1929.
O'Dea, Thomas F. *The Mormons.* Chicago: University of Chicago Press, 1957.
Pivar, David J. *Purity Crusade: Sexual Morality and Social Control, 1868-1900.* Westport, Connecticut: Greenwood Press, Inc., 1973.
Quint, Howard H.; Cantor, Milton; and Albertson, Dean, eds. *Main Problems in American History.* 2 vols. 2nd. ed. Homewood, Illinois: The Dorsey Press, 1972.
Rauschenbusch, Walter. *Christianity and Social Crisis.* Edited by Robert D. Cross. New York: Harper and Row, 1964.
__________. *A Theology for the Social Gospel.* New York: Abingdon Press, 1945.

Reorganized Church of Jesus Christ of Latter Day Saints. Book of Doctrine and Covenants. Independence, Missouri: Herald Publishing House, 1952.

__________. The Book of Mormon. Authorized ed. Independence, Missouri: Herald Publishing House, 1955.

__________. *General Conference Resolutions, 1852-1915.* Lamoni, Iowa: Herald Publishing House, n.d.

__________. *The Hymnal.* Independence, Missouri: Herald Publishing House, 1957.

__________. *The Priesthood Manual.* Independence, Missouri: Herald Publishing House, 1964.

__________. *Rules and Resolutions.* Independence, Missouri. Herald Publishing House, 1964.

Ross, Dorothy G. *G. Stanley Hall: Psychologist As Prophet.* Chicago, Illinois: University of Chicago Press, 1972.

Sills, David A., ed. *The International Encyclopedia of the Social Sciences.* 17 vols. New York: The Macmillan Co. and the Free Press, 1968.

Smith, Elbert A. *On Memory's Beam.* Independence, Missouri: Herald Publishing House, 1946.

Smith, Frederick M. *The Higher Powers of Man.* Lamoni, Iowa: Herald Publishing House, 1918.

Smith, Heman C.; Smith, Joseph III; and Edwards, F. Henry. *The History of the Reorganized Church of Jesus Christ of Latter Day Saints.* 8 vols. Independence, Missouri: Herald Publishing House, 1976.

Smith, Joseph Jr., et al. *History of the Church of Jesus Christ of Latter-day Saints,* 12 vols. Salt Lake City, Utah: The Deseret Book Company, 1961.

Smith, Ruth Lyman. *Concerning the Prophet: Frederick Madison Smith.* Kansas City: Burton Publishing Company, 1924.

Soule, George. *Prosperity Decade: From War to Depression, 1917-1929. The Economic History of the United States,* vol. 8. New York: Harper and Row, 1947.

Sproat, John G. *"The Best Men:" Liberal Reformers in the Gilded Age.* New York: Oxford University Press, 1968.

Thelen, David P. *The New Citizenship: Origins of Progressivism in Wisconsin, 1885-1900.* Columbia: University of Missouri Press, 1972.

Timberlake, James H. *Prohibition and the Progressive Movement, 1900-1920.* Cambridge, Massachusetts: Harvard University Press, 1963.

Troeltsch, Ernst. *The Social Teaching of the Christian Churches.* Translated by Olive Wyon. 22 vols. New York: The Macmillan Co., 1931.

Tyler, Alice Felt. *Freedom's Ferment: Phases of American Social History from the Colonial Period to the Outbreak of the Civil War.* New York: Harper and Row, 1962.

Ward, John William. *Andrew Jackson: Symbol for an Age.* New York: Oxford University Press, 1962.

White, Ronald C. and Hopkins, C. Howard. *The Social Gospel: Religion and Reform in Changing America.* Philadelphia: Temple University Press, 1976.

Wyllie, Irwin G. *The Self-Made Man in America: The Myth of Rags to Riches.* New York: Macmillan Co., 1954.

Yarrington, Roger. *The Auditorium.* Independence, Missouri: Herald Publishing House, 1962.

Pamphlets

Church of Jesus Christ of Latter-day Saints. *Appeal of Frederick M. Smith to President Joseph F. Smith for Unlimited Use of the Meeting Houses of the Latter-day Saints and His Reply.* Salt Lake City: Deseret Publishing Co., 1905.

First Presidency. *An Open Letter to "Protesting Saints" and all Other Interested Parties.* Independence, Missouri: Reorganized Church of Jesus Christ of Latter Day Saints, May 18, 1926.

__________. *An Open Letter to the Saints.* Independence, Missouri: Reorganized Church of Jesus Christ of Latter Day Saints, July 26, 1926.

__________. *Changes and Innovations: An Open Letter to the Reorganized Church of Jesus Christ of Latter Day Saints.* Independence, Missouri: Reorganized Church of Jesus Christ of Latter Day Saints, October 1, 1926.

Independence Institute of the Arts and Sciences. *Articles of Incorporation.* Independence, Missouri: n.p., 1923.

__________. *Independence Institute of the Arts and Sciences: Seasons of 1917-1918.* n.p., n.d.

__________. *Bulletin of the Independence Institute of the Arts and Sciences: Announcements of Courses for 1922-1923.* n.p., n.d.

Long, E. E. *The De Kalb Agreement.* n.p., n.d.

__________. *Minority Rights or in the Footsteps of the Fathers: The Protesting Saints Declare Themselves.* Independence, Missouri: n.p., n.d.

McGuire, Benjamin R. *Some Interesting Facts Relating to the General Conference Auditorium*. Independence, Missouri: Herald Publishing House, 1924.

McGuire, Benjamin R.; Keir, James F.; and Smith, Israel A. *The Unbroken Chain: A Treatise on the Law of the Lord as Relating to the Work of the Bishopric*. Independence, Missouri: n.p., n.d.

McGuire, Benjamin R.; Keir, James F.; and Smith, Israel A.; Rushton, John W.; Williams, T. W.; Karlstrom, A. V.; and May, Roderick. *Protest Against "Supreme Directional Control."* Independence, Missouri: n.p., n.d.

McKim, B. L. *An Appeal*. Independence, Missouri: n.p., 1940.

__________. *Explanation and Statement*. Independence, Missouri: n.p., 1943.

__________. *Has the Church a Prophet at Its Head?* n.p., n.d.

__________. *Where Does the Church Stand?* Ogden, Utah: privately published, 1920.

Quorum of Twelve. *Brief Submitted by the Quorum of Twelve*. n.p., 1919.

Reorganized Church of Jesus Christ of Latter Day Saints. *The Lamoni Order of Enoch: Articles of Association and By-Laws*. Lamoni, Iowa: Herald Publishing House, 1914.

Sheehy, F. M. *Nothing Done Until Done Right*. Independence, Missouri: n.p., 1924.

Skinner, Hubert M. *An Old Poem Re-Studied*. Chicago, Illinois: Lincoln-Jefferson University, June 10, 1909.

Smith, Elbert A. *The True Philosophy of Church Government*. Independence, Missouri: Herald Publishing House, 1924.

Smith, Frederick M. *An Address to the Priesthood*. Lamoni, Iowa: Herald Publishing House, 1917.

__________. *Address to the Seventy-First Conference of the Reorganized Church of Jesus Christ of Latter Day Saints*. Independence, Missouri: Herald Publishing House, 1926.

__________. *The Church and Change*. Independence, Missouri: Herald Publishing House, 1944.

__________. *Church-Industry-Society*. Independence, Missouri: Herald Publishing House, 1937.

__________. *The Elements of a Christian Peace*. Independence, Missouri: Herald Publishing House, 1945.

__________. *Foundations of Zion*. Independence, Missouri: Herald Publishing House, 1951.

__________. *Kirtland Centennial, March 27-29, 1936*. Independence, Missouri: n.p., January 1, 1936.

__________. *Marriage and the Church.* Independence, Missouri: Reorganized Church of Jesus Christ of Latter Day Saints, 1929.

__________. *A Message from the Seed of Joseph the Seer to the People of the Church of Jesus Christ of Latter Day Saints.* Indedependence, Missouri: Herald Publishing House, ca. 1905.

__________. *A Message to the Young People of the Church.* Lamoni, Iowa: Herald Publishing House, 1922.

__________. *Our Social Ideals.* Independence, Missouri: Herald Publishing House, 1923.

__________. *The President's Message to Conference, 1919, Lamoni, Iowa.* Lamoni, Iowa: Herald Publishing House, 1919.

__________. *The Sublimation of Labor.* Independence, Missouri: Herald Publishing House, 1926.

__________. *With the Quorum.* Independence, Missouri: Herald Publishing House, 1943.

Smith, Frederick M.; Briggs, George N.; Macgregor, Daniel; Trowbridge, G. S.; and Smith, Mrs. F. M. *Report of the Coordinating Committee.* Lamoni, Iowa: Herald Publishing House, 1918.

Smith, Frederick M. and Carmichael. *The Making of a Steward.* Independence, Missouri: Herald Publishing House, 1929.

Smith, Frederick M.; McGuire, Benjamin R.; and Rushton, John W. *The Disaffection of R. C. Evans.* Independence, Missouri: Herald Publishing House, n.d.

Smith, Israel A., et al. *In Memory of Frederick Madison Smith.* Independence, Missouri: Herald Publishing House, 1946.

__________. *Let the Facts Be Known.* Independence, Missouri: n.p., n.d.

Succession of Ministerial Authority: Where to Be Found? Independence, Missouri: n.p., n.d.

Trowbridge, Richard. *Facts Which People Should Know and Earnestly Consider.* Independence, Missouri: n.p., 1927.

Williams, Thomas W. *The "New" Social Program of the Church.* Independence, Missouri: n.p., n.d.

Yates, James E. *Refusal to Sustain Doctrine of Supremacy of Church President.* Independence, Missouri: n.p., 1925.

Scholarly Articles

Aiken, John R. and McDonnell, James R. "Walter Rauschenbusch and Labor Reform: A Social Gospeller's Approach," *Labor History* 2 (Spring, 1970): 131-150.

Andrist, Ralph K. "Paladin of Purity," *American Heritage* 24 (October, 1973): 4-7, 84-88.

Arrington, Leonard J. "Early Mormon Communitarianism: The Law of Consecration and Stewardship," *Western Humanities Review* 7 (Autumn, 1953): 341-69.

Davis, David Brion. "The New England Origins of Mormonism," *New England Quarterly* 26 (June, 1953): 147-68.

Flanders, Robert B. "The Kingdom of God in Illinois: Politics in Utopia," *Dialogue: A Journal of Mormon Thought* 5 (Spring, 1970): 28-36.

Glad, Paul M. "Progressives and the Business Culture of the 1920s," *Journal of American History* 53 (June, 1966): 75-89.

Handy, Robert T. "Christianity and Socialism in America," *Church History* 21 (March, 1952): 39-54.

Hansen, Klaus J. "The Political Kingdom as a Cause for Mormon-Gentile Conflict," *Brigham Young University Studies* 2 (Spring-Summer, 1960): 241-60.

James, William. "The Energies of Men," *Philosophical Review* 16 (1907): 1-20.

Mulder, William. "Mormonism's 'Gathering:' An American Doctrine with a Difference," *Church History* 23 (September, 1954): 248-64.

O'Dea, Thomas F. "Mormonism and the Avoidance of Sectarian Stagnation: A Study of Church, Sect and Incipient Nationality," *American Journal of Sociology* 70 (November, 1954): 285-93.

Rader, Benjamin G. "Richard T. Ely: Lay Spokesman for the Social Gospel," *Journal of American History* 53 (June, 1966): 61-74.

Schlesinger, Arthur M., Sr. "A Critical Period in American Religion," *Massachusetts Historical Society Proceedings* 64 (June, 1932): 523-47.

Starbuck, Edwin Diller. "The Life and Confessions of G. Stanley Hall: Some Notes on the Philosophy of Genius," *Journal of Philosophy* 21 (March 13, 1924): 149-50.

Szasz, Ferenc M. "The Progressive Clergy and the Kingdom of God," *Mid-America: An Historical Review* 55 (January, 1973): 3-20.

Thelen, David P. "Robert LaFollette's Leadership, 1891-1896: The Old and the New Politics and the Dilemma of the Progressive Politician," *Pacific Northwest Quarterly* 62 (July, 1971): 97-108.

Vlahos, Clare D. "The Challenge to Centralized Power: Zenas H.

Gurley, Jr. and the Prophetic Office," *Courage: A Journal of History, Thought and Action* 1 (March, 1971): 141-58.
Welter, Barbara. "The Cult of True Womanhood," *American Quarterly* 18 (Summer, 1966): 151-74.

Theses, Dissertations, and Unpublished Papers

Bitton, Davis. "Lyman Wight: Wild Ram of the Mountains." Unpublished paper presented to the John Whitmer Historical Association, Lamoni, Iowa, April 17, 1975.
"Digest of the Development and History of the United Order of Enoch at Independence, Missouri." Unpublished typescript, Office of the Presiding Bishopric, Reorganized Church of Jesus Christ of Latter Day Saints, Independence, Missouri.
Flanders, Robert B. "The Mormons Who Did Not Go West: A Study of the Emergence of the Reorganized Church of Jesus Christ of Latter Day Saints." Master's thesis, University of Wisconsin, 1954.
"History of the Atherton Stewardship Experiment." Unpublished typescript, Library-Archives of the Reorganized Church of Jesus Christ of Latter Day Saints, Independence, Missouri.
Howard, Richard P. "Utopia and the Church." Unpublished paper presented to the John Whitmer Historical Association, Lamoni, Iowa, Spring, 1975.
Hutchins, Robert D. "Joseph Smith III: Moderate Mormon." Master's thesis, Brigham Young University, 1977.
Independence Institute of the Arts and Sciences. "Tentative Working Program." Unpublished typescript, Library-Archives of the Reorganized Church of Jesus Christ of Latter Day Saints, Independence, Missouri.
__________. "The Campus." Unpublished loose-leaf binder, 1927-1928. Library-Archives of the Reorganized Church of Jesus Christ of Latter Day Saints, Independence, Missouri.
"Story of the Atherton Adventure." Unpublished typescript, Office of the Presiding Bishopric, Reorganized Church of Jesus Christ of Latter Day Saints, the Auditorium, Independence, Missouri.
Tickemyer, Garland E. "The Philosophy of Joseph Smith and Its Educational Implications." Ph.D. dissertation, University of Texas, 1963.
Vlahos, Clare D. "Images of Orthodoxy: Self-Identity in Early Reorganization Apologetics." Unpublished paper presented to the Mor-

mon History Association, Logan, Utah, May 6, 1978.
Warner, Edward A. "Mormon Theodemocracy: Theocratic and Democratic Elements in Early Latter-Day Saint Ideology, 1827-1846." Ph.D. dissertation, University of Iowa, 1973.

Interviews and Correspondence

Cheville, Roy A. Former Presiding Patriarch, Reorganized Church of Jesus Christ of Latter Day Saints, Independence, Missouri. Interview, February 21, 1975.
__________. Letter to the writer, October, 1972.
Edwards, Alice M. Daughter of Frederick M. Smith, Independence, Missouri. Questionnaire Interview, Spring, 1972.
Hamilton, Millard D. Recorder, Ararat Shrine Temple, Kansas City, Missouri. Letter to the writer, October 6, 1972.
Howard, Richard P. Church Historian, Reorganized Church of Jesus Christ of Latter Day Saints, Independence, Missouri. Letter to the writer, March 15, 1973.
Larsen, Edward. Son-in-law to Frederick M. Smith, Independence, Missouri. Interview, November 25, 1972.
Larsen, Lois. Daughter of Frederick M. Smith, Independence, Missouri. Interview, November 15, 1972.
Livingston, Henry M. Bishop, Reorganized Church of Jesus Christ of Latter Day Saints, Independence, Missouri. Interview, October 10, 1975.
Love, Devere. Recorder, Mizra Temple, Ft. Scott, Kansas. Letter to the writer, November 1, 1972.
Negaard, Leland A. Former Professor of Religion, Graceland College, Lamoni, Iowa. Letter to the writer, March 26, 1974.
Recorder of Orient Lodge No. 546, A.F. & A.M., Kansas City, Missouri. Letter to the writer, January 12, 1976.
Runkle, Jerry C. Bishop, Reorganized Church of Jesus Christ of Latter Day Saints, Lamoni, Iowa. Interview, February 14, 1975.
Tickemyer, Garland E. Former pastor of the Stone Church congregation, Reorganized Church of Jesus Christ of Latter Day Saints, Independence, Missouri. Interview, November 25, 1973.

Public Document

Kansas City Board of Public Welfare. *Annual Report of the Board of Public Welfare of Kansas City, Mo., April 21, 1913-April 20, 1914*. n.p., n.d.

Newspapers

Annual. 1924-1925. Publication for High Priesthood of the Reorganized Church of Jesus Christ of Latter Day Saints.

Ararat Shrine News. 1941.

Autumn Leaves. 1896, 1915-1916, 1926. Publication for the youth of the Reorganized Church of Jesus Christ of Latter Day Saints.

Evening and Morning Star. 1833. Official publication of the early Mormon Church.

The Examiner. 1914, 1921, 1923, 1925. A daily newspaper, Independence, Missouri.

Journal of History. 1908, 1912, 1918-1920, 1922-1924. Organ for official treatment of historical material, Reorganized Church of Jesus Christ of Latter Day Saints.

Kansas City Journal. 1913.

Kansas City Star. 1912, 1914-1915.

Kansas City Star Magazine. 1925.

Kansas City Times. 1915, 1946.

Liberty Street Bulletin. 1943-1946. Publication by the Liberty Street Congregation of the Reorganized Church of Jesus Christ of Latter Day Saints, Independence, Missouri.

Masonic World. 1936.

Messenger. 1925-1927. Publication by the protesting congregations of the Reorganized Church of Jesus Christ of Latter Day Saints, 1925-1927.

One. 1919. Publication for the priesthood of the Reorganized Church of Jesus Christ of Latter Day Saints.

Priesthood Journal. 1922-1923, 1935-1937, 1943. Publication for the priesthood of the Reorganized Church of Jesus Christ of Latter Day Saints.

Reorganized Church of Jesus Christ of Latter Day Saints. *General Conference Minutes.* 1903, 1906-1907, 1909, 1911-1912, 1914-1915, 1917-1920, 1922-1923, 1925-1927. Lamoni, Iowa, and Independence, Missouri.

Saints' Herald. 1873, 1879, 1889, 1893, 1895-1896, 1898-1899, 1901, 1903-1906, 1908-1909, 1911-1945, 1957, 1959-1960, 1962, 1966. Official publication of the Reorganized Church of Jesus Christ of Latter Day Saints.

Stone Church Bulletin. 1943-1946. Publication by the Stone Church Congregation of the Reorganized Church of Jesus Christ of Latter Day Saints, Independence, Missouri.

Times and Seasons. 1840, 1844. Publication of the early Mormon Church.
True Latter Day Saints' Herald. 1860, 1869-1870. Official organ of the early Reorganized Church of Jesus Christ of Latter Day Saints.
Unity. 1917-1918. Publication for the priesthood of the Reorganized Church of Jesus Christ of Latter Day Saints.
Zion's Advocate. 1925. Publication of dissenters from the Reorganized Church of Jesus Christ of Latter Day Saints.
Zion's Ensign. 1908, 1911, 1915-1922. Missionary organ of the Reorganized Church of Jesus Christ of Latter Day Saints.
Zion's Progress Bulletin. 1945. Publication by Lee Davis in protest against the stewardship policies of the Reorganized Church of Jesus Christ of Latter Day Saints.

Unpublished Manuscripts

Independence, Missouri. Library-Archives of the Reorganized Church of Jesus Christ of Latter Day Saints. Clipping file.
__________. Library-Archives of the Reorganized Church of Jesus Christ of Latter Day Saints. William H. Kelley Papers.
__________. Library-Archives of the Reorganized Church of Jesus Christ of Latter Day Saints. Order of Enoch File.
__________. Library-Archives of the Reorganized Church of Jesus Christ of Latter Day Saints. Letter File.
__________. Library-Archives of the Reorganized Church of Jesus Christ of Latter Day Saints. Garland E. Tickemyer Papers.
__________. Henry L. Livingston Papers. In his personal possession.
__________. Office of Presiding Bishopric, Reorganized Church of Jesus Christ of Latter Day Saints. A. J. Yarrington Letters, September 6, and March 28, 1928.
__________. Frederick M. Smith Papers. In the possession of Frederick Niels Larsen. Part of these papers have been microfilmed and are housed in Lamoni, Iowa. Mormon History Collection, Graceland College.
Kansas City, Missouri. Ararat Shrine Temple. "Minutes for the Years 1941-1942."
Lamoni, Iowa. Paul M. Edwards Private Collection. F. Henry Edwards Private Correspondence.
__________. Graceland College, Mormon History Collection. Rebecca Weld Noland Papers.
Worcester, Massachusetts. Clark University. Clark University Library Papers, Frederick M. Smith Student File.